ESSAY AS ENABLER IN YVES BONNEFOY
CREATING THE GOOD READER

LEGENDA

LEGENDA is the Modern Humanities Research Association's book imprint for new research in the Humanities. Founded in 1995 by Malcolm Bowie and others within the University of Oxford, Legenda has always been a collaborative publishing enterprise, directly governed by scholars. The Modern Humanities Research Association (MHRA) joined this collaboration in 1998, became half-owner in 2004, in partnership with Maney Publishing and then Routledge, and has since 2016 been sole owner. Titles range from medieval texts to contemporary cinema and form a widely comparative view of the modern humanities, including works on Arabic, Catalan, English, French, German, Greek, Italian, Portuguese, Russian, Spanish, and Yiddish literature. Editorial boards and committees of more than 60 leading academic specialists work in collaboration with bodies such as the Society for French Studies, the British Comparative Literature Association and the Association of Hispanists of Great Britain & Ireland.

The MHRA encourages and promotes advanced study and research in the field of the modern humanities, especially modern European languages and literature, including English, and also cinema. It aims to break down the barriers between scholars working in different disciplines and to maintain the unity of humanistic scholarship. The Association fulfils this purpose through the publication of journals, bibliographies, monographs, critical editions, and the MHRA Style Guide, and by making grants in support of research. Membership is open to all who work in the Humanities, whether independent or in a University post, and the participation of younger colleagues entering the field is especially welcomed.

ALSO PUBLISHED BY THE ASSOCIATION

Critical Texts
Tudor and Stuart Translations • New Translations • European Translations
MHRA Library of Medieval Welsh Literature

MHRA Bibliographies
Publications of the Modern Humanities Research Association

The Annual Bibliography of English Language & Literature
Austrian Studies
Modern Language Review
Portuguese Studies
The Slavonic and East European Review
Working Papers in the Humanities
The Yearbook of English Studies

www.mhra.org.uk
www.legendabooks.com

RESEARCH MONOGRAPHS IN FRENCH STUDIES

The *Research Monographs in French Studies* (RMFS) are selected, edited and supported by the Society for French Studies. The series seeks to publish the best new work in all areas of the literature, language, thought, history, politics, culture and film of the French-speaking world and to cover the full chronological range from the medieval period to the present day. Proposals are accepted for monographs of up to 85,000 words, while proposals for 'short' monographs (50,000–60,000 words), a traditional strength of the series, are still welcomed.

❖

PUBLISHED IN THIS SERIES

www.rmfs.mhra.org.uk

Essay as Enabler in Yves Bonnefoy

Creating the Good Reader

❖

LAYLA ROESLER

l

LEGENDA
Research Monographs in French Studies 67
Modern Humanities Research Association
2022

Published by Legenda
an imprint of the Modern Humanities Research Association
Salisbury House, Station Road, Cambridge CB1 2LA

ISBN 978-1-83954-046-2 *(HB)*
ISBN 978-1-83954-047-9 *(PB)*

First published 2022

Copy-Editor: Charlotte Wathey

CONTENTS

❖

To my Parents:
in memoriam

L.R., Lyon, October 2022

A NOTE ON THE DIFFERENT EDITIONS
OF *L'IMPROBABLE*

❖

This note is intended to clarify the interlocking relationship between the texts which correspond to Bonnefoy's title *L'Improbable*. That title, in fact, refers to a pluri-edition work, and instead of pointing to a single textual object, it has come over time to resemble the ever-widening circles produced by a stone dropped into water. The original nucleus — the 'stone', as it were — is the 1959 collection of eight essays plus a poem ('Dévotion') called *L'Improbable*. This, the first *Improbable*, was published by Mercure de France. A second, stand-alone volume of essays appeared roughly ten years later. Titled *Un rêve fait à Mantoue* (1967), it contained thirteen essays plus a highly poetic narrative text that reads much like a prose poem ('Sept feux'). In 1980, Bonnefoy consolidated these two essay collections into a single volume, which he entitled *L'Improbable, suivi de Un rêve fait à Mantoue*. This second expanded but also heavily revised book is the second *Improbable*. Two other distinct volumes of essays were to follow over the next twenty years: *Le Nuage rouge* (1977) and *La Vérité de parole* (1988). In the latter, Bonnefoy reveals in a discreet endnote that all four volumes of essays are part of a larger structure that he identifies as *L'Improbable*. Though never published as a single volume, this four-volume supra-structure to which he alludes can be identified as the third *Improbable*. (There is also a 1990 reprinting of *L'Improbable, suivi d'autres essais*, but it is not materially very different from the 1980 edition and is therefore peripheral to this demonstration.) The three different *Improbables* thus reflect three broadening textual scales. Schematically, the three versions of *L'Improbable* look like this:

1. *L'Improbable* (1959)
2. *L'Improbable* (1959) + *Un rêve fait à Mantoue* (1967)
3. *L'Improbable* (1959) + *Un rêve fait à Mantoue* (1967) + *Le Nuage rouge* (1977) + *La Vérité de parole* (1988)

Finally, an additional level of paratextual complexity stems from the fact that although all these books initially appeared in Mercure de France, they were subsequently republished in more accessible Gallimard 'livre de poche' editions, further expanding the textual information given. The present book shows how these publishing choices contribute to representing Bonnefoy's struggle not only to express the arc of his intellectual and philosophical position, but also to carve out a space for the author and the writing individual.

A NOTE ON
TRANSLATIONS AND QUOTATIONS

❖

Many of the primary and secondary materials quoted in this book are in French. In order to provide readers with a more fluid reading experience, primary materials (texts by Bonnefoy himself) are quoted in French and followed immediately by an English translation. Translations of these texts are most often my own. However, where English translations by other translators do exist, I provide those rather than retranslating myself. This is especially the case for the translations by Galway Kinnell, John Naughton, and Richard Stamelman, in as much as Bonnefoy provided some input into their translations. There are, however some instances where I do not agree with the published translation and in those cases, I retranslate. Unless otherwise indicated, all translations are my own. By contrast, citations from secondary material eschew the more cumbersome double text used for the primary material and are directly translated into English. Again, all translations are my own.

Quotations from frequently cited texts by Bonnefoy are referenced by abbreviations and page numbers in the main text, as follows:

APP   *The Act and the Place of Poetry*, trans. by John T. Naughton (Chicago: University of Chicago Press, 1989)

D   *On the Motion and Immobility of Douve*, trans. by Galway Kinnell (Newcastle upon Tyne: Bloodaxe Books, 1992)

E   *Entretiens sur la poésie (1972–1990)* (Paris: Mercure de France, 1990)

I   *L'Improbable, suivi de Un rêve fait à Mantoue* (Paris: Gallimard, 1983; repr. 1992)

NR   *Le Nuage rouge: essais sur la poétique* (Paris: Mercure de France, 1977; repr. 1992)

P   *Poèmes: Du mouvement et de l'immobilité de Douve, Hier régnant désert, Pierre écrite, Dans le leurre du seuil* (Paris: Mercure de France, 1978)

VP   *La Vérité de parole* (Paris: Mercure de France, 1988)

YB   *Yves Bonnefoy: poésie, art et pensée. Colloque international 9–11 mai 1983*, ed. by Yves-Alain Favre (Pau: Publications de l'Université de Pau et des pays de l'Adour, 1983)

INTRODUCTION

❖

A veces creo que los buenos lectores son cisnes aún más tenebrosos y
singulares que los buenos autores.

[At times I think that good readers are swans which are even more
shadow-ridden and singular than good authors.]

— Jorge Luis Borges[1]

Borges's almost facetious little quip from *Historia universal de la infamia* serves as a
guide to my contention that one of the significant *raisons d'être* for the work of Yves
Bonnefoy lies in providing a means for his readers to become better readers. But
better readers of what? The question is quite legitimate, for most readers encounter
Bonnefoy through his rich poetry, whose density and grave tone accentuate its
universal dimension. Those who venture into his essays encounter texts that
explain and reinforce the absolute need for poetry, as in a sentence where Bonnefoy
writes: 'Il y a dans la poésie moderne française un cortège du Graal qui passe, les
objets les plus vifs de cette terre — l'arbre, un visage, une pierre — et ils doivent
être nommés. Il en va de notre espoir' [Passing in front of us, there is in modern
French poetry a Grail procession that contains the most vital objects of this earth:
a tree, a face, a stone. They must be named. The whole of our hope hangs on
this].[2] The urgency of this comment invites, even exhorts, readers to see poetry as
a union composed of naming and hope. Complementarily, the allusion to Chrétien
de Troyes's *Perceval* tale through the reference to the Grail procession serves as a
reminder that Perceval's error upon beholding the procession was to remain silent
and not ask about it. Had he spoken, he would have healed the Fisher King, keeper
of the Grail. The message is clear: silence is anathema; words have the power to
heal; poetry is hope. And if this improbable concatenation of elements is cited
here, that is because they mirror the central concerns of Bonnefoy's written work,
as appears clearly in his programmatic call to arms: 'Je voudrais réunir, je voudrais
identifier presque la poésie et l'espoir' [I would like to bring together, almost to
equate poetry and hope] (*I*, 107).

Yet, despite the high value that he gives to the very notion of poetry, what is
perhaps most striking for Bonnefoy's readers is that he did not confine his writing
to poetry alone. On the contrary, one of the most marked aspects of his *œuvre* is the
double path he followed, continuously maintaining a difficult equilibrium between
two seemingly opposite poles: on the one hand, poetry and its translation, and on
the other, a substantial number of thought-provoking essays.[3] Although Bonnefoy's
poetic production remained relatively modest, he was a prolific writer of essays
covering a broad range of subjects and appearing in a variety of textual media.

Paradoxically, however, he never subjected his essays to the same keen analysis that he gave to poetry or to translation. For a writer as self-aware as he was, this invites scrutiny, and provides the central dynamic of this study, to wit, the singularly neglected question of the place of the essay in Bonnefoy's work. Its ubiquity is striking, giving rise to a number of questions. Why indeed would a poet who specifically extols the unique ethical value of poetry feel the need to accompany his poetic texts with such a massive body of essays? Can there be a connection between essay and poetry? What, in short, does the essay *do* for him that poetry cannot?

The great number of these essays confronts his readers with a conundrum, partly because of his silence on their role, but partly also because of the problem of reconciling his essayistic production with his philosophical engagement with poetry. Indeed, careful readers of his work cannot long remain unaware of his deep-seated commitment to the theo-philosophical notion of *présence*. In numerous texts and interviews he defended, at times vehemently, the idea that poetic praxis can, and indeed must, allow access to the experience of *présence*, a position that greatly contributes to the specificity of Bonnefoy who, well before his death in 2016, had earned in France the laconic though eloquent title 'poète de la présence'. The fusion he created between poetry and *présence* so completely determined his own interpretation of his work that it has mobilized a substantive amount of critical attention, leading in turn to academic corroboration of Bonnefoy's position by the frequent reiteration of the connection between poetry and *présence*.[4] Moreover, the strength of his position is closely tied to a commensurate rejection of the siren call of aestheticism. For him, the poem cannot merely be the inert object of aesthetic admiration. On the contrary, poetry is invested with a much higher mission. As the title of the essay 'L'Acte et le lieu de la poésie' [The Act and the Place of Poetry] suggests, it must act, its function being to transform, almost 'convert' (in the theological sense of *metanoia*) the reader.[5] This notion of function, or purpose, enters into dialogue with different positions that have come into conflict from the nineteenth century onward. On many points, Bonnefoy's stance clearly rejects the *beau* extolled, for example, by Mallarmé and the *Parnassiens*. However, he also had difficulty in adhering to the literature imbued with political function that was advocated by Romantic poets such as Victor Hugo. Bonnefoy's position clearly reflects a larger debate: between the nineteenth and twentieth centuries, the place of aesthetics in literature underwent a radical transformation, shifting, for instance, from the autotelic insistence on *l'art pour l'art* by the *Parnassiens* evoked above, to Theodor Adorno's oft-cited remark from *Kulturkritik und Gesellschaft*, 'No poetry after Auschwitz'.[6] Very naturally then, a fundamental question becomes that of the increasingly problematic value of poetry. Indeed, as Benoît Denis argues in his study of 'la littérature engagée', the idea of writing that is more focused on the political and existential condition of society than on form is one of the central themes of twentieth-century literature.[7] Poetry appears to be the form most antithetical to that ambition of political commitment, as Denis indicates when he describes it as:

> A closed and autonomous form which is its own principle and its own end; in poetry, language closes in on itself, becoming its own object, expressing

nothing more than this auto-reflexive process. Poetry, the very summum of intransivity, resists *engagement* with its entire being.[8]

The crux of the matter lies in the value of this intransivity. Indeed, the problem, as many now point out, is that the closure and autotelism that have long been associated with poetry have shifted in value, and instead of revealing poetry's connection with philosophy and a higher, more truthful form of expression (precisely the point Heidegger seems so frequently to be making) the poem is losing, or has lost, its power to point not only to truth in general, but also to the inner truth of the writing subject. That is certainly what Bonnefoy seems to confirm with some disquiet when he remarks that 'aujourd'hui, en effet, la poésie est problématique par nature. Celui qui parle n'a plus l'impression que ce qu'il va donner à lire sera l'expression transparente de ce qu'il est' [Today, poetry is indeed inherently problematic. He who speaks no longer has the impression that he is providing readers with the transparent expression of who he is].[9]

The problem is clearly one of poetry, and though Adorno's uncompromising statement cannot, of course, have been known by Bonnefoy in the immediate aftermath of the the Second World War, he does quote it in the 1986 essay 'Poésie et vérité'.[10] Indeed, his earliest poetry, dating from the mid-1940s, and including texts such as 'Anti-Platon' or the 'Traité du pianiste', was still heavily influenced by the surrealist movement to which he had briefly belonged, but abandoned because of a philosophical difference of opinion. Still, the successive revelations of the horrors or the war had a significant impact on the intellectual scene of the time, leading to a shocked questioning of the role of literature. Bonnefoy recalls this discomfiture in a later essay: 'How, indeed, in the aftermath of the war, when everything cried out for reappraising every level of the discourse of a civilisation on the verge of going under, could one still find meaning in Surrealism?'.[11] His celebrated 1953 poem cycle, *Du mouvement et de l'immobilité de Douve* (hereafter *Douve*), thus signalled the beginning of his developing realization that post-war poetry could not longer rely solely on aesthetic value in order to engage writer and reader. But what, concretely, was needed to navigate between the Scylla of an impotent *beau* and the Charybdis of a surrealism widely criticized for an apolitical stance symbolically reinforced by André Breton's wartime flight to the United States in 1941? Bonnefoy's choice, whether by personal inclination or by moral orientation, was to eschew the more explicit socio-political goals embraced by mid-century contemporaries such as Louis Aragon or René Char, and to seek change through a more profound transformation grounded in philosophical reflection. This is seen in the intellectual training he chose to engage in. His studies at the Sorbonne in the late 1940s brought him into contact with Gaston Bachelard, and also with Jean Wahl and Jean Hyppolite, both well-known Hegelians. Wahl also introduced Bonnefoy to the writings of Kierkegaard, whose work provides the grounding ideas both for *Douve* and for *L'Improbable* (1959), Bonnefoy's first collection of essays. This philosophical dimension, so patent in Bonnefoy's writing, also has its roots in the phenomenological currents of thought present in the Paris of the 1940s and '50s. Initially grounded in a rejection of idealism that is reflected in the title of his early poem 'Anti-Platon', Bonnefoy's philosophical questioning of conceptual thinking ('rien n'est moins réel que le concept' [nothing is less real than the concept], *I*, 19) eventually gave birth to his signature notion of *présence*, which was itself patiently constructed in opposition to a triumvirate of Bonnefoyian antagonists: 'concept', 'ce qui est', and 'la mauvaise présence'. What *présence* is, for Bonnefoy, is substantively defined by how it is *not* these things. But as he ruefully recognized, the problem of *présence* is that it is an experience of immediacy that translates imperfectly into the deferred reality of writing. This problem requires a solution, so the second characteristic of Bonnefoy's work lies in strategies and tools he put into place not only to circumvent the intrinsic 'unsayability' of *présence*, but also to reveal the contours of the path allowing access to *présence* itself, while carving out a terrain within which the poetic 'I' could regain a place of value in the eyes of the community. Among those strategies, the most important are, as the present work argues, his extensive use of the essay. In many ways, however, the essay is merely the tip of an iceberg containing a wide-ranging intellectual structure that federates theology, linguistics, philosophy, and allegoresis. And though the pedestrian, prosaic essay is commonly perceived to be at the polar opposite of the literary spectrum from poetry, a more informed study of its characteristics suggests that the distance between them is not as great as customarily imagined. The genre, as Chapter Two shows, can house a convincing rationale for *présence* while providing a robust rhetorical scaffolding by which to obtain the adherence of readers.

More broadly, because Bonnefoy's work coalesces the problems confronting twentieth-century poetics, analysing it provides an excellent 'laboratory' in which to examine some of the more pressing issues confronting contemporary poets. His lifelong quest to make *présence* textually available allows us to observe directly how his solutions map onto a transformation of the literary paradigms that are still active today. While his choice of the notion of *présence* as well as his use of the essay clearly represent responses that are consonant with the larger perspectives informing the intellectual history of the twentieth century, his preferences concerning aesthetics, literary genre, and language are undoubtedly determined by his personal affinities, as indeed is suggested by comments he made during a 2009 interview given to Laurent Lemire for *Amateur idées*. There, he describes his 'detestation' of the diary form because of its impressionistic potential for 'auto-satisfaction' [complacency]. Simultaneously, however, he also rejects 'synthesizing' textual forms because they disallow the personal reactions of the individual subject.[12] These two extremes of his disaffection provide a good picture of his quest for a common ground located between those two poles. It is the essay, with its mixture of individual proximity and analytic distance, that provides that common ground. The balance found in the essay between an omnipresent, though understated subjectivity is reinforced by Bonnefoy's reiterated invocation of allegory in his descriptions of *présence*, both elements providing a crucial key to understanding the global arc of his work and thus becoming better readers ourselves. Indeed, reading his collected essays in the light of a message that affirms the value of text, author, and past is the only means satisfactorily to understand them.

However, before we can address the question of the structure of Bonnefoy's essays, we need to return to source-definitions not only of the theo-philosophical dimension of *présence*, but also of the intellectual tools Bonnefoy marshalled to provide a grounding and a space for this *présence*. These tools comprise the essay, of course. To it, we must add Bonnefoy's reliance on linguistics and rhetoric, particularly through his use of deixis and allegory. My goal, however, particularly for the notion of *présence*, is not to propose yet another set of definitions describing 'Bonnefoy's presence'. That task has already been successfully accomplished in an ample body of research. Rather, it is important to tackle the problem from an earlier vantage point. First, a consideration that might seem obvious: Bonnefoy was a reader before he was a writer. Like any reader, he absorbed definitions and characteristics through what he read. The questions of 'why *présence*?', 'why the essay?' must therefore be turned around to reflect the meanings that they might furnish for any reader, the salient point being that neither of those elements were created by him *ex nihilo* to serve his own purposes. On the contrary, they were conscious choices that mirrored his own understanding of what they mean and how they might further his own project. My second point is linked to what that project might be. I would suggest that like all contemporary poets, Bonnefoy grappled with a harsh, yet seemingly incontrovertible fact: the diminishing readership that poetry musters in today's world. At a very fundamental level, the cardinal difficulty is simply that of bringing readers to poetry. At a higher level, readers must be brought to understand the complexities and the capacities of the poetic text: they must become those *good* readers of poetry that Borges brings to our attention. His comment is perhaps far truer for readers of poetry than other forms of writing.

Given this situation, it is perhaps easier to see the problems that confronted Bonnefoy. On the one hand, his long-standing intellectual investigations that hovered on the cusp of theology and philosophy brought him to his adamant position regarding the crucial importance of the notion of *présence*, both in real life and, more problematically perhaps, in writing. On the other hand, he was faced with the dilemma of trying to convey this notion of *présence* through a medium, poetry, that appeared rapidly to be losing, or even have already lost, its pre-eminent literary position. My objective in this work is to show how the essays of Bonnefoy confront these challenges by providing a way of 'creating' good readers and thus counter the fact that readers of poetry in contemporary society have dwindled to vanishingly small numbers, leading ineluctably to the increasing difficulty poetry has in finding an audience.

Indeed, perhaps one of the most surprising aspects of research into Bonnefoy's writing is that although much work has been done to define what constitutes his idea of *présence*, very little has been done to examine the reasons for his allegiance to the notion. Similarly, virtually nothing has been done to appraise the reasons for his steadfast choice of the essay form. There are, as yet, few book-length studies on the specificity of the essay in Bonnefoy's work. In her monograph on his work, Concetta Cavallini devotes a single chapter to Bonnefoy as an essayist, showing essentially how he takes up the mantle of Renaissance essayism. She does, however, remark in passing that while critical work on Bonnefoy overwhelmingly strives to label his essays, qualifying them as oriented either toward 'art criticism' or 'literary criticism', there are very few studies devoted to his essays qua essays.[13] Even Daniel Acke's densely researched *Bonnefoy essayiste*, the single critical volume wholly devoted to Bonnefoy's essays, does not address the problem of the essay as a specific genre. Acke focuses rather on the problem of how Bonnefoy's idea of *présence* responds to the crisis of modernity and its well-known doubt about the capacity for language to express thought. For Acke, Bonnefoy's essays provide 'a prime testimony to the difficult problem of the relationship between philosophical thought and literature'.[14] His brief comment demonstrates the persistence of the idea that Bonnefoy's essays can only be analysed as derivative, as witnesses to another battle, but not themselves producers of something new.

It is certainly true that many readers come late to Bonnefoy's essays. Seduced by the verse of Bonnefoy the poet, they come slowly to the essays to discover the thinker behind the poetry. For that approach, we feel intuitively, defines the essays of poets: prose that reveals the working of a mind that would otherwise remain hidden behind the scrim of poetic language. The reader of Bonnefoy's essays is not disappointed, for his essays do indeed reveal the intellectual, even philosophical, structures that inhabit his poetry. Yet, the complexity of the thought they reveal exacts a price: his essays have the popular reputation of being 'complicated', 'obscure', certainly, as numerous critics have suggested, far from transparent. Even Bonnefoy seems to concur with the description saying, 'Je suis surpris d'entendre parler de limpidité à mon propos' [I am surprised to hear people speak of limpidity with reference to my work] (*E*, 63). Indeed, at first (even second and third) reading, his essays do seem dense and difficult, uniting complex abstract concepts with a rich, poetic language that deals in paradox and syntactic complexity. A good example of this is seen when Bonnefoy creates an exact equivalence between *l'improbable* and *ce qui est* in his dedication to the 1959 essay collection, *L'Improbable*: 'Je dédie ce livre à l'improbable, c'est à dire à ce qui est' [I dedicate this book to the improbable, that is to say, to that which is]. Bonnefoy subsequently foregrounds this connection radically by giving his four essay collections the supra-title, *L'Improbable*.

Nonetheless, despite his essays' complexity and depth, a legitimate focus on Bonnefoy's poetry has all too frequently led critics to read his essays in a somewhat reductive manner, often describing them as no more than obscure but necessary companion pieces to his poetry. In keeping with that perception, shortly after the 1959 publication of *L'Improbable*, Olivier de Magny described it as an *ars poetica* consonant with 'the great didactic texts of Reverdy, Breton, and Jouve'.[15] The term *ars poetica* is probably a good description of Bonnefoy's essays. Still, the term also implies a need to explain and thus, by extension, anxiety regarding the reader's potential incomprehension, a fact that is picked up by Daniel Leuwers when he writes that Bonnefoy is 'a poet who is never quite sure of being completely understood through his poems alone, and [...] needs to accompany them with oblique texts'.[16] Leuwers's statement points toward the question that engendered the present work, that is, why the preponderance of essays within Bonnefoy's work?

What is their relationship to a poetry that he presents as the only vector of *présence*? Can they indeed be read as some form of anxiety regarding a message that might not be transmitted by the poetry alone?

Indeed, a shorthand definition of his essays would argue that their principal characteristic is their organization around the quest for *présence*, seen in things both ordinary and extraordinary: in the broken leaf dying on the ground, as well as in the most painstakingly created work of art. In other words, while Bonnefoy's essays address a great variety of subjects — ranging from mortuary ornaments in 'Les Tombeaux de Ravenne' [The Tombs of Ravenna] to Yeats and the notion of place in 'Byzance', or temporality in the paintings of Quattrocento artists — their central question is always this: has this work of art, this artist, this object, this person accounted for *présence*? If so, how? And if not, where has he, she, or it failed? Specifically, this serves, of course, to situate Bonnefoy's position. At the same time, however, the fact that all meaning rests upon one word underscores the idea that *présence* represents in a telegraphic manner the whole of Bonnefoy's intellectual and philosophical interaction not only with the natural world, but also with its representation through the art and writing. And it is precisely the ubiquity of the notion of *présence* which brings us to its universality in Bonnefoy's work. By universality, I mean something quite specific, which is that *présence* functions both as *telos* and as tool for Bonnefoy. Let me expand: *présence*, particularly in poetry, can be seen as the quiescent subject underlying each poetic image, in the sense that Bonnefoy wants us to see his poems as places of access to *présence*. In parallel, and more frequently used thus in the essays, *présence* also appears as the tool with which he analyses the cultural corpus contained in his essays. The general orientation of the essays is thus determined by Bonnefoy's attempt to investigate, develop, and finally express the specificity of this position. Still, the path is not immediately perceptible. That uniting of hope and poetry we saw earlier ('Je voudrais réunir, je voudrais identifier presque la poésie et l'espoir') reveals the tension at the heart of Bonnefoy's work. While the gist of the statement suggests that the essay must de facto be considered as inferior to poetry because it cannot attain the privileged status associated with the term 'hope', paradoxically, the very equating of poetry and hope is found in a prose sentence embedded in an essay.

Concerning that hierarchization — and the commensurate special status of poetry — it must be said that Bonnefoy clearly felt himself to be first and foremost a poet whose mission was to render unto poetry the ancient transformative power it once held. As the title of his essay 'Sur la fonction du poème' suggests, poetry has a function and thus a purpose, indeed, an ontological being that sets it apart from other literary forms; it has a power that transcends the limited intellectual nature of words agglomerated on a page. Poetry is, in fact, almost a belief akin to Pascal's leap of faith, which states that beyond rational understanding there exists a world which is no less real and true for not being immediately comprehensible: 'tout ce qui est incompréhensible ne laisse pas d'être'.[17] Parenthetically, perhaps, it must be said that certain aspects of the Pascalian position hover at the surface of Bonnefoy's consciousness. In a curious, quasi-apologetic footnote where he wonders if he has been too critical of Paul Valéry, he describes the private, internal battle against writers that 'exist *in us*', concluding that 'c'est peut-être un pari, dans le sens un peu grave que l'on donne à ce mot' [it is perhaps a wager, in the rather serious sense given to the word] (*I*, 105, n. 1). Bonnefoy's use of 'wager' evokes Pascal's 'pari sur l'existence de Dieu'; this, coupled with the fact that Pascal's name is not mentioned, seems to confirm his 'internalization'. The idea of a world not immediately accessible to us meshes well with the familiar idea that poetic language is somehow different from the ordinary 'mots de la tribu' that Mallarmé famously invokes in 'Le Tombeau d'Edgar Poe'.[18] It also harks back to a long-standing French critical tradition which has had a significant influence on the contemporary understanding of poetry. This tradition, reading Baudelaire's *Salon* pieces, or the texts of Mallarmé, Valéry, Reverdy and others, subordinates the essays of poets to their poetic production, using well-worn arguments such as the idea that prose is always more limpid, almost facile, when compared to the so-called 'difficult' or 'obscure' poetic text, and that a clear and discernible distinction always exists between prose and poetry. These statements are, of course, mere generalizations, but as such they contain a grain of truth: poetry is notorious for its perceived hermeticism, whereas it is rather rarer, though not of course impossible, to find prose that suffers from the same perception of disrepute. These distinctions have long been well-anchored: using the essayistic text to explain unclear elements of the poetry is an attitude at least partially engendered by the Romantic vision of the poet as a sort of divine oracle, a mouthpiece for poetry that comes from elsewhere. That mechanism is thematized very early in Bonnefoy's work. In the 1953 *Douve* cycle, he writes in the section tellingly entitled 'Douve parle':

> Pourtant ce cri sur moi vient de moi,
> Je suis muré dans mon extravagance.
> Quelle divine ou quelle étrange voix
> Eût consenti d'habiter mon silence?
>
> [And yet the cry comes from myself,
> I am walled up in my extravagance.
> What divine or what strange voice
> Would have agreed to live in my silence?][19]

The possibility of an exterior voice, foreign to the speaking 'I', is central in the poem. And though it is rejected there, comments made elsewhere by Bonnefoy indicate that the matter continued to haunt him, as he said in a 1979 interview: 'from my side of the poem', 'j'ai surtout l'expérience d'images qui me viennent obscures et qui le restent, et de contradictions que je n'arrive pas à lever' [I experience above all images that appear obscurely to me and remain so, contradictions that I cannot resolve] (*E*, 63). Thus, the Romantic view that the relationship between the poet and his poetry is governed by a form of scission renders the inferior status of the essay more comprehensible: because the poetic text is generated by an inspiration that remains exterior to the poet, he must himself become the critic of his own poem, since it remains potentially as opaque for him as for any other reader.

In parallel, and precisely because he understands this language as powerfully imposed from elsewhere, Bonnefoy can contend that *présence* is not merely symbolically constructed in language but can really inhabit certain poetic words, giving them a substance which contributes to the direct experience and potential transformation, not only of the reader, but of the writer himself. He writes:

> Les pouvoirs de la langue, c'est qu'elle peut rebâtir une économie de l'être-au-monde, une intelligence de ce qu'il est par rapport au regard désincarné de la science; c'est qu'il y a dans ses mots fondamentaux une incitation à se souvenir qu'il peut y avoir de l'être c'est-à-dire du sens, des lieux, de la présence et non de l'absence. (*E*, 21)

> [The power of language lies in the fact that it can rebuild an economy of being-in-the-world, an understanding of what it is, as opposed to the disembodied gaze of science; Contained in fundamental words is the incitement to remember that there can be being, that is, meaning, places and presence, not absence.]

What makes Bonnefoy's work so interesting is that he is not content to simply make such pronouncements. On the contrary, he musters the scientific rigour of linguistics to back up his philosophical intuition. Thus Florence de Lussy's description (written in close collaboration with him) demonstrates the 'technical' reasons for the primacy of poetry:

> La représentation détruit la présence, mais la poésie est justement ce qui veut briser cette clôture, sous l'effet de laquelle s'efface de la mémoire cette transcendance du monde sur le signe que l'on a nommé le divin. La poésie veut briser cette clôture, et elle le peut, parce que son recours à la part sonore du mot lui vaut de neutraliser dans la phrase, devenue vers, le système de représentations et de notions dont se compose 'l'image', le monde-image. Ce qui permet une entrevision, à tout le moins, du monde au-delà des mots : non comme figure, cette fois, mais comme 'présence'.[20]

> [Representation destroys presence, but poetry is precisely that which can abolish this closure, which erases from memory that transcendence of the world over the sign that we call the divine. Poetry seeks to overcome this closure; it can do so because it appeals to the sound-element of the word, thus allowing it, in a sentence that has become verse, to neutralize the system of representations and notions that compose the 'image', the world-image. This, at least, allows us a glimpse of the world beyond the words, not as figure this time, but as 'presence'.]

De Lussy's comment indicates that the very collision between the different material aspects of language gives poetry the possibility of abolishing the mental — hence conceptual — image created by words, thus consolidating the adamant distinction Bonnefoy makes between poetry and prose. 'La parole,' he writes, 'peut bien, *comme je le fais maintenant*, célébrer la présence, chanter son acte, nous préparer en esprit à sa rencontre, mais non pas nous permettre de l'accomplir' [Speech can indeed, *as I'm doing right now*, celebrate presence, sing its act, prepare us mentally to encounter it, but it cannot allow us to attain it] (*I*, 126, my emphasis). The phrase I have emphasized, 'as I'm doing right now', can be seen as designating the realm of essayistic prose that Bonnefoy is engaged in, indicating thereby that in the context of the essay, *parole* has no capacity to create a linguistic space within which prose could access *présence*, for granting it this capacity requires the intervention of the poetic act. As the following chapters show, I find this clear distinction to be deeply problematic.

Still, Bonnefoy's marginalization of his essays, whereby they become handmaids to the central poetic enunciation, itself derives from an implicit theoretical position. Alex Argyros, though he does not subscribe to the idea that a system of binary oppositions can explain the relationship between Bonnefoy's poetry and his essays, essentially presents the problem as it stands when he writes, 'For the most part, the poetry of Yves Bonnefoy has been read as an application of Bonnefoy's numerous theoretical statements concerning the function of poetry'. Hence the normative critical tendency has been to situate Bonnefoy's poetry and essays within a mechanism characterized by the opposition of two terms. Consequently, Argyros continues:

> Critical work on Bonnefoy [...] has operated within the horizon of one of the fundamental binary oppositions of Western esthetics: pure idea/ its reification [...] Specifically, the theory/ application couplet makes a number of implicit assumptions. It assumes the possibility of a clear demarcation between two identifiable realms: the realm of theoretical prose and that of its realization in verse.[21]

By seeing the poetry as the application of a theoretical precursor, Argyros reverses the direction that Bonnefoy himself gives to the genesis of his work. The point merits attention despite the fact that it is essentially an insoluble, chicken-and-egg problem of origin: which came first, the poetry oriented toward ontological concerns, or the ontological concerns which took the shape of poetry?

From a critical point of view, the very existence of essays within the context of Bonnefoy's explicit laudation of poetry creates a conundrum: do they really represent, as Leuwers suggests, some uncertainty regarding the transmission of a message through poetry? Certainly, Leuwers's hypothesis seems to be corroborated by the fact that Bonnefoy explicitly links his four first volumes of poetry with four specific essays: the *Douve* poem cycle with the essay, 'Les Tombeaux de Ravenne'; *Hier régnant désert* with 'L'Acte et le lieu de la poésie'; *Pierre écrite* with 'La Poésie française et le principe d'identité'; and finally, *Dans le leurre du seuil* with 'Baudelaire contre Rubens'. He describes the shift from poetry to essay as 'a use [*emploi*] of the categories of thought that had emerged from the writing of the poems'.[22] Implicit in the comment are certain assumptions that allow appreciable insight into Bonnefoy's understanding of the relationship between essay and poetry. A first significant point is that he explicitly associates each major volume of poetry with its 'own' essay. Although there can be no doubt about his sincerity in giving us this information, his linking of specific essays to companion pieces of poetry is a double-edged sword, for while it doubtless gives useful insight into his own understanding of his writing, it also has the latent function of orienting the reading of the essays and their corresponding poetic texts in the direction he would have us take. This caveat notwithstanding, the point to retain is that his own clear perception of a pattern of co-existence between poetry and essay hints at a symbiotic relationship between the two kinds of writing. This interconnection is further highlighted by his reference to the 'categories of thought', which suggests the existence of a semantic content which is both independent and transmissible, since it clearly has been transposed from the poetry into the essays. Particularly prevalent in the *Douve* poems and the essays of *L'Improbable*, the displacement of content from poetry to prose is highly pertinent to the question of the function of Bonnefoy's essays. For if his statement indicates that he believes his essays to carry on the intellectual work initiated in his poetry, by conjoining poetry and essayistic prose into a unified intellectual framework, Bonnefoy reveals two of the vital elements that shape his work: first, that both prose and poetry are a means to a greater end; and second, that both partake of a similar creative impulse rooted, naturally enough, in a single *imaginaire* — an *imaginaire*, nonetheless, that is characterized by its hierarchical structure. In his pairings, Bonnefoy carefully establishes his position by associating the essay with 'un emploi de' [a use of]. The term *emploi* is significant because it opposes poetry and prose by stressing the functional capacity of the latter, a notion that is further substantiated by his vehement 'justement, la poésie n'est pas un "emploi" de la langue' (*I*, 247), which suggests that to see poetry as a mere use of language is to debase it, to disallow its higher purpose.

In sum, then, faced with the specific problem of the essays, it would seem that Bonnefoy believes, and would have us believe, that his essays represent a struggle to understand the categories of thought generated by his poetry. Certain critics, most notably Gérard Gasarian, have already pointed out the difficulty of accepting that explanatory relationship. He writes:

> Even though they are more or less contemporaneous with the poetry, the essays do not explain the poems; rather, they complicate them, transferring their difficulty into a register that though it is more discursive, is not clearer. [...] The essays can be read independently from the poems [...], they convey not an exegetic thought process but a reflection that is itself poetic.[23]

Gasarian's reading goes to the heart of the problem that interests me. It suggests that far from being merely derivative, the essays obey their own creative impulses, and thus have their own purpose that can also be seen as poetic. Indeed, one of the specific characteristics of Bonnefoy's essays is that they resist the prose/poetry categorization, and consistently escape the model that Bonnefoy proposes for them. Rather than a clear and constant distinction between his poetry and his essayistic prose, what we see instead is a permeable and fluctuating boundary; and this for two very good reasons: first, is the idea that poetry and essay are two facets of a single higher goal, which is expressing *présence* through language; the second, though no less important point is that prose might, in fact, be necessary to convey the complete notion of *présence*. The latter idea is confirmed by Bonnefoy's acknowledgement that the capacity of poetry to be open to *présence* can also fail: 'le poème achevé ne parle pas, il *est*' [the finished poem does not speak, it *is*].[24] This, in turn, leads Argyros to write that:

The difference between a 'vrai lieu' and the poem as text, what Bonnefoy calls a 'poème achevé', is that while the former is a window to absolute plenitude, the latter does not serve as a sign announcing the extra-linguistic; it simply is.[25]

My goal is to investigate whether his essays really are limited to the activity of clarifying, or even dismantling, the zone of shadows produced by the poetry. For while Bonnefoy's essays do derive their meaning, and indeed, their rationale from his poetry, they are also unique in that they represent a specific response to the aesthetic and philosophical concerns which are central to his *œuvre*. In other words, his essays, precisely because they are essays, have a crucial role to play. They are a response to a plurality of needs that poetry cannot adequately fill, notably its holistic capture of *présence*. To adequately broach this notion, it is useful to bring in the idea of parergon, or 'addition' to the work (*ergon*), evoked both by Georg Lukács and Jacques Derrida. The theoretical usefulness of the parergon lies in its inherent quality of supplemental 'not-yetness' which causes Lukács to describe the essayist as a John the Baptist preaching in the wilderness about another yet to come. That 'other', for Lukács, is a unified aesthetic theory, a 'longing for value and form' that is the intrinsic desire of the essay.[26] In Bonnefoy's case, that 'other' translates to accessing *présence* through poetry. However, that access remains problematic, and it is Derrida's theorization of the parergon that provides an understanding of what the essay might be doing in Bonnefoy's work. Parerga, by definition, are external to the work, but as Derrida points out, they occupy a specific form of exteriority which 'touches', 'presses against', and adjoins the interior inasmuch as parerga are a response to the fact the inside is 'missing something'. Derrida adds, 'the parergon is against, beside, and above and beyond the ergon, the work accomplished, the accomplishment of the work. But it is not incidental; it is connected to and cooperates in its operation from the outside'.[27]

It thus follows that to study Bonnefoy's essays as mere adjuncts to his poetry is to do disservice to the totality of his project. As I suggested earlier, such an approach has not yet been fully explored; in the main, Bonnefoy's critics have tended to relegate his essays to the position of satellites revolving around the poetic centre, using them mainly to illuminate and clarify certain poetic problems and to demonstrate the theoretical position from which his poetry derives. My intent is to go beyond these critical positions and show that in Bonnefoy's work, transmitting the value both of *présence* and of subjectivity, is not the sole province of poetry. On the contrary, it is equally, if not more so, a philosophical ambition that Bonnefoy, using the tools of language, rhetoric, and form, attempts to delineate and express in his essays. In order to address this goal efficiently, my focus on Bonnefoy's essays is very much guided by the strategies he himself put into place to convey his message. Thus an important first point to note is that within the abundant and scattered corpus of Bonnefoy's essays, a number of them have a particular status inasmuch as they were gathered, organized, and presented as self-contained collections by the poet himself. For though the main body of his essays was given the general title of *L'Improbable*, that supra-title consists of four independent volumes: *L'Improbable* (1959), *Un rêve fait à Mantoue* (1967), *Le Nuage rouge* (1977), and *La Vérité de parole*

(1988). Though the critical essays contained in these volumes are generally unified by the fact that they remain firmly rooted in the problems and imaginative spaces of the Western cultural tradition, they can literally be read as a single unified structure. In a bibliographic note to the last volume, *La Vérité de parole*, Bonnefoy clearly indicates the relationship between the different volumes when he says that *La Vérité de parole* is the third volume of *L'Improbable*, a collection of essays on poetics whose first two parts are *L'Improbable* (along with *Un rêve fait à Mantoue*) and *Le Nuage rouge*.[28] The most important information revealed by his statement is the architecture of the whole structure.

In the present work, though I use all four of the volumes collected under the general title of *L'Improbable*, I focus more specifically on those contained in the 1980 *L'Improbable*. That volume provides material that is particularly interesting in establishing the generic parallels between poetry and essay because Bonnefoy explicitly combines there essayistic prose with poetic texts. Additionally, the essays collected there have a greater degree of textual existence as integrated structures because they have repeatedly been reprinted as such, at times with substantial modifications, thus more clearly demonstrating Bonnefoy's on-going intellectual structuring of the essays.[29] Indeed, the 1980 edition combines into a single volume two texts that were originally stand-alone books, *L'Improbable* and *Un rêve fait à Mantoue*. It bridges them with four additional essays entitled 'Quatre notes', while inserting two new essays into the *Un rêve fait à Mantoue* section of the volume. This careful construction demonstrates the functional ambitions Bonnefoy attributes to his essays, and drives my analysis of their purpose. For though the unifying theme of the collections as a whole is a reflection on poetics, in *L'Improbable* essay and poetry really do merge, not only through their common projection of the core ideas structuring Bonnefoy's writing, but also through the literal integration in each case of identifiably poetic texts: 'Dévotion' for *L'Improbable*, and 'Sept feux' for *Mantoue*. Further, essay and poetry also fuse through the indubitably poetic qualities of their language as well as the continuous interplay of the images that cross and re-cross the highly permeable boundary between them. Finally, though it is clear that Bonnefoy took considerable pains to construct them as volumes, this structuring has not yet been the object of critical study. This is clearly a lacuna, for Bonnefoy's use of individual essays to complement the poetic transmission of *présence* is no less significant than the choice to select, collect, and organize a number of essays and then present them in structured groups. Clearly, this purposeful decision is of significance.

The present work is organized into four chapters that seek to understand the place and function of Bonnefoy's essays in the body of his work, starting from the observation that neither *présence* nor the essay are elements that Bonnefoy created *ex nihilo* for his own communicative purposes. The first two chapters emerge from the initial questions that motivated my inquiry — why *présence*? why the essay? — and try to move beyond Bonnefoy's choices to perceive the outlines of his intellectual project. Chapter One strikes out beyond the normative descriptions of *présence* that have been such a ubiquitous component of much of the critical analysis of Bonnefoy's work, starting instead from the fact that as a theological and philosophical construct, *présence* is a notion that far antedates his use of it. It is also a hybrid notion, both experience and idea, and is inherently linked with the deictic *origo* that figures so prominently in his writing. The chapter thus focuses on the reasons that might have brought him to build his entire poetics on this cornerstone, and examines how he uses rhetorical tools such as deixis to mould *présence* to fit his own purposes. Indeed, if the theological dimension of *présence* allows Bonnefoy to claim a sense of moral gravity and desire for communion and community, its phenomenological axis allows him to mount a defence against the challenge brought to *présence* by postmodern and deconstructionist analyses of language.

Chapter Two, in tackling the question of 'why the essay?', describes the hierarchization that explicitly places Bonnefoy's essays at an inferior level with respect to his poetry. As the chapter shows, this distinction stems from the supposedly self-evident nature of the essay: just as with the notion of *présence*, everyone 'knows' what an essay is. At a primary level, this familiarity undoubtedly factors into Bonnefoy's frequent use of the genre. The chapter shows, however, that the attraction for the essay also plays out at a more subliminal level connected with notions of individuation and immediacy that concatenate with the characteristics of *présence*, particularly that experience/idea duality mentioned above. While conveying concepts, the essay also reproduces that immediacy, using the deictic 'I', 'here', and 'now' in ways that many other forms of writing cannot broach as naturally. Its strength also lies in its propensity to speak from a seemingly tentative, subjective point of view that explicitly presents itself as non-narcissistic. What the essay can *do* lies thus at the core of why Bonnefoy chooses it to parallel his poetic production. The chapter thus examines the essay from the perspective of the essayist — who, inevitably, is also a reader — to see how its various rhetorical and functional characteristics (stylistic malleability, absence of rhetorical constraints, 'truth' potential, but also community-building and didacticism) create a literary space that matches the *présence* that Bonnefoy urgently needed to communicate.

Chapter Three returns to the double qualities of *présence* to address the role the essay plays in fulfilling Bonnefoy's goal of synthesizing concept and experience to transmit *présence*. It engages with the theoretical and rhetorical parallels that exist between essay and poetry to explain how, despite Bonnefoy's dispraise of the essay, the latter actually has more functional usefulness for him in conveying the duality of *présence*. Indeed, in contradistinction to his poetry, it is only in the essay that Bonnefoy gives imaged descriptions of *présence*. In part, this is, as I show, because many of the defining elements that seem proper to poetry can transfer with minimal difficulty to the essay. Both genres, for instance, have an identical predilection for a voice that takes the experience of the speaking 'I' as the central dynamic. Both genres also explicitly work to demonstrate the truth potential of any subject, no matter how trivial. The chapter thus uses Bonnefoy's two notable descriptions of *présence* (the 'leaf' and the 'salamander' episodes) to show how they play into the didactic ambitions that are a latent characteristic of the essay and its possibility for furthering a teleological goal that might even function better by remaining subliminal.

Finally, Chapter Four focuses on Bonnefoy's collected essays to show how he uses both the genre's proximity to *présence* and its unassuming claim to truth to engage in a high degree of structuring that counteracts the fragmentary character of the essay. The genesis of these collections derives from the conscious ordering of extant pieces and reveals an authorial hand whose goal of transmitting *présence* is subliminally rendered by the fact that each essay shows a moment that allowed him to construct his own understanding. These combined factors allow Bonnefoy's collected essays to be read cartographically as the itinerary showing how he arrived at his own understanding of *présence*. Such a structuring, I argue, reveals a latent autobiographical function linked to the often-unexpressed didactic ambitions that subtend Bonnefoy's essayistic work. This reading is based on theories of postmodern allegory, which suggest that its function is to point to and reinforce the figure of the author. The proto-autobiographical nature of the essay can easily be demonstrated, inasmuch as both genres merge author, narrator, and character. At the same time, however, the rhetorical identity of the essay deconstructs its autobiographical potential by highlighting its tentative nature and downplaying the focus on the 'I'. This strategy requires the reader to engage in a form of allegoresis to recognize the full dimension of Bonnefoy's intent. Indeed, the teleological objective of showing *présence* imperfectly masks the broader purpose of making a mark on, and perhaps even transforming, readers in order to return them to poetry. Thus the trope of the itinerary is motivated by its purpose: allowing us to become the 'better readers' that Borges evokes, for the goal of describing the itinerary is to provide some form of guidance that becomes available only if the reader can be brought to read the collected essays through the matrix of allegoresis, and to make use of the map that they indicate.

Notes to the Introduction

1. Borges, Jorge Luis. *Historia universal de la infamia* (Madrid: Alianza, 1998), front matter.
2. Yves Bonnefoy, *L'Improbable et autres essais, suivi de Un rêve fait à Mantoue* (Paris: Gallimard, 1983), p. 126. All further quotations from this work are from this edition, hereafter referenced as *I* in the main text.
3. A lesser strand of his work includes short pieces of philosophical fiction he called 'dream-narratives'.
4. See, for example, Gérard Gasarian, *Yves Bonnefoy: la poésie, la présence* (Seysell: Champ Vallon, 1986), or the work of John Jackson, Richard Vernier, Richard Stamelman, John Naughton, and others.
5. Μετάνοια, a transformation of the mind.
6. This English translation is a frequently cited approximation of 'nach Auschwitz ein Gedicht zu schreiben ist barbarisch'. Theodor Adorno, *Prismen: Kulturkritik und Gesellschaft* (Munich: Deutscher Taschenbuch, 1963), p. 26.
7. Benoît Denis, *Littérature et engagement: de Pascal à Sartre* (Paris: Seuil, 2000), p. 19.
8. Ibid., p. 71.
9. *Yves Bonnefoy: poésie, art et pensée. Colloque international 9–11 mai 1983*, ed. by Yves-Alain Favre (Pau: Publications de l'Université de Pau et des pays de l'Adour, 1983), p. 5. This written compilation of talks delivered at a symposium at which Bonnefoy was present includes Bonnefoy's own talk, as well as his reactions to each talk, hereafter referenced as *YB* in the main text.

10. Yves Bonnefoy, *Entretiens sur la poésie (1972–1990)* (Paris: Mercure de France, 1990), p. 273 (hereafter referenced as *E* in the main text).

11. Yves Bonnefoy, 'Le Carrefour dans l'image', in Arnaud Buchs, *Yves Bonnefoy à l'horizon du surréalisme: la réalité à l'épreuve du langage* (Paris: Galilée, 2005), pp. 11–32 (p. 12).

12. Laurent Lemire, 'Interview d'Yves Bonnefoy, poète', *Agitateur d'idées*, 23 March 2009 <http://www.agitateur-idees.fr/Site/suite.php?art=86>.

13. Concetta Cavallini, *Langage et poésie: lire Yves Bonnefoy* (Millau: Alain Baudry, 2009), p. 140.

14. Daniel Acke, *Yves Bonnefoy essayiste: modernité et présence* (Amsterdam & Atlanta, GA: Rodopi, 1999), p. 5.

15. As quoted by F. C. St. Aubyn in 'Yves Bonnefoy: First Existentialist Poet', *Chicago Review*, 17. 1 (1964), 118–29 (p. 118).

16. Daniel Leuwers, *Yves Bonnefoy* (Amsterdam: Rodopi, 1988), p. 62.

17. Blaise Pascal, *Œuvres complètes* (Paris: Seuil, 1963), p. 530 (frag. 230–430 *bis*).

18. Stéphane Mallarmé, *Poésies* (Paris: Gallimard, 1979), p. 94.

19. Yves Bonnefoy, *Poèmes: Du mouvement et de l'immobilité de Douve, Hier régnant désert, Pierre écrite, Dans le leurre du seuil* (Paris: Gallimard, 1982), p. 79 (hereafter referenced as *P* in the main text); *On the Motion and Immobility of Douve*, trans. by Galway Kinnell, (Newcastle upon Tyne: Bloodaxe Books, 1992), p. 91 (hereafter referenced as *D* in the main text).

20. Florence de Lussy and Yves Bonnefoy, *Yves Bonnefoy: livres et documents*, exhibition catalogue (Paris: Bibliothèque nationale de France, 1992), p. 155.

21. Alex Argyros, 'The Topography of Presence: Bonnefoy and the Spatialisation of Poetry', *Orbis Litterarium*, 41 (1986), 244–64 (p. 244).

22. de Lussy and Bonnefoy, *Yves Bonnefoy*, p. 166.

23. Gasarian, *Yves Bonnefoy*, p. 10, n. 1.

24. Yves Bonnefoy, *Le Nuage rouge: essais sur la poétique* (Paris: Mercure de France, 1977; repr. 1992), p. 271 (hereafter referenced as *NR* in the main text).

25. Argyros, 'The Topography of Presence', p. 251.

26. Georg Lukács, *Soul and Form*, trans. by Anna Bostock (Cambridge, MA: MIT Press, 1974), pp. 16, 17.

27. Jacques Derrida, 'The Parerga', trans. by Craig Owens, *October*, 9 (1979), 3–41 (pp. 21, 20).

28. Yves Bonnefoy, *La Vérité de parole* (Paris: Mercure de France, 1988), p. 331 (hereafter referenced as *VP* in the main text).

29. The Mercure de France edition of *L'Improbable* has been printed three times (1959, 1980, and 1992), the Gallimard/Folio edition twice (1980, 1992).

CHAPTER 1

❖

Why 'présence?'

L'objet sensible est présence. Il se distingue du conceptuel avant tout par un acte, c'est la présence.
Et par un glissement. Il est ici, il est maintenant.

[The sensate object is presence. It differs from conceptuality above all by an act, which is presence. And by a shift. It is here, it is now.] (*I*, 26)

The notion of *présence* is of such pivotal importance in Bonnefoy's poetics that hardly any critic studying his work fails to give at least a sketchy definition of what the word means and how the poet uses it.[1] While it is true that it is virtually impossible to understand Bonnefoy's work without understanding the term, its ubiquity there has transformed it into a sort of intellectual shorthand that circumvents deeper reflection on what it might mean. Further, in the light of that recurrent use, many critics have very naturally focused on discussing how *présence* appears in Bonnefoy's writing without necessarily seeking to examine the reasons subtending his determination to construct his position around the word. They are supported in this approach by the idea that the notion appears so transparent that it hardly needs any further explication: everyone knows what *présence* means. In reality, however, the notion obeys a sort of rule that seems to govern simple things: the more one looks at them, the more complex they turn out to be. Hence, *présence* is a much more enigmatic and multifarious notion than appears at first glance, and this even within Bonnefoy's own appreciation of the term, which underwent notable modifications over the course of his career.

Indeed, it is telling that the earliest incarnations of the web of interlocking ideas and experiences that would eventually become Bonnefoy's *présence* had different names: *le sensible* [the sensate] and *la substance*, both of which he abandoned in favour of the term which is so familiar to his readers.[2] In a 1972 interview, he explains why he eschewed *le sensible*:

C'est un mot [le sensible] que je n'emploie plus, car on pourrait le comprendre comme signifiant 'concret', 'réservé à la pratique des sens', alors qu'il ne s'agit pas pour moi de la simple apparence, de la texture du monde, mais de ce qui, au contraire, échappe à la perception, quitte à lui conférer en retour son intensité, son sérieux. (*E*, 57–58)

[It is a word that I no longer use, because it might be understood as meaning 'concrete', 'limited to the use of the senses'. But I'm not referring just to the appearance, the texture of the world, but to that which, on the contrary, escapes perception, even if only to re-endow it with its intensity, its gravity.]

A comparison of the 1959 and the 1980 editions of *L'Improbable* renders this comment even clearer. In the 1980 version of the essay 'Paul Valéry', Bonnefoy writes a condemnatory phrase which strikes at the core of his criterion for judgment: the all-important notion of *présence*: 'Valéry a méconnu le mystère de la présence' ['Valéry failed to understand he mystery of presence'] (*I*, 100). In 1959, by contrast, that sentence read: 'Valéry a méconnu le mystère de la substance'.[3] The substitution of the newer term points to a dematerialisation of the original notion, taking it beyond the passive thingness of matter toward a more dynamic notion of being. It also allows us to glean a notion of what *présence* is not, insofar as one understands that it is not only the natural quality of the world, but rather something which lies beyond perception, while acting on this very perception to give it a resonance stronger that a mere physical experience of the world.

However, in the rush to bind *présence* to Bonnefoy, what has often been side-lined is the fact that the word is an appropriation, a borrowing both from theology and from philosophy. That this borrowing is conscious is clearly indicated in the Bibliothèque nationale's description of its 1992 Yves Bonnefoy exhibition. Discussing Bonnefoy's readings of Plotinus, Shestov, and others, the text asks whether these 'books that mattered' belonged in the categories of philosophy or theology. The answer is telling: 'The most important ones lay on the boundaries between the two'.[4] These two vectors of Bonnefoy's work are pervasive enough to have each been the object of critical analysis, but they have rarely been addressed together. Yet, they interlock, for they both encapsulate the struggle to arrive at an ontological understanding of reality. This single goal perhaps crystallizes best the usefulness of *présence* for Bonnefoy and underscores the idea that his *présence* is a hybrid distillation, a fusion not only of the two currents of thought that have fed into it historically, but also of its own inherent duality, which combines concept and experience. Recognizing these underlying theo-philosophical anchors enables us to grasp the gravity with which Bonnefoy approaches the issues that are at stake for him. These stakes are necessarily high, because he is striving to transmit a position that contains an ontological, even profoundly moral dimension.

The object of this chapter is to examine how Bonnefoy's development of his own hybrid notion of *présence* is intellectually grounded in the theological and philosophical dimensions of the term. These axes are important, for they determine the tools he adopted to transmit *présence*, among the most important of which are the various literary forms used — essay, poetry, and narrative — as well as his reliance on linguistics, as seen through a co-opted structuralist lexicon and the insistent mobilizing of deixis. Commensurately, his grappling with the language-oriented thinking of philosophers and phenomenologists such as Hegel, Husserl, Heidegger, Saussure, and Derrida contributed heavily to his construction of his own vision of *présence*, as did his brief passage through the winds of surrealism. This double strand is clearly evident in his comment that 'après le surréalisme ce furent précisément ces pages de la *Phénoménologie de l'Esprit* qui ont été un des ébranlements fondateurs de ma réflexion poétique, ces pages sur l'ici-et-maintenant' [after surrealism, it was precisely those pages on the here-and-now in the *Phenomenology of the Spirit* that rocked the foundations of my poetic thinking] (*YB*, 45). This chapter thus functions chronologically, dealing first with the theological roots of *présence* and their correlation with Bonnefoy's use of deixis, and then focusing on the pivotal place *présence* has occupied in the phenomenological currents that swirled through twentieth-century philosophy and culminated in the deconstructionist challenge to the very notion.

★   ★   ★   ★   ★

A first question: why spend time on the theological foundations with respect to a poet who overtly disclaims his own adhesion to Christian doctrine, saying most notably in *Entretiens sur la poésie*, 'je ne suis pas chrétien. [...] je n'ai pas de foi' [I am not Christian. [...] I have no faith] (*E*, 46)? Indeed, Richard Vernier describes Bonnefoy's theological stance as one of 'subversion radicale', warning readers of the danger of any hasty assimilation of Bonnefoy's position to that of a 'chrétien qui s'ignore' [a Christian unaware of his Christianity].[5] Nevertheless, Bonnefoy's work is riddled with allusions to elements of Christian theology and is permeated with a sort of nostalgia for religion, a feeling he defends by pointing out that both poetry and religion address the same life-issues, each providing answers that are necessarily related.[6] And though Vernier's point is well-taken, it is indeed the Christian paradigm that provides a first step in understanding the particularity of Bonnefoy's *présence*. The poet explains the double poles of his attraction to and rejection of Christianity by locating the difficulty of modern poetry in the fact that it must simultaneously define itself through Christianity and against it (*I*, 122). This is because Christianity hinges upon the suffering of a specific individual, Jesus Christ, at a specific time and place, thus giving dignity and worth to the singularity of each being. And yet, Bonnefoy says, 'le christianisme n'affirme qu'un court instant l'existence singulière. Chose créée, il la reconduit à Dieu dans les voies de la Providence et voici *ce qui est* privé une fois encore de sa valeur absolue' [Only for a brief instant does Christianity affirm singular existence. Once created, that existence is returned to God through the paths of Providence, leaving *that which is* once again bereft of its absolute value] (*I*, 122).

Statements such as this have provided fertile terrain for a more explicitly religious interpretation of Bonnefoy's work, and a number of critics have shown how his use of the word *présence* recapitulates some of the more 'technical' aspects of its theological roots. Ronald Gérard Giguère suggests this parallel, explaining that in Christian dogma Jesus incarnates both the Father and the Verb, which are doubly given to the world through the Gospels and the person of the Christ. He equates Bonnefoy's work to this, asking whether his poetry 'is not an attempt to give the world back poetic language through its ability to incarnate reality'.[7] His comment recapitulates a goal that underpins much of Bonnefoy's commitment to a *présence* that would inhabit poetry through the latter's capacity to show reality through language. This goal, however, is an ideal whose realisation is always in doubt, for the fraught question of whether the type of transcendence suggested by the term *présence* can be obtained through language is precisely the central problem of

Bonnefoy's work. This residual anxiety pierces through much of his writing and serves as catalyst for my main argument, which is that his essays are the tangible, material demonstration of his subterranean fear that poetic language might not suffice to invoke *présence*; that some other form of writing might be needed to transmit his ontological position. And the essays are, in fact, suffused with language clearly consonant with a theological lexicon ('salvation', 'original sin', 'communion', 'sacrifice', 'negative theology', etc.), even if his use of this vocabulary deviates explicitly from its religious anchors. A case in point is Bonnefoy's frequent use of the deictic expression *hic et nunc*. The expression is closely connected to a theological past, as indeed Jean-Pierre Jossua, who has written extensively on the relationship between Bonnefoy and Christian theology, reminds us when he says that:

> The expression *hic et nunc* is [...] Christian and theological. Indeed, while the combining of the adverbs — absent the copula — is not unknown in classical Latin, it is characteristic of Christian Latin, in which the ordinary meaning ('in the present circumstances') is often invested with a precise connotation: on this earth, as opposed to eternity and beyond.[8]

Bonnefoy's use of such a highly connoted vocabulary strongly suggests that the historically theological dimension of *présence* is substantively assimilated into his own form of it, as indeed is confirmed by statements such as his 'qu'on le sache ou non, qu'on le veuille ou pas, on est toujours engagé dans ce qui est par essence contradictoire, et qu'il faut bien appeler, d'un mot aujourd'hui suspect, notre dimension religieuse' [whether we are aware of it or not, whether we like it or not, we are always engaged in something that is essentially contradictory, and which we must call, using an expression that has now become suspect, our religious dimension] (*E*, 41).

Beyond vocabulary, however, Bonnefoy's writing is imbued with a lucid under-standing of the figures and narrative elements of Christian tradition as, for example, when he analyses the hopefulness of what he calls 'the myth of the Nativity', only to conclude that it gives him 'not faith, of course, but faith in the possibility of faith' (*E*, 46). Similarly, the emblematic attention he gives in 'Les Tombeaux de Ravenne' to a broken leaf explicitly makes of it the very figure of a form of salvation. Clearly, what Bonnefoy rejects is the purely theological proposition that makes salvation accessible solely through the dogmas of faith. It is, in fact, the rejection of this proposition that allowed him to develop his own position, forging it first out of the rejection of surrealism and then honing it through the tools provided by linguistics, language, and genre.

★   ★   ★   ★   ★

As concerns surrealism, there is certainly no question about Bonnefoy's temporary allegiance to the movement: it has been examined by a number of critics (Buchs, Jackson, and others), and the poet himself addresses the vital importance that surrealism had for his younger self in a series of interviews reprinted in *Entretiens sur la poésie*. However, as early as 1947, Bonnefoy took his distance from surrealism in reaction to his nascent realization that the exclusive attention to the imagination preached by the more dogmatic surrealists might not suffice to maintain the links between the individual and the world.[9] When he finally refused to sign the 1947 surrealist manifesto *Rupture inaugurale*, the divergences between Bonnefoy and the surrealists were already sufficiently established so that the final break was hardly the occasion of high emotion. In a later interview with John E. Jackson (1976), Bonnefoy states that neither drama nor insults marked the event, Breton simply refusing to shake hands at the end of the meeting (*E*, 71).

What then did Bonnefoy take from surrealism? In an early piece published in *La Révolution la nuit*, his journal of short duration (two issues, 1945–46), Bonnefoy grappled with the relationship between surrealism and science. Impressed with the then-recent discoveries in the physical and biological sciences, Bonnefoy was nonetheless perturbed to find that the scientific eye penetrates the real objects of the world, discarding their holistic *présence* in order to address their particular or atomic existence. He recalls his discomfiture in *Entretiens sur la poésie*, where he notes that contrary to the modern sciences, 'l'ancienne science' could maintain all aspects of reality in an integrated network of correspondences (*E*, 73). By contrast, then, with the blindness of science to the reality perceived on a human scale through the apparatus of the human senses, Bonnefoy appreciated in surrealism the hallmark term of *le merveilleux*, or attentiveness to the juxtapositions and coincidences connecting the things of the world, which was clearly a first step toward *présence* (*E*, 90).

And yet, surrealism also failed Bonnefoy. The 'network of correspondences' turns out to be as absent from the surrealist vision as it is from the scientific approach to reality. More precisely, the problem of surrealism lay in what Bonnefoy perceived as its inadequate grasp, or even distortion, of reality. Daniel Leuwers describes Bonnefoy's position: 'The Surrealist image or object claim to seek reality, but in the end, they do no more that cut a hole out of reality, thus diminishing reality itself'.[10] Leuwers's rather abstract position is rendered clearer when juxtaposed with Bonnefoy's appreciation of certain surrealist works. Although he admired Breton's *Les Vases communicants* and *L'Amour fou*, his disappointment with *Nadja* derived from his perception that instead of being attentive to the reality and rhythms of other individuals, *Nadja* was rather a solipsistic imposition of Breton's own viewpoint on the personality of the main character. Breton, Bonnefoy averred, was completely caught up in an illusory supremacy; though he believed he saw Nadja as a free presence, he did not, in reality, allow her her own truth, which was too simple, too banal (*E*, 123). The reference here is, of course, to Breton, in *Nadja* bitterly reproaching the young woman for giving free rein to her 'idle chatter rather than the other remarks which were so important to me'.[11] From this type of comment, one easily gleans the fact that Breton constructed reality instead of reading it and this, in Bonnefoy's eyes, was a perversion of the attitude we should have toward the world. Finally, in his later description of his break with surrealism, it is noteworthy that the clearest element of Bonnefoy's opposition is based neither on a point of poetic technique, nor on definitions of poetry, but on the failure of surrealism to understand the grounding unity of the world, a failure he couches in explicitly

religious terms, writing that it was an underlying idea of 'unity' that he describes as
'religieux', 'le sacré en puissance', that engendered his rejection of surrealism, 'dont
l'erreur fut au total de ne pas avoir foi dans les formes simples de la vie, préférant
le déploiement de l'imaginaire au resserrement de l'évidence, la roue du paon aux
pierres du seuil' [whose error, in the end, lay in its inability to have faith in the
simple things of life, preferring the unfurling of the imagination to a centring on
reality, the fanning of the peacock's tail to the stones of the threshold] (E, 82).

   In this text, Bonnefoy accuses surrealism of not having kept the faith because
of its fundamental incapacity to perceive the unity that forms the linking web of
reality; however, the theological axis to Bonnefoy's thought is broader and lies not
so much in the narratives and symbols of Christianity, but rather in the fact that his
writing addresses notions of transcendence and communion that are generally more
germane to a religious viewpoint. He writes in *Entretiens sur la poésie*:

> Que je dise: *le pain, le vin*, ces deux mots seulement, et l'on aura tout de suite à
> l'esprit, je pense, un certain type de relations essentielles entre les êtres [...], ce
> sont là des mots pour la communion, des mots qui font souvenir que la langue
> n'est pas vouée seulement à décrire les apparences, mais à nous tourner vers
> autrui pour fonder avec lui un lieu et décider de son sens. (E, 21)

> [If I say, *bread, wine*, just those two words, immediately, I believe, one thinks of
> certain types of essential relationships between beings [...]; those are the words
> of communion, words that remind us that the task of language is not simply to
> describe appearances, but to turn us towards others in order to create together
> a place and decide its meaning.]

Unsurprisingly then, critic Svein Eirik Fauskevag attributes to Bonnefoy's poetry a
Eucharistic function, writing that 'its goal aims at expressing ontological presence
both universally and plurally'.[12] Symbolically, its association with a core element of
Christian theology certainly contributes to legitimating the gravity of Bonnefoy's
tone, as well as the moral imperative toward *présence* that emanates from his writing,
emerging in sentences such as 'une intention de salut [...] est le seul souci du poème'
[an intention of salvation [...] is the poem's only concern] (I, 252). This meshes well
with the Eucharist, for of the Christian sacraments, the Eucharist and the idea of
communion it proposes is the one most closely associated with the notion of *présence*.
It is also the one has posed the greatest difficulty throughout the centuries. The
underlying question — can something truly be present in something else? — is one
that has continued to haunt the human psyche, gradually evolving from a purely
religious matter to a broader philosophical questioning of the capacity of language
to contain meaning. More concretely, the Eucharist is grounded in a celebrated
deictic phrase that has historically engendered much theological furore: *hic est corpus
meum*. As it happens, this double use of deictics (*hic* and *meum*) is of direct import to
the Bonnefoy reader because the frequent use of deixis is a prominent characteristic
of his work. Strikingly present in one of his earliest poems, 'Anti-Platon' (1947), it
continued to inform his thinking throughout his career, for in an email to me (17
June 2010), he indicated that 'la deixis est le porche de la création poétique' [deixis
is the antechamber to poetic creation]. Along with the essay and the lexicon of

structuralism, deixis is one of the key tools Bonnefoy mustered with the double goal of both allowing concrete access to *présence* and intellectually grounding the argument describing this possibility. This, of course, begs the question of why deixis should be so useful for Bonnefoy.

⋆   ⋆   ⋆   ⋆   ⋆

Karl Bühler's influential *Sprachtheorie* (1934) provides one theoretical description of deixis which is central to the very words and expressions that so constantly appear in Bonnefoy's writing. As we will see, it also sheds light on his predilection for the essay. Bühler proposes the notion of a deictic *origo* at the intersection of three axes defined as temporal, spatial, and subjective. His *origo* is a 'zero point', or a fixed instance that involves positing the time of utterance as 'now', the place as 'here', and the speaker as 'I'. What is remarkable about these three terms as acoustic phenomena, suggests Bühler, is their requirements: 'schau auf mich als Augenblicksmarke das eine, als Ortsmarks das andere, als Sendermarke (Sendercharakteristikum) das dritte' [see me as the mark of the moment, for the first, as the mark of the place, for the second; and for the third, as the mark of the sender].[13] He thus posits all speech as a series of modulations based on the central triplet of *ego*, *hic*, and *nunc*. In various forms, these terms reverberate throughout Bonnefoy's work. His early poem, 'Hic est locus patriae', for example, explicitly thematizes the notion of place. Even more telling is a statement from the essay, 'Paul Valéry', where Bonnefoy uses italics to put 'ce que Valéry croit réel, *la* mer et *l'*olivier et *le* vent' [that which Valéry believes to be real, *the* sea, *the* olive tree, and *the* wind] into vivid opposition with a more terrestrial form of reality embodied by 'cet olivier, mais dans sa différence profonde, son existence de *hic et nunc*, son être qui sous la hache ou l'incendie le perdra' [this olive tree, in its profound difference, its *hic et nunc* existence, its being, which the axe or fire will strip from it] (*I*, 100).

Beginning with subjectivity, Bühler's '*origo*' model allows us to see how temporality, spatiality, and subjectivity concatenate with what Bonnefoy is trying to achieve through the deictic markers so prevalent in his poems and essays. Though Bühler suggests that *ego*, *hic*, and *nunc* are inextricably simultaneous, the notion of subjectivity would nonetheless appear to be coterminous with the very possibility of a deictic enunciation. Indeed, in order to localize and project a stable *hic* and *nunc*, an anchoring *ego* must determine the loci of the deictic words used. Now while this primary occurrence of a person materially able to project a subjective self is primordial in an ordinary speech act — seen, for example, in the ostensible conflation between the speaker and the user of the word 'I' — this same projection of the self becomes infinitely more complicated in the act of writing where deictic subjectivity arguably becomes a sort of fiction. It is precisely this relationship between language and subjectivity posited by deixis that lies at the heart of Bonnefoy's preoccupations. Indeed, the necessity for the subject to find an authentic and individual 'I' in spite of the prison of linguistic structures, comes through in his insistence on appropriating language through individual speech-acts, through what might be more familiar to the reader as the Saussurean term *parole*. In Bonnefoy's view, it is only when the structure of language has been individuated by the speaker that *présence* can inhabit the text and become accessible to the reader. Commensurately, his constant shifting between the highly subjective genres of poetry and essay suggests the great significance he attaches to establishing the subject qua subject at the centre of the utterance. Bonnefoy frequently reiterates the idea that poetry must seek to show, creating a direct connection with the reader through a perception of immediacy. The essay, as the following chapters demonstrate, contains the same mimetic form of interaction between writing subject and reader.

Beyond subjectivity, however, it is in the way the *nunc* and the *hic* axes of deixis relate to the act of writing and reading that we can more clearly grasp the fundamental importance that deixis might have for Bonnefoy's goal of overcoming the barriers between language and reality. As concerns the *nunc* axis, although its expression of a 'now-ness' seems in a true discourse situation to be wholly bound to the moment of enunciation, the parameters again change radically in writing, for the temporal standpoint is transformed by the dynamics of reading: the 'now' of the author and the 'now' of the reader are indubitably non–identical, clearly pointing to two distinct moments in time. Paradoxically, however, through the dynamic act of reading, the reader is always engaged in a present moment that replicates the moment of writing, thus suggesting the engagement of the reader in what is potentially a collaborative effort of writing and interpretation. This point meshes well with Bonnefoy's claim that poetry can provide an access to *présence* that cannot — and indeed *must* not — be limited to the passive reception of a finished text but is obtainable only through a specific process defined as an 'act' undertaken by both the writer and the reader.

This dynamic process of interaction between writer and reader is reiterated in the *hic* dimension. Considered at its originary, pre–writing level, the *hic* aspect of deixis has driven a number of philosophers, Bühler included, to posit that subjectivity itself is grounded in a perception of the boundaries of one's own body. This reference to the creation of place via one's corporeal existence cannot but resonate for readers of Bonnefoy, who are familiar with the expression *vrai lieu*, or 'true place' that navigates almost obsessively throughout his poetry and his essays. His often-cited phrase, 'le vrai lieu est toujours un ici' (*I*, 22) consolidates the deictic quality of poetry as a 'here' which *présence* might occupy. However, if a concrete verbal exchange between two people can easily allow us to conceptualize how a feeling for the *présence* of an object or a subject can occur within the immediacy of the physical space, once again, it is more difficult to see how such a feeling might emanate from a written text. The seemingly transparent connection Bonnefoy makes between 'here' and *présence* via the link of the *vrai lieu* challenges us to confirm the paradigm by examining how the written text modifies the notion of spatial deixis in his work. A good example is found in the 'Dédicace' to *L'Improbable*, where the literary space of the dedication and the space of the text to come are related through the spatiality of writing. When Bonnefoy writes in that striking opening statement, 'je dédie ce livre à l'improbable, c'est-à-dire, à ce qui est', the sentence coalesces both a metaphorical and a physical dimension. Indeed, one can legitimately consider that a written text quite literally creates a physical space concretely inhabited by symbols, which are, again, also of a physical nature (e.g. shape, style, typography, etc.). The textual 'here' of the writer thus becomes a deictic 'here' that uses words as symbols pointing not to an extra-linguistic reality, but rather toward the space within the text. In the Dédicace, 'l'improbable' is an idea, of course, but it is also literally 'ce qui est', i.e. the book it points to, in the sense that the writer's deictic 'here' becomes, through the act of reading, a 'here' for the reader as well, precisely because of the conjoined attention — or intentionality, as we will see — that both writer and reader give to the physical space constituted by the written text. Finally, regarding its physical materiality, the *hic* dimension has another role to play through its potential for iterating experience from one reader to another. Seen from this perspective, the written text is the creation of another type of virtual space, a material 'here' shared by the writer and any number of readers, a 'com-union', if we return to the root of the word. A corollary to that notion of shared space is the enlarged scope of the transmission: because of its physical nature, a written text has the capacity to expand the experiences it generates to a potential community of readers. By extension, thus, it even might be said to create such a community where none had previously existed, a point which echoes the connection between *présence* and the Eucharistic notion of community and which is fundamental to the theorisation of the essay.

★   ★   ★   ★   ★

As a linguistic marker gesturing specifically to that which is extra-linguistic, deixis introduces several interlocking notions that play an important role in Bonnefoy's ontological project. As concerns language, one of the obvious consequences of using indexical markers lies in their self-referential capacity. The inherently 'empty' nature of deicticals points back to their function within the system of language. To repeat the example used previously, the coded definition of the word 'I' is something along the lines of 'this word designates the speaker speaking about him or herself'. In the absence of a speaker, the word cannot be actualized, and is thus shorn of the more significant part of its meaning. One of the consequences of this dependency on context is that the use of deictics draws attention to the function of language as a tool, more specifically, as an inadequate tool. Bonnefoy, in a radical form of re-orientation, assigns this inadequacy a positive value: the potential incompleteness of indexicals constitutes a breach in the system of referential markers. Indeed, their existence points to the incapacity of language to be a totalizing system, able to faithfully and completely reproduce the referential world. And if we accept the deconstructionist view of language as a system which constrains speakers by making them use pre-established mental constructions, indexicals potentially allow the speaker to break out of the dominant structure and become master of his or her own language.

The notion of mastery over individual expression leads to Bonnefoy's attempt to extract — or 'salvage', to co-opt his own word — parts of his writing from the constraints that language in general, but written language in particular, seems to impose on the freedom of the individual. The title of one of Bonnefoy's late collections of essays, *Le Siècle où la parole a été victime*, metaphorizes the notion of 'saving' the speech act from attack, which can be considered as a form of riposte to Derrida. Indeed, deconstructionism notwithstanding, writing has long been perceived as a sort of 'congealed' form of speech serving to preserve something which is, by its very nature, evanescent and fragile. One can consider Bonnefoy's insistence on incorporating deictic words into written structures as a sort of anti-Derridian rhetorical trope that functions as a trap, undoing writing and returning the written text to its origin as speech, and at times casting even further back in search of the origins of speech. Again, the evocation of 'trap' and 'speech origin' immediately resonates with Bonnefoy's own use of these words, either as titles ('L'Origine de la parole', in *Dans le leurre du seuil*) or integrated into essays where he describes, for instance, poetry as a positively charged space with the potential to 'snare' *présence*.[14]

Finally, the issue of deixis and totalization most notably concerns context. Many theoreticians evoke the idea of the semantic deficiency of deixis and its implications upon the respective roles of speaker and listener. For if we return to the root notion of deixis, that is, to the act of pointing, the deictic word itself stands for a gesture. And if we then take the demonstrative 'this' as an example, the vacuity of the word used within a physical exchange serves to draw the attention of the interlocutor to the gesture that accompanies it. Stephen Levinson refers to Peirce's understanding of the relationship between the sign and the thing indicated, writing, 'The magical ingredient is the direction of the addressee's attention to some feature of the spatio-temporal physical context'. He adds that 'indexicality [i.e. *deixis*] is both an intentional and an attentional phenomenon, concentrated around the spatial-temporal center of verbal interaction'.[15] This perception of indexicals dovetails particularly well with the importance Bonnefoy gives to the idea of poetry as an act, in the sense that a true deictic always requires action from the interlocutors: its very use generates an act by focusing the attention of speaker and listener on the element intended by the speaker. This key element, intent, can draw the reader into sharing the intention at the origin of the text and thus vanquish the explicit absence of a shared physical environment.

It would be difficult to overstate the importance of this notion in Bonnefoy's work, because the implications that derive from it are closely connected to the implicit 'truth-value' of a text, and this has a vital role in the writing of essays. Levinson provides a mechanism for understanding the relationship between deixis and intention. He writes:

> When I point and say 'I mean that' I intend to invoke in you a referent-isolating thought just by virtue of your recognising that that is what my intention is [...]. In this way gesture — and arguably deixis in general — is crucially intentional: you cannot say 'False!' to my utterance 'I am referring to that'.[16]

Continuing this logic, it can be argued that when using deixis, the writer invites the reader into a construction that is, at least in part, not imaginary, but real and true at the level of intent. Thus, when Bonnefoy writes, not once, but twice, in 'Anti-Platon', 'il s'agit bien de *cet* objet', even if the 'objet' evoked is only accessible through the imagination, there is no gainsaying the truth of the indication itself. Strangely, thus, deixis appears to concatenate two almost contradictory definitions. The written deictic, which initially appeared as the very figure of an imaginary construction, since the reader and writer could not possibly meet the deictic precondition of sharing the same physical or temporal space, appears instead to exist as a small space of reality carved out of the vast structure of the fictional universes created through writing. It appears as the very figure of truth.

Paradoxically, however, deixis is held as the very exemplar of non-truth because of the impossibility for a deictic utterance to enunciate a philosophical truth. This goes to the heart of Bonnefoy's equivocal relation with language and philosophy and, a fortiori, to the way these can inhabit the essay. Western philosophical tradition teaches that truth can only be expressed by a statement whose value is independent of the accidents of its production. The *summum*, thus, of absolute truth lies in mathematical statements, which remain true regardless of individual assertion. Again, Levinson provides us with an interpretation of the truth-value of deictical statements that resonates for Bonnefoy. He indicates that 'any sentence with indexicals [...] cannot directly express a proposition, for in any doctrine, a proposition is an abstract entity whose truth-value is independent of the times, places, and persons in the speech event'.[17] The deictic statement is thus antithetical to the possibility of introducing pure concepts into language. This seemingly simple statement is of capital importance for readers of Bonnefoy, for, as is clearly seen in his early essays, notably those of *L'Improbable*, *présence* is constructed in vehement opposition to the notion of the concept.

★   ★   ★   ★   ★

Generally speaking, it is difficult to deny the ubiquitousness of the concept, which has so long formed the cornerstone of Western philosophy that it has become inextricably enmeshed in our understanding of the very functioning of thought. In the development of a specifically Bonnefoyian philosophy, the notion of concept, along with the attendant idea of *ce qui est*, relies in part upon the work of Leo Shestov. Indeed, one of the essays Bonnefoy chose to include in *L'Improbable* is 'L'Obstination de Chestov'. When I first began studying his work, Bonnefoy specifically directed me to Shestov's *Le Pouvoir des clefs* in order to better understand his own intellectual position. Shestov, in essence, is bitterly opposed to the fact that Western thought has erected Reason as the supreme — indeed, the only — virtue. 'L'Ανάγχη ("necessity") est invincible' he writes, and philosophy does no more than teach us to submit to this necessity.[18] This impassioned 'revolt against scientism and philosophical rationalism' has, suggests philosopher Bernard Martin, repelled many of Shestov's readers and led to his relative obscurity in modern philosophical circles.[19] And yet Bonnefoy says of Shestov's writing that it 'touches' and 'impresses' him, evoking in him 'profound echoes' (I, 284). Indeed, it is difficult not to see reverberations of Shestov in Bonnefoy's uneasiness regarding 'le parler scientifique' and the disjunction he observes between modern science and the lived experience of human beings.

The obstinacy to which Bonnefoy refers in the title of his essay derives from Shestov's radical existentialism, his insistence on the idea that faith alone can allow man to break free of the iron grip of the rationally possible and regain his essential freedom. For if man, and God himself, are subject to the apparently immutable physical laws that condition our existence then, perforce, it is these laws that dictate the limits of the possible and the impossible, not the will of God. Against this, Shestov affirms the need for a faith so entire that it rends the veils that we take for self-evident truth. Faith, for him, suggests Martin:

> Is not 'a weaker form of knowledge (knowledge, so to speak, 'on credit,' for which proofs, though presently unavailable, are anticipated at some future time), but rather [...] a conviction that all things are possible even, for instance, the negation of the laws of identity and temporality that form the bedrock of science and philosophy.[20]

Martin is at pains to point out that Shestov's dismissal of science is far from being a rabid and unconsidered rejection of scientific knowledge per se, pointing to Shestov's explanation, in *In Job's Balances*, that science and truth must not be considered on the same plane:

> However much we may have attained in science, yet we must remember that science can give us no truth because, by its very nature, it will not and cannot seek for the truth. The truth lies there where science sees the 'nothing,' in that single, uncontrollable, incomprehensible thing which is always at war with explanation, the 'fortuitous'.[21]

Clearly, Shestov's embracing of the 'fortuitous' and his concomitant struggle against the conceptual abstractions that science reifies as self-evident truths are significant markers on Bonnefoy's own path toward *présence*. An echo of them is clearly perceptible in the high value Bonnefoy imparts to the term *improbable*. But because his attention does not focus on the question of unconditional faith, Bonnefoy constructs a more restricted polarity than that of Shestov, limiting it to the opposition between *présence* and concept. Bonnefoy evokes the reasons for their antagonism when he suggests that 'l'idée d'un être [...] implique son existence, et cela vainc le concept, qui doit abolir celle-ci pour que ses formules prospèrent' [The idea of a being [...] implies its existence, and this vanquishes the concept, which must abolish that existence in order to flourish] (*I*, 251). The opposition between concept and *présence* thus lies in the fact that in order to function meaningfully, the concept needs intellectually to reduce a being to its most general component parts. Consequently, the concept eschews completely those aspects which are the sources of any being's specific reality. With this perspective in mind, Bonnefoy makes no bones about the fact that his own writing is the development of an intellectual rejection of the concept because of the latter's own rejection of reality. His position is most clearly evoked in 'Les Tombeaux de Ravenne' where he writes, 'nothing is less real than the concept' (*I*, 19) and leads us through a litany of real things which can impinge upon us, but which cannot be conceptually expressed: 'Y a-t-il un concept d'un pas venant dans la nuit, d'un cri, de l'éboulement d'une pierre dans les brousailles? De l'impression que fait une maison vide? Mais non, rien n'a été gardé du réel que ce qui convient à notre repos' [Is there a concept for a footfall in the night, for a cry, for a stone tumbling in the undergrowth? Of the impression given by an empty house? Of course not, nothing has been preserved of reality except that which contributes to our peace of mind] (*I*, 15).

It is not by accident that 'Les Tombeaux de Ravenne' contains the most precise evocation of Bonnefoy's difficulty with the notion of the concept. That essay, standing in proemial position to his collected essays, is the initial call to action where he presents for the first time his repudiations and affinities. And as concerns the concept, Bonnefoy connects its experiential inadequacy to the fear of mortality: 'la peur de la mort [...] est le secret du concept' (*I*, 28). Essentially, his argument rests on the idea that the concept is a philosophical creation whose function is to attenuate and mask the brutal reality that we, that everything that lives in this world, also dies: 'Parce qu'on meurt dans ce monde et pour nier le destin l'homme a bâti de concepts cette demeure logique, où les seuls principes qui vaillent sont de permanence et d'identité' [It is because we die in this world, and in order to negate destiny that man has built out of concepts this logical dwelling that values only the principles of permanence and identity] (*I*, 14). For it is clear that the concept has no reality of its own outside the meandering paths of an intellectual apprehension of the world. Its function, at least philosophically, is evident: it allows us to think in general and to manipulate ideas by abstracting from all things their particularity. Hence, to take a banal example, the existence of the concept allows us to think about tables or trees generally, without needing to refer to specific tables or trees. The concept is thus a powerful tool for abstract thought, but Bonnefoy follows Shestov in affirming that the problem lies precisely in this power of abstraction:

> De quelle chose sensible, d'ailleurs, de quelle pierre qui soit au monde le concept n'est-il détourné? Ce n'est pas seulement de la mort qu'il se sépare, c'est de tout ce qui a visage, de tout ce qui a chair, pulsation, immanence et qui est ainsi, il est vrai, pour sa secrète avarice, le danger le plus insidieux. (*I*, 20)

> [Is there any tangible thing, any stone of this world from which the concept does not shrink? It preserves itself not only from death, but from everything that has flesh, pulsation, and immanence, and which thus presents, it is true, the greatest danger to its secret avarice.]

But what is this insidious danger of which he speaks, and why in fact would it be a danger? What is the risk involved? I would argue, as Bonnefoy himself will in later essays, that if the material reality of things presents a danger to the concept, the real danger is to us, but only indirectly, through language, and this because the power that accrues to the concept is in large part derived from its symbiotic relationship with language. In a sense, there can be no concept without language, and, perhaps, no language without concepts. It is precisely at this intersection that Bonnefoy's writing carves out its space, setting *présence* both as a poetic *telos,* and as a goal of poetic communion that, paradoxically perhaps, opposes it to certain philosophical paths.

Still, despite his hostility to the concept, the dense quality of Bonnefoy's writing has frequently caused readers to describe it as 'philosophical'. Regarding his poetry,

Jean-Claude Pinson invents a portmanteau word, 'poésophie', to represent it. With respect to his essays, David Jasper is even more explicit when he says that Bonnefoy's attachment to philosophical thinking shifts 'through Husserl and Heidegger towards an ethics of reading the "other" in a hidden narrative whose possibility is "conditional on the unconditional responsibility of *being-for-the-other*"'.[22] Indeed, it is clear that Bonnefoy's *présence* has a philosophical specificity that takes it beyond the purely theological definition given to the word. John Naughton compares it with the *punctum* that Roland Barthes evokes in *La Chambre claire* and says that '"presence" is precisely what is beyond, or outside of, conceptual categories or a conditioned perception'.[23] To most attentive readers of Bonnefoy, this is an accurate definition of *présence*. Closer examination, however, reveals it to be somewhat tautological, in that it essentially describes *présence* as indescribable. Naughton, in a later publication, notes the difficulty in pinning down an exact definition of *présence*, writing that:

> Although the term is clearly the cornerstone of [Bonnefoy's] entire poetics, the idea is never defined once and for all, and this is one reason why it has become the object of considerable discussion in analyses of his work. It seems to me, furthermore, that there is a certain evolution and development in Bonnefoy's own understanding and use of the term, and that this in part explains why there should be some confusion and disagreement about its meaning and validity.[24]

Certainly, Naughton's point about the evolution of Bonnefoy's *présence* merits careful attention. I would argue, however, that it is less its meaning that was subjected to shifts and realignments, but rather a double problem that is linked first to the complicated relationship between *présence* and *ce qui est*, and then to the no less important questions of whether *présence* can find expression in language, and if so, how? The re-evaluation of language is a significant turning-point in Bonnefoy's understanding of *présence*. In his earlier essays, he demonstrates a profound ambivalence regarding the capacity for language to communicate being. In the 1959 essay 'L'Acte et le lieu de la poésie', Bonnefoy sharply criticizes Mallarmé's belief that words can contain the very kernel of being and thus be a point of access to an ideal form of beauty that becomes the objective of poetry. His judgement seems irrevocable: 'Language is not the Word. However distorted, however transformed our syntax might be, it will always remain merely a metaphor for the unachievable syntax, signifying only exile'.[25] Significantly, however, his position later changed, and a sentence from the 1967 essay 'Baudelaire parlant à Mallarmé' sheds some light on the matter:

> Autrefois je croyais que les mots, brûlés par leur emploi conceptuel, ne disaient pas la présence, n'en pouvaient permettre à jamais que la "théologie négative". Maintenant je pressens qu'une archéologie est possible qui dégagerait par fragments les voûtes de notre forme.[26]

> [Previously I believed that words, scorched by their conceptual use, could not tell of presence, that they could never do more than allow a 'negative theology'. Now, I sense that an archaeology is possible which would reveal by fragments the vault of our form].

This change could perhaps be assimilated to a sort of natural evolution over time. I would suggest, however, that it was motivated more by Bonnefoy's fundamental opposition to deconstuctionist re-evaluations of language and is clearly marked by his strong opposition to those who would see in poetry nothing more than a mere 'effet de présence' (NR, 270). His discovery, sometime in the 1960s, of a way to use the tools provided by Saussurian structuralist linguistics to rationalize the possibility for expressing *présence* changed his attitude toward language.

Beyond that, clearly, the question of *présence* extends far beyond Bonnefoy's work: as a philosophical object, it has long had a central position in the phenomenological currents and the 'philosophies of existence' that emerged over the past century. It lies at the heart of a signal conflict of perceptions on how philosophy can truly describe the reality of human thought and experience. And while Bonnefoy himself explicitly claimed not to be a philosopher, he was an extremely well-informed and constant reader of philosophical texts, citing his indebtedness to, among others, Kierkegaard, Hegel, and Plotinus, but also to Georges Bataille, Etienne Gilson, Henri-Charles Puech, and, of course, Lev Shestov (E, 77).

More formally, Bonnefoy studied the philosophy of science with Gaston Bachelard at the Institut d'histoire des sciences, commenting much later of these classes that contrary to Bachelard's classes at the Sorbonne, they were almost private lessons since there were so few other students.[27] The two continued to correspond until the Bachelard's death in 1962. Bonnefoy also studied Hegel with Jean Hyppolite and Jean Wahl, writing for the latter a thesis conjoining poetry and philosophy entitled 'Baudelaire et Kierkegaard'.[28] Rather naturally, what Bonnefoy took from his readings in philosophy filtered into his work, and thinkers such as Plotinus, Plato, Nietzsche, but also the theologian St Jean de la Croix, constantly crisscross the pages of Bonnefoy's writing; the epigraph to *Douve*, for example, is drawn from Hegel.

That said, it must be noted that much like his position regarding theology, Bonnefoy projects a certain ambivalence toward philosophy as, for example, when he writes in *L'Improbable*:

> Je ne poserai pas de quelque façon philosophique le problème du sensible. Affirmer, tel est mon souci. [...] Je ne sais, je ne veux pas dresser la dialectique du monde, placer le sensible dans l'être avec cet art minutieux de la patiente métaphysique: je ne prétends que nommer. Voici le monde sensible. Il faut que la parole, ce sixième et ce plus haut sens, se porte à sa rencontre et en déchiffre les signes. Pour moi, je n'ai de goût qu'en cette tâche, recherche du secret que Kierkegaard n'avait plus. (I, 23)

> [In no philosophical way whatsoever will I pose the problem of the sensate. Affirming is my concern. [...] I have neither the knowledge nor the desire to set forth the dialectic of the world, to place the sensate within being with the artful precision that patient metaphysics has: I claim only to name. Behold the sensate world [*le monde sensible*]. Speech [*la parole*], our sixth and highest sense, must meet it and decipher its signs. As for me, I have no taste for anything else but this task, the quest for the secret that Kierkegaard lost.]

It would be difficult to imagine a clearer repudiation of philosophy. Despite his disavowal, however, Bonnefoy builds his utterance around an explicitly philosophical lexicon through his use of the terms 'la dialectique', and 'la métaphysique', or even 'speech', and 'signs'. And of course, his specific reference to Kierkegaard sets the reader even more firmly on the terrain of philosophy. Still, by redefining *parole* [speech] as a sense, Bonnefoy equates it with a means of apprehending the world, and this, of course, is a radical departure from traditional metaphysics. Concurrently, evoking the term 'speech' also carries semantic weight for those who are as familiar as Bonnefoy was with the very specific vocabulary of structuralism. Indeed, his definition of *la parole* as the highest of the human senses relies on the nomenclature used by structuralist thinkers, while removing the act of speaking from the system of language where structural linguistics locates it, to place it in a wholly Bonnefoyian association with the physical senses. This shift is not insignificant: co-opting a structuralist vocabulary that he redefines to align to his own purposes is one of the incisive strategies Bonnefoy uses to anchor his position to the seemingly unassailable scientific ground occupied by linguistics. Finally, 'the sensate world' (*le monde sensible*) serves as a reminder that in the archeology of Bonnefoy's work, *le sensible* was the archaic name for *présence*.

The ambivalence contained in the passage between an explicit desire to reject philosophy, and the philosophical lexicon used, figures the importance of the essay in his work inasmuch as the opposition between philosophizing and affirming stands for the real tension at the core of Bonnefoy's thought, namely the way his rejection of conceptual systems dovetails with his simultaneous need for those same systems in order to communicate his ideas. Along those lines, his use of the word *affirmer* is noteworthy. Naughton stresses the fact that 'Bonnefoy's idea of poetry is inseparable from a certain form of affirmation and hopefulness' (*APP*, xvii). Indeed, *affirmer* presupposes the existence of the thing, state, or condition being affirmed, and thus connects with Bonnefoy's ontological focus on being, as shown, in particular, through *ce qui est*, the crucial construction which so frequently serves as a foil to the notion of *présence* in his work. Tellingly, however, with respect to the essay, *affirmer* also intimates a didactic function, inasmuch as the act of affirming supposes something that one is convinced of, or that one wishes to convince others of. Recognizing its didactic potential is essential to fully understanding the essay's capacities and seeing that it can take on tasks that other forms of writing struggle to address as efficiently. Finally, the opposition between the dynamic affirming and the conceptual philosophizing is linked in large part to the *telos* of expressing *présence* through writing. And as Bonnefoy himself is painfully aware, the experiential quality of *présence* cannot be fully mediated by language. 'What can words retain, or say, when *présence* is given in the universe of the moment?', he writes (*I*, 126). Insurmountably, however, Bonnefoy is forced to use language, the problematic crux, indeed, of a philosophy of *présence*.

★   ★   ★   ★   ★

Regarding the percolation of the term *présence* into Bonnefoy's own environment, what is important is the philosophical trend particular to the Paris of the first half of the twentieth century, the time when he was developing his own writing and thinking (Bonnefoy settled in Paris in the early 1940s). The impact of phenomenology on what has been called the 'Continental' current of philosophy is considerable, particularly since the work of Husserl and Heidegger, but also of Hegel and Lévinas, was broadly disseminated in French intellectual circles during this period.[29] Various connections made by *passeurs* Jean Wahl and Jean Hyppolite — thinkers principally known for their translations and transmission of ideas — but also by philosophers in their own right such as Jean-Paul Sartre and Maurice Merleau-Ponty, or even Gaston Bachelard and Paul Ricœur, enabled these ideas to gain significant intellectual ground. Some years later, though still firmly anchored in the same current of thought, Jacques Derrida's analysis of Husserl's vision of phenomenology challenged the primacy of the notion of *présence* in Western philosophical thinking, questioning its very possibility. Regarding these various actors on the French philosophical scene, it is notable that with few exceptions, all were people with whom Bonnefoy had direct personal or intellectual contact. Thus even though his position shows a clear demarcation from a number of the philosophical conclusions of his peers, there can be no doubt that phenomenology had an impact on the manner in which he constructed his own vision of the world.

Though Heidegger and Derrida seem obvious choices to discuss with respect to Bonnefoy's *présence* — Heidegger because of his focus on poetic language and 'Being', and Derrida because he questions the very possibility of *présence* — Husserl must be evoked because his philosophical rehabilitation of the individual subject is the substratum on which so much else is built. As Derrida censoriously points out, the notion of the *présence* 'of the self to itself' is one of the false presuppositions undergirding Husserl's work.[30] That said, it is useful to bear in mind that Husserl's main object in engaging his reflection of Cartesian metaphysics was the desire to reinterpret radical doubt, more firmly establishing thereby a sort of *mathesis universalis*, or all-encompassing knowledge. As it happens, this desire to erect some form of method is not alien to Bonnefoy's own preoccupations, even though he deliberately reorients his practice along the lines of what might be described as a 'methodless method'. This latter 'unmethod' emerges particularly clearly in his essays, which can be read as prototypical exempli, furnishing a sort of a blueprint to guide the reader's reflection. This strategy is even more apparent at the level of his collected essays, where it becomes clear that if each essay conveys an intuition, an experience, or a reaction, the collected essays construct something that transcends the immediacy of *présence*, and is more akin to a method.

More 'technically', a number of the tools Husserl developed illuminate vital aspects of Bonnefoy's *présence*. Among these is an attachment to phenomena, both material or conceptual, which is a guiding principle of Bonnefoy's poems — indeed, of contemporary poetry in general. It is also, as we will see, a grounding element of the essay. Husserl explicitly highlights the independent existence of objects: 'Through [...] the different ways of sensory perception, corporal things somehow spatially distributed are for me simply there, in verbal or figurative sense "present", whether or not I pay them special attention'.[31] This recognition of the independent reality of material things is echoed in Bonnefoy's praise for Baudelaire's poem 'À une passante' about which he writes: 'Baudelaire does not create this Andromache, he "thinks" about her; this means that being exists outside consciousness' (I, 115). Of equal relevance in Husserlian phenomenology is the co-equal importance given to the thinking subject and the objective world, as well as the crucial value of the subject as the sole agent able to effect the eidetic transformations and reductions leading to an awareness of the essence of the objects of reflection.

Husserl places the subject at the epicentre of the phenomenological method, a focus that comes in opposition to objective philosophical systems based on the idea that reality can only accurately be appraised by excluding those specific, contingent moments of its perception by individuals. This is clearly anathema, both to phenomenology and to Bonnefoy. For both, the focus on the subject and its relation to the other is axiomatic. As James Edie writes, 'For phenomenology, the subject is the zero-point of a system of coordinates, the necessary centre of all experience, around which the world of objects is arraigned as in an indefinite horizon'.[32] The subject must assume this crucial role because, Husserl suggests, individual consciousness is the only pathway through which phenomena can obtain their transcendental meaning. On this subject, Heidegger will go even further and contend that it is the specific role of man, even his duty, to enable the existence of phenomena, a moral imperative that has strong echoes in Bonnefoy's thought and conditions his use of the essay form. The phenomenological subject thus has a decisively dynamic role: it makes itself receptive to phenomena in order to extract from them an understanding of their essential nature. This is rendered possible by the notion of 'intentionality', or 'aboutness', i.e. the means by which a subject broaches all objects, whether these be physical (that table over there) or mental (the most suitable table for my future house), and allows them to enter into consciousness by 'thinking about them'.

Concretely, what Husserl proposes is not only a description of a philosophical enterprise, but also the manner in which such an enterprise might take place. This is the celebrated *epoché*, or 'bracketing' of all prior knowledge regarding the phenomena that appear to the subject. Although similar at first glance to the familiar Cartesian step of rejecting the very existence of the world in order to discern the *res cogitans* as the thinking subject, the Husserlian technique is radically different in that it accepts the existence of the world, simply 'excluding' and 'bracketing' the knowledge furnished by it for the purposes of the phenomenological reduction. François Lyotard equates this position with the deliberate refusal to take a position, whether of radical doubt, or of acceptance.[33] The objective is to reveal the residual being that remains after bracketing and eidetic reductions, and which can be understood as the transcendental truth inherent not only in the object, but also in the observing self. In essence, this consists in mentally varying the characteristics of the phenomenon observed until a contradiction is reached regarding its temporal or spatial existence. To give a banal example, if we take a common table as an observable phenomenon, we can mentally vary its characteristics, making it change in colour, height, width, surface quality, and so on. We could also attempt to locate it mentally in another time: last week, tomorrow, in the next century, etc. None of these manipulations would seem to alter the so-called 'tableness' of the table. *A contrario*, if we imagine it surfaceless, or without some sort of supporting structure like an *n* number of legs, we reach a mental contradiction which no longer allows us to identify it as a table. This contradiction is what allows for the disclosure of the *aeterna veritas* of the object.[34] The influence of these eidetic transformations seems particularly apparent in Bonnefoy's earlier collections of poetry. In *Douve*, for example, the central character of Douve is described in a multitude of different manners, from landscape, to female figure, to corpse, to various animal forms. All these infinite variations in the character seem to point the reader toward its truth, an idea substantiated by the fact that unlike the later volumes of poetry, *Douve* contains a significant number of poems incorporating the words *vérité* and *vrai* in their title. More importantly with respect to Bonnefoy's essays, this type of eidetic transformation bridges the gap between his poetry and prose, for a number of very concrete images that appeared initially in the poetry — the ivy, the orangery, etc. — are later carried over to the essays, thereby reinforcing the blurring between the genres that we will examine in the following chapters. The most significant of these emigrations is doubtless the image of the salamander, which figures in a number of the *Douve* poems before reappearing in the essay, 'La Poésie française et le principe d'identité', where Bonnefoy develops what is clearly a phenomenological investigation by examining the chance encounter with a salamander through all possible vectors of interpretation.

Husserl's positions notwithstanding, it is the work of his student, Heidegger, that likely had a greater influence on Bonnefoy, despite his clearly-voiced reticence acknowledging an adhesion described as 'merely aesthetic or intellectual' in spite of his admiration for Heidegger's introduction of death into philosophical debate, thus 'giv[ing] life to time, which orients being' (*I*, 14). Indeed, the perception of poetic language that Heidegger projects — most notably in *Poetry, Language, Thought* — intersects well with the type of praxis that emerges in Bonnefoy's essays, particularly in their blurring, mentioned above, of clear distinctions between prose and poetry. A number of the crucial points of Heideggerian inquiry contribute not only to shaping the contours of Bonnefoy's *présence*, but also point to a latent moral imperative that can be found in the genre of the essay. Three Heideggerian postulates foreshadow Bonnefoy's *présence*: first, the question of 'Being', which necessarily subtends any notion of *présence*; then, the philosophical consideration of death; and finally, the question of language.

Concerning the first, Richard Cohen remarks, 'The most important, deepest founding question of philosophy is for Heidegger the "question of being"'.[35] To address this, Heidegger rejects the Aristotelian principle of man as a rational animal, rejecting, in other words, the idea of man as a natural entity to which something — rationality — has been added. He builds upon Husserlian phenomenology and the cardinal importance it gives to the thinking subject, suggesting that it is the very function and nature of humans to discern and show the being of all things. Humans, for him, differ from all the other beings in their capacity to consciously reflect upon Being. This causes them to stand out from Being, conferring upon them the quality of what he calls 'ek-sistence'. This function, he suggests, completely reorients the position of man: 'man,' he writes in the *Lettre sur l'humanisme* originally addressed to Jean Beaufret, 'is not the master of that which is.[36] Man is the shepherd of being'.[37] Co-extensive with the call to duty given by the image of the shepherd, that of man as keeper of Being reinforces the latter's exterior, independent nature. J. Glenn Gray highlights the nature of this relationship by pointing out that 'Man does not create Being, but he is responsible for it since, without his thinking and remembering, Being has no illumination, no voice, no word'.[38] Heideggerian phenomenology seeks to counteract the fact that traditional metaphysics has long veiled and forgotten authentic Being. Crucially, the trajectory toward Being, that is, toward an understanding of the fundamental truth of those things that *are*, is materialized in the act of disclosure by which the Being that always inherently inhabits the phenomenological object is unveiled, its truthful essence standing forth and becoming present to the observer.

This position has substantive echoes in Bonnefoy's work. Indeed, disclosure, the unveiling and 'making-present' of Being, can be thought of as a dynamic gesture, an act whose function is to show a truth that is inherently static in nature. This idea is seen in the explicit distinction Bonnefoy's work makes between *présence* and *ce qui est*, with the two terms interacting in a relation that could almost be qualified as symbiotic in the sense that *ce qui est* cannot be accessed without the act that is *présence*. By the same token, *présence* can have no significance without the underlying stability of the *ce qui est* to which it points. The phrase itself merits attention, for it appears with great frequency, most notably in the 'Dédicace' to *L'Improbable*, which opens with that apparently paradoxical statement: 'je dédie ce livre à l'improbable, c'est-à-dire, à ce qui est'. While the expression itself has clear roots in Bonnefoy's early interpretation of Kierkegaard, whom he identifies as 'l'inventeur de *ce qui est*', he later expanded the expression, writing, '*ce qui est, c'est la finitude*', giving us thus to understand that the phrase is linked to the passage of time, to inevitable endings, to death (*E*, 82).[39] This cycles back to Heidegger, for the question of death is another important point of contact between Bonnefoy and Heidegger. The latter radically transforms death, taking it out of the realm of the incidental, where metaphysics has traditionally placed it, and bringing it to the centre of philosophical reflection. And though the notion of death might appear to be less immediately pertinent to definitions of *présence* per se, the two notions are highly interdependent, as Cohen explains:

> Mortality, [...] far from being the sort of thing the philosopher must flee or dismiss for the sake of purified intellection and eternal truth, is to the contrary, the most philosophical of all moments. It is only in being-toward-death that the temporality of one's own being, and the historical-ontological context within which one's own being finds its ultimate sense, are disclosed.[40]

Given Bonnefoy's conscious and deliberate integration of death, particularly in early texts such as the *Douve* poem cycle and the essay 'Les Tombeaux de Ravenne' in *L'Improbable*, Heidegger's perception constitutes a significant substratum in Bonnefoy's position. Cohen very cogently breaks the relationship between the Heideggerian *Dasein* and death down into a number of descriptive points, writing that 'because being-toward-death is not a self-understanding that Dasein can maintain at all times, when Dasein does realize itself this way it enters into the back and forth movement of "fallen" (*Verfall*) or "inauthentic" Dasein and authentic Dasein'.[41] This point has a strong bearing on Bonnefoy's vision of *présence* and its materialization in writing, particularly in the opposition between *présence* and the *mauvaise présence* that he describes in the salamander image of the essay 'La Poésie française et le principe d'identité'.

Finally, Heidegger's conviction that poetic language is instrumental in the gesture of unveiling resonates strongly in Bonnefoy's work and is particularly visible — paradoxically, perhaps — in his essays, whose language frequently demonstrates identifiably poetic qualities. Again, the 'Dédicace' provides a good example of this, with parallel forms of assonance unifying precisely the very sentence within which poetry is thematized: 'A une po*é*sie d*é*sirée, de plu*i*es, d'*atten*te et de v*ent*' (I, front matter). Heidegger indeed places language squarely at the centre of man's relationship with his world. As Gray notes:

> Language is conceived by Heidegger in a way directly contrary to most modern thinking. It is no mere tool or instrument, nor does its essence consist entirely in being a means of transmitting information. Language is the supreme event of human existence because it enables man, in the words of the poet Hölderlin, 'to affirm what he is'.[42]

As Heidegger himself repeats insistently, 'Language speaks' and has the power to invoke absent things, making them present here. He writes, 'The call does indeed call. Thus it brings the presence of what was previously uncalled into a nearness'.[43] These considerations shed light on vital markers of Bonnefoy's work: a theological grounding enacted in a specific lexicon, an explicitly ontological orientation, and the evocation of the deictic indicators, seen in the 'hereness' of *présence*. Taken together, these factors demonstrate the general environment within which our experiential relation to *présence* can emerge. More importantly, however, for the development of Bonnefoy's 'methodless method', his essays clearly serve also to orient our understanding of *présence* through the triangulation he seeks to create between *présence*, *ce qui est*, and *mauvaise présence*.

Like the term *présence*, *ce qui est* clearly serves for Bonnefoy as a form of moral benchmark to appraise the work of other artists. Though his appreciation can be negative, as we saw earlier ('Valéry a méconnu le mystère de la présence'), it can also be positive, as in an essay where Baudelaire's attachment to *ce qui est* is described as a form of salvation: 'Baudelaire sensed at the very core of that which exists [*ce qui est*], through its death and because it must die, that it may prove our salvation' (*APP*, 108). Here, through a clearly theological lens, Bonnefoy correlates *ce qui est* with contingency and death. That is one aspect. In an essay on the poems of Gilbert Lély

('La Cent vingt et unième Journée'), the contingency of *ce qui est* is also associated with place, with being, and with time — in other words, with all the elements that constitute the object of deixis (*I*, 88). These parallels bring together *présence* and *ce qui est* as standards for moral judgement. It is noteworthy, however, that they are by no means equivalent terms for Bonnefoy. On the contrary, the difference between them can be correlated to the phenomenological action of disclosure or unveiling, for Bonnefoy repeatedly states that *présence* is an act and not the passive reception of an experience: 'The sensate object is *presence*. It is differentiated from the conceptual above all by an act, which is presence' (*I*, 26). Authentic *présence*, thus, can only be experienced as an encounter characterized by intention. However — and this is an element that has always remained at the margins of critical analysis of Bonnefoy's *présence* — if *présence* is construed by him as an act, a dynamic gesture that occurs in the moment, the object of this revelation, *ce qui est*, is a far more stable form of reality. 'Dans un moment d'irréalité,' he writes, 'de libre décision quant à la chose physique, nous pourrons arracher *ce qui est au sommeil de ses formes stables*, qui est le triomphe du néant [In a moment of unreality, of free choice regarding the physical world, we can wrench '*ce qui est*' *from the slumber of its stable forms*, a slumber where nothingness triumphs' (*I*, 127, my emphasis).

This point is capital from several perspectives. First, the fact that that stability can be put into parallel with the independent existence of objects, which, as we saw, is an important substructure of Husserlian phenomenology. For Bonnefoy, there can be no doubt that an entire world exists beyond the subject. Access to this world, however, is not something that can be complacently considered as given; it is rather something that can only be obtained through constantly renewed efforts made to make oneself available. Bonnefoy's *présence* is the emblem of this effort, and *ce qui est* its object. The second significant point lies in the absolute quality of *ce qui est*, a quality that links it to the notion of unity that was so instrumental in Bonnefoy's rejection of surrealism, but connects it also to more widespread perceptions. Maurice Blanchot, for instance, makes a very similar analogy between *ce qui est* and a sort of unifying continuity that would be the very essence of reality, writing in *L'Entretien infini* that this postulate of unity is as ancient as thought itself.[44] The tenor of this comment, coupled with his work on the fragment, is perhaps what led Mario Maurin to remark in 1958 that the intellectual parallels between Blanchot and Bonnefoy are such that 'to look at [Blanchot's] essays is to discover [...] the central problem and sometimes the very wording of Bonnefoy's poetry'.[45] Indeed, Blanchot's comment clearly associates the idea of unity with more ancient currents of philosophy which see the true nature of world as one of absolute underlying unity. The idea can somewhat transparently be compared to Plotinus's 'One', or to Parmenides's 'Way of Aletheia', both of whose influence Bonnefoy explicitly acknowledges: Parmenides, he says, 'was one of the starting points of my thinking [when I was writing *Pierre Ecrite*]' (*YB*, 195). Similarly, Bonnefoy's engagement with Plotinus has been noted by a number of critics, including Daniel Lançon, who, in his talk 'Alchimie et couleur dans l'œuvre d'Yves Bonnefoy', connects Bonnefoy's explicit Plotinian references to 'l'Un' with 'the experience of something more central, more profound, more true' (*YB*, 194).

And yet, despite the stability he associates with *ce qui est*, it would be a mistake to equate the expression with some variant of a conceptual understanding of the world. On the contrary, somewhat later in his writing, Bonnefoy will come to recognize that the problem lies not in the existence of the concept itself, but in the relation between language, concept, and the possibility of true representation. In a letter to critic John Jackson, he equates his initial thinking with the use of an inappropriate terminology, and writes that 'je réduisais alors le péril des mots à celui du concept, et nommais gauchement "objet" ce qu'aujourd'hui je dirais "présence"' [at that time, I reduced the peril of words to that of the concept, and awkwardly called 'object' what I would now name 'presence'] (*E*, 133). This comment demonstrates that for Bonnefoy, the real impediment to *présence* is 'le péril des mots', that is, the power language has to give the appearance of pointing to reality even as it lets this same reality escape. The cataclysmic endpoint of this type of situation is a point that Bonnefoy names 'la mauvaise présence', whose negative intensity links it to *présence*, but seen darkly through its frightening opposite: meaninglessness.

We will return in greater detail to this wholly Bonnefoyian notion in Chapter Three. Suffice here to say that Bonnefoy describes the *mauvaise présence* as that through which *ce qui est* 'becomes absent at the very moment when it appears to us, and closes itself off from our reading' (*E*, 76). This clearly stated opposition between *présence*, *ce qui est*, and *mauvaise présence*, crystallizes the triangular relation between the three terms. Tellingly, it is at this juncture that Bonnefoy begins to associate the problem of access to *ce qui est* with the use of language. For the idea of something becoming 'closed off to our reading' focuses attention on an interaction that appears primarily to take place through language. Indeed, the 'salamander episode' analysed in Chapter Three describes an experience wherein an object becomes so completely consumed by language that the perceiving subject, despite his or her concerted efforts, is frighteningly cast adrift in a world where access to meaning, to the reality of *ce qui est* is no longer possible because language has sealed off this path to unity, leaving only the arbitrary quality of its relation to reality.

The problem of language thus becomes the main issue confronting Bonnefoy's philosophy of *présence*. Unsurprisingly, this complexity, which is inherent to the experiential and conceptual double nature of *présence* is exacerbated by the development of deconstructionist theories and their challenge to *présence*. Therefore, before closing this section on the philosophical definitions that influenced Bonnefoy's choice of the term *présence*, attention must be given to the Derridian counter-position. Indeed, inasmuch as it is generally considered to be opposed to the very possibility of a stable and unvarying *présence*, the intransigence of Jacques Derrida's position contributed, potentially, to Bonnefoy's desire to 'salvage' (borrowed again from Bonnefoy's frequently used *sauver*) the notion from the violence done to it by the deconstructionist model. As noted by a number of critics and readers, Derrida's position was never very far from Bonnefoy's thinking. Alex Argyros, for example, suggests that for both, 'Presence is the possibility of integrity, of propriety (the proper, property — a "vrai lieu" — etc.) and access which allows for the erection of truth as a normative principle'.[46] Bonnefoy himself is clearly aware of the potential for the conflation of his thought with that of the deconstructionists when he comments that:

> La parole se laisse enfermer dans la création de mondes-images, systèmes de représentations, de notions, de valeurs, de règles de conduite, qui privent le sujet parlant d'une expérience de la réalité en ce que celle-ci a d'immédiat, d'"indéfait', mais qui le séparent tout aussi bien d'autrui et, en dernière analyse, de soi-même.[47]

> [Speech allows itself to be closed up in the creation of image-worlds, systems of representation, notions, values, rules of behaviour that cut the speaking subject off from an experience of reality in its immediacy, its 'un-dismantledness', but also separates him/her from others and, *in fine*, from himself/herself.]

'These considerations,' he adds, 'might seem akin to deconstructionist thought, inasmuch as it also sees in the system of signifieds which composes a state of language an unreal representation whose absolutization would be ideology and falsehood].[48] Certainly this, along with a number of statements made elsewhere by Bonnefoy, indicates that he is not viscerally opposed to the deconstructionist re-examination of the speaking subject and its expression in writing. At times, he seems even to espouse the notion that we are more shaped by the structures of our language than masters of our expression, as when he writes:

> On a compris aujourd'hui, par opposition radicale à la pensée romantique, que le 'moi' qui semblait maître de sa parole n'est qu'un effet de la langue, une cristallisation de forces qui dans les mots, par les mots, viennent d'ailleurs que de lui, disent autre chose que nous, se composent tout autrement que nous le pensions ou le voudrions : et c'est là ce que j'ai retrouvé pour ma part [...] dans ma pratique propre de l'écriture depuis *Douve*. (*E*, 152)

> [In radical opposition to Romantic thought, we understand today that the 'I' which seemed to be master of its speech is no more than an effect of language, a crystallisation of forces which, in words, through words, come from elsewhere, say other things than we do, come together in ways that are different from what we thought or wanted; this has been my experience [...] in my own writing, ever since *Douve*.]

Bonnefoy's attitude indicates a level of acceptance that is not unique to him. Indeed, even in the face of an eventual refusal, intellectual honesty forces opponents to acknowledge the strength of the positions evoked by deconstructionist thought. George Steiner, whose close attention to the notion of *présence* and its relation with art and literature parallels some of Bonnefoy's positions, demonstrates a similar respect, writing in *Real Presences* that '*on its own terms and planes of argument*, terms by no means trivial if only in respect of their bracing acceptance of ephemerality and self-dissolution, the challenge of deconstruction does seem [...] irrefutable'.[49]

And yet, though Bonnefoy accepts deconstructionism's emblematic challenge to the centrality of the author, its position on the auto-referentiality of language, the absence of truth, of self-presence, he follows up immediately with:

> Ce défi ne pourra être maintenu, il faudra bien que notre fondamental libre-arbitre soit reconnu dans son rôle, qui est de décider qu'il y a du sens, il faudra

que l'auteur se réaffirme, sinon dans les méandres de l'écriture, du moins dans son rapport avec son œuvre, dont il a le devoir de faire du sens. (*E*, 176)

[This challenge cannot be maintained. The role of our fundamental free will to decide that meaning exists must be recognized; the author must reassert himself, if not in the meanders of writing, at least in his duty to give meaning to his work.]

Such statements lend credence to the idea that Bonnefoy's strong adhesion to the notion of *présence* might also be anchored in a form of resistance. For despite their undoubted merit in forcing reflection on matters that had seemed thereto to have escaped critical analysis, the ideas proposed by Derrida also met with general incomprehension and even fierce opposition.

For Derrida, *présence* lies at the heart of a substratum of thought that informs all of Western metaphysics. The notion is, as John Sallis points out, crucial in establishing the building blocks that define Derrida's work: 'It is with the question of the meaning of presence that one can begin to construct the deconstructive square'.[50] The challenge here is to extract from the large body of writing by and about Derrida, a schematic indication of those elements that have a bearing on Bonnefoy's adhesion to the idea of *présence*, especially insofar as they might be experienced by him as a sort of pre-emptive antidote to certain post-modern positions, notably concerning truth and reality. Three axes are of particular significance for Bonnefoy: the first is philosophical, and lies in the Derridian challenge to the very notion of *présence*; the second is linguistico-semiotic and is related to the no less important problem of how language interacts with *présence*, particularly through the agency of *parole*, or speech; the third concerns a specific negation of community that would seem to be the endpoint of certain deconstructionist positions.

Like Heidegger, Derrida grounds his thought on Husserlian phenomenology, initially seeing it a positive light. In a sentence that parallels many of Bonnefoy's preoccupations, he writes in his introduction to Husserl's *L'Origine de la géométrie*: 'The phenomenological attitude is first of all the availability of attention for the coming of a truth that has always lain in waiting'.[51] However, his criticism of Husserl grows out of the very question of *présence*, as David Allison shows succinctly: 'the systematic development of Husserl's phenomenology [is] best demonstrated not in terms of a particular problem, but by the examination of a certain *prejudice* — namely, the epistemological and metaphysical value of *presence*'.[52] How does this prejudice function? Put simply, the phenomenological gesture, as we saw earlier, purports to reveal the essential truth of a being, as received by the subject. In order for this action to function, however, both subject and object must *be*. And this being has, according to Derrida, always been conceived as a form of *présence*, not only the presence of the object to the thinking subject, but also, the self-presence of the subject to itself: in order to receive the truthful essence of the real or virtual object I am contemplating, not only must it become present to me, but I must also be present to myself. For Derrida, these unexamined presuppositions generate in their wake a series of binary oppositions that, he contends, are the subliminal fundamentals of Western metaphysics. More troublingly, they imply a value-laden relationship wherein one of two terms is positively perceived at the expense of the other: the grounding notion of being, for example, cannot avoid conceptually implying its negative obverse, not-being. Presence and absence thus form the matrix of metaphysics, but this pairing of opposite terms, as Allison reminds us, is replicated in a number of such sets: 'among the many conceptual oppositions to be found there are those of matter (*hyle*) and form (*eidos*, idea), corporal and incorporeal, body and soul, animate and inanimate, signifier and signified'.[53] To this we can also add the crucial pair, speech and writing, and the broader question of language.

The pre-eminence of speech over writing, but also the pairing of signifier and signified are easily recognizable elements of the Saussurian paradigm. Indeed, Derrida uses tools derived from the structuralist toolbox to challenge both the unexamined nature of Husserlian *présence*, and the centrality of individual subjectivity as the origin of knowledge and thought. For Husserl, thought within solitary mental life (when one 'speaks' to oneself) points to the real identity, or *présence* of the object and is a pure signified (*signifié*). Because it remains ideal, this meaning is untainted by the use of the signifiers needed for communication through language. To understand this position more effectively, we must refer to Saussure's well-known insight into language, which showed that although the link connecting the signifier and the signified is always arbitrary, the relationship between each signifier and its corresponding signified is unique, and relies on difference, which is the fundamental condition of meaning ('In language itself,' Saussure writes, 'there are only differences [...] Although in general a difference presupposes positive terms between which the difference holds, in a language there are only differences, *and no positive terms*').[54] In other words, although there may be a plurality of apparently identical signifiers, each of them is differentiated from the others by its co-presence in several paradigms (phonic, semantic, etc.) and thus by the unique link it has with its signified. To take an example, the signifier 'bear' can point to an animal or to a variety of different actions, carrying, giving birth, tolerating, etc. In each case the sign 'means' something specific because the signifier is associated with a different signified. Simultaneously, however, the Saussurian system postulates the stable and unvarying presence of the signified that the signifier points to: at the end of the noun 'bear' there is always a specific type of animal that can itself be identified by the eidetic reduction proposed in the Husserlian model.

Using the Saussurian model as a springboard, Derrida revisits the Saussurian notion of difference, positing that it characterizes not only the relationship between different signs, but also, more crucially, the relationship between signifier and signified. Using the neologism 'différance', he pushes structuralist reasoning further by proposing the disorienting reflection that the signifier points not to a stable unique signified, but to a plurality of other signifiers, thus constantly differing meaning to the point where it becomes inaccessible. Lucie Guillemette and Josiane Cossette give a particularly illuminating example of how this process works by analysing the indeterminate signified 'water'. Reading the word, they suggest, we may think of raindrops, a lake, or a chemical symbol (H_2O). We are not necessarily given an immutable mental image. Each signifier can thus call up another signifier.

The effect of this, they say, is the creation of an unending chain of signifiers that displaces and dissolves the boundaries of the text.[55] Consequently, Derrida re-evaluates the Husserlian idea that the signified is that part of the sign that must simply *be* inasmuch as the eidetic reduction has eliminated all the contingent aspects that have historically accrued to the object and revealed its authentic *présence*. He writes, 'what Saussure does not say would have to be said: there is neither symbol nor sign, but becoming-sign of the symbol'.[56] In other words, once it is admitted that their arbitrary relationship precludes any homogeneous unity allowing the signifier to call the signified into presence, it must also be admitted that their true relationship is one of non-presence: the sign is thus the place that marks the absence of identity between the signifier and signified. Gayatri Spivak expresses this quality particularly effectively, writing: 'such is the strange "being" of the sign: half of it always "not there" and the other half always "not that"', meaning that the signified is never there because it is only imagined to be present in the concept we mentally create, while the signifier is obviously vastly different from the thing itself.[57] In the final analysis, then, the deconstructionist model upsets the very grounds of metaphysical investigation by indicating that the signified to which the signifier points can never be attained; its reality is always deferred in an endless web of signifiers. By the same token, there can be no *présence*, because 'Derrida shows that the relation between eidetic reduction and the absolute origin is one of repetition [...] This origin is produced only retrospectively through the act of repetition, signalling to a presence that never existed'.[58]

Clearly, Bonnefoy is morally opposed to Derrida's attack on the very possibility of *présence* and origin. As in the case of surrealism, an apparent initial adherence to deconstructionist positions rapidly gives way to a strongly expressed condemnation. The moral dimension of his position is emphasized by the fact that Bonnefoy's condemnation revolves around the oppositional poles of *espoir* and *désespoir*, and is particularly evident when one compares the sentence cited in the Introduction ('je voudrais réunir, je voudrais identifier presque la poésie et l'espoir', *I*, 107) with his description of deconstructionism as 'un désespoir qui n'espère pas [...] une atonie généralisée' [hopeless despair [...] boundless inertia] (*E*, 39). His criticism is construed along a strongly moral axis engaging not only the individual, but all of society. Bonnefoy writes:

> Si la déconstruction de l'antique visée ontologique peut apparaître, à un certain plan, un impératif de la connaissance, voici en tout cas que son affaiblissement dans des situations concrètes s'accompagne d'un risque de décomposition et de mort pour la société tout entière.[59]

> [If deconstructing the age-old ontological goals might seem at a certain level necessary for knowledge, their weakening in concrete situations goes along with a risk of decomposition and death for society in its entirety.]

However, this despair and inertia to which Bonnefoy refers is only the hypothetical endpoint of the deconstructionist position taken to its logical extreme. Clearly, no writer who continues to write can have wholly accepted it, and Bonnefoy, although he has long meditated on the Rimbaldian experience of a complete refusal of writing, in fact uses Rimbaud's silence to re-invest poetry with meaning for himself (*E*, 32). And precisely because deconstructionism frames the problem as emanating from language, Bonnefoy seeks a solution that is rooted in language, while also providing a modern echo to the theological question of how *présence* can, as Heidegger says, be 'called into being'.

Though meticulously grounded, all of this leaves the question of how such a project might be accomplished. While Bonnefoy takes from deconstructionism useful ways to re-evaluate the relationship between writer, writing, and meaning, in reality many of the fundamental building blocks of his re-evaluation of language are the result of the work of Saussure and structural linguistics, as indeed is made abundantly clear by the terminology Bonnefoy uses to defend language's ability to integrate *présence*. And while it is doubtless true that structuralism has been largely discredited by more contemporary linguistic theories, it remains a vibrant source of mental imagery and reference, and this perhaps even more so for a writer of Bonnefoy's generation, who clearly acknowledges Saussure's contributions, as when he writes that 'Saussure et ceux qui l'ont suivi ont montré que le signe est déterminé par une structure, ainsi ont-ils ajouté une dimension nouvelle à la signification et, [...] à la connaissance des œuvres' [Saussure and those who followed him showed that the sign is determined by a structure; they thus added a new dimension to meaning and [...] to the understanding of written works] (*I*, 247). And yet, as is clearly visible in the description he gives of his poetic ambitions, the role of the speaking subject and its access to *présence* are the axes around which Bonnefoy's opposition to structuralism (and, a fortiori, deconstructionism) revolves:

> Je ne voulais pas signifier mais faire d'un mot en somme quelconque l'agent de la désagrégation de ces systèmes que les signifiants — comme nous disons aujourd'hui — ne cessent de mettre en place. Je voulais lui assurer la capacité d'être cette fois non la notion, la figure, mais au-delà, c'est-à-dire dans l'immédiat, et directement, pleinement, le contact avec l'Un, ce que j'appelle *présence*. (*E*, 140)

> [I wanted not to signify, but to make of an ordinary word the agent that disintegrates those systems that the signifiers — as we say nowadays — continuously put into place. I wanted to give it the possibility this time to go beyond being notion, figure, but directly, immediately connect it with the One, with what I call *presence*.]

Here, Bonnefoy's conviction that any ordinary element of language can be the focal point of an experience of *présence* is clear, couched as it is in that very notion of unity that mandated his rejection of surrealism. Equally clear from his tone is the considered distance he maintains from Saussurian linguistics. Despite this, several important points emerge. First, a seemingly pragmatic acceptance of the idea of structure postulated by Saussure: 'la poésie qui dénie l'empire du signe, a tout intérêt à en connaître les lois' [poetry which denies the empire of the sign had better know its laws].[60] A second important point lies in the expression 'what I call presence'. That seemingly innocuous statement reveals a particularly powerful modus operandi that can be seen at many levels of Bonnefoy's thought. This process, of which he was perhaps unaware, involves modulating ideas and incorporating them so thoroughly into his own thought patterns that he is unselfconsciously able to claim their ownership, as he does with 'I call presence'. This co-opting plays a central role in his ambivalent interactions with structuralism which shift from adopting its premises to rejecting its conclusions, while simultaneously reconfiguring and incorporating its lexicon.

Succinctly, we could say that the greatest impact on Bonnefoy's positions came from Saussure's view of language as a structure whose terms can be understood only in relation to other terms within the system: 'my definition of language presupposes the exclusion of everything that is outside its organism or system'.[61] By extension, this points to the notion that no external measure can establish the coherence and 'truth' of a given system, since meaning cannot exist prior to or outside the interconnections within a system. It is, by definition, relative. Here, we already begin to see the outlines of the divergence that will eventually pit Bonnefoy against the philosophical notions derived from structural linguistics. For as we saw in the discussion on the implications of the phrase *ce qui est*, the unity that Bonnefoy proposes is not relative. It is absolute, immutable, and completely central, in the sense that whether we realize it or not, all meaning and even all sense of self, derives from the existence of an underlying unity which forges us and allows us to fully exist. He writes, for example, in his letter to John Jackson, 'Dans l'expérience de la finitude [...] le sujet humain est au monde, il participe de l'unité de cet Univers qui lui est alors immanent et lui assure d'emblée son épaisseur d'être, sa substance' [It is in the experience of being finite [...] that the human subject is in the world; he participates in the unity of this universe which is then immanent in him and confirms his existence, his substance] (*E*, 92).

But if the philosophical points of Bonnefoy's opposition to structuralism are apparent, the matter is quite different as concerns the mechanics and vocabulary of the Saussurian system. As shown by the Bonnefoy statement on *les signifiants*, his adoption of the Saussurian lexicon suggests that he found the structuralist framework useful enough to integrate it seamlessly into his own discourse. Three iconic elements are of particular interest. The first is the signifier/signified tandem grounding Saussure's conception of the sign. Second are the relations within the celebrated triad: *langage, langue*, and *parole*.[62] The third is the Saussurian development of the notion of *différence*. Bonnefoy's incorporation of these terms is complete, but not unproblematic, as Bruno Gelas indicates when he writes that Bonnefoy's '*langue/parole*' opposition does not properly map onto Saussure's distinction between 'virtual' and 'realized', and thus elicits the question of why Bonnefoy uses the terminology.[63] The answer, I would suggest, lies in Bonnefoy's need to rationalize the possibility for *présence* within the poetic text.

In point of fact, what has interested me is not only that Bonnefoy uses terms that are such clear codes of a structuralist outlook, but, as we saw with the phrase 'I call presence', that he integrates them so totally into his own position that he seems to completely forget their 'adopted' origin. This strategy is recurrent, as we see in the response he gives to an analysis of his work, where he says that he has to transcribe it into *'mon langage personnel,* qui passe par les catégories de *'présence',* de *'langage',* de *'parole'"* (*YB*, 132, my emphasis). Explaining his position further, Bonnefoy shows that this appropriation is not a mere borrowing but a real transformation, insofar as it takes on explicitly theological overtones:

> Cela aussi peut se traduire dans mon langage. La parole n'est qu'un état-limite. Elle a besoin, pour consumer la langue, de la langue même. [...] le péché originel est de systématiser les notions, c'est la langue, par opposition à la parole ; et la poésie c'est se délivrer du péché originel. (*YB*, 134)

> [This too can be translated into my language. The speech-act is no more than a borderline. In order to consume language, it needs language itself. [...] the original sin lies in systematizing notions, in language rather than the speech-act; poetry [by contrast] frees us from original sin.]

Needless to say, the association of *langue* with original sin is completely absent from the original Saussurian model, whose ambition rather was to establish a scientific basis for the study of language, thus uncoupling it from the historical and analogical models prevalent at the time.

The only way to understand Bonnefoy's incorporation of these more affective modes of thought into a purely scientific model is to examine them in relation to the value Saussure himself gave them. Hence, regarding the notion of the sign, for example, linguists generally acknowledge Saussure's unique contribution in creating an unambiguous vocabulary by proposing to 'replace *concept* and *sound-image* respectively by *signified* and *signifier*; the last two terms have the advantage of indicating the opposition that separates them from each other and from the whole (*sign*) of which they are parts'.[64] This statement makes clear the precision of the vocabulary Saussure developed. By contrast, a passage describing a young reader confronting a great book for the first time demonstrates Bonnefoy's re-appropriation and deviation of the very same lexicon:

> Les mots sont bien là pour [le jeune lecteur], il en perçoit les frémissements, qui l'incitent à d'autres mots, dans les labyrinthes du signifiant, mais il sait un signifié parmi eux, dépendant d'aucun et de tous qui est l'intensité comme telle.[65]

> [Words are indeed there for [the young reader]; he perceives their quivering, which leads him toward other words in the labyrinths of the signifier. But he knows that there is one signified among them that depends on none and on all, and is intensity itself.]

Bonnefoy's deflection of the terminology is most evident in his curious comment about 'a signified which is intensity itself'. Indeed, Saussure is very clear about the fact that the signified has no existence prior to the sign that emerges from its contact with the signifier. His opposition to any form of nomenclature has been evoked by a number of commentators, such as Richard Otheguy, who underlines the fact that 'the central holding of Saussure's theoretical position is that there are no ideas to encode independently of language, that there are no antecedent concepts for language to express, in short *that language is not a nomenclature*'.[66]

Yet, in contra-distinction to Saussure's very clear delimitations of the scope of the signified, Bonnefoy pointedly selects a specific signified which emerges from the 'labyrinths of the signifier' and is invested with extraordinary impact. And unlike the Saussurian signified, which is always completely engaged in the structure that it is a part of, the Bonnefoyian signified exists simultaneously inside and outside the structure ('which depends on none and on all').[67] In other words, the horizontal, analogic relationship linking the signifiers in a web of associative connections is, for Bonnefoy, subject to the primacy of a unique, immeasurable signified. Undoubtedly, this 'signified which is intensity itself' is another expression for *présence* and its shadowy avatar, *ce qui est*. Numerous statements found in Bonnefoy's essays and interviews demonstrate his insistence on the fact that poetic language can literally incarnate *présence*, thus conferring on poetry its serious, high purpose. Saussurian linguistics allows Bonnefoy a rational means of concretely determining — and clearly demonstrating — how language can give access to *présence*. This point, it must be said, is rendered clearer by Saussure's description of the structure of language.

Of Saussure's tripartite structure for language (*langage, langue,* and *parole*), not all elements have equal importance in Bonnefoy's *imaginaire*. Indeed, he refers infrequently to *langage*, that is, human capacity for speech, but *langue* and *parole*, the two symbiotically linked terms derived from *langage* are vital for him. In the Saussurian model, these two terms are conceptualized as oppositional. Whereas *langue* (language) is an abstraction, a sort of collective mental storehouse containing the structures needed to produce communication, *parole* refers to a concrete activity that is strictly individual. Saussure refers to it as the 'execution' of language, writing, 'execution is never carried out by the collectivity. Execution is always individual, and the individual is always its master: I shall call the executive side *speaking* [*parole*]'.[68] The importance for Bonnefoy of this third element of the Saussurian triangle cannot be overstated inasmuch as *parole* points to the essential contribution of the individual speaking being, which he emphatically claims for us when he states:

> En fait, la parole est plus vaste que la langue, et elle porte ce que la langue ne porte pas, c'est-à-dire l'espérance d'un avenir, le mouvement vers d'autres états de la relation du sujet parlant à lui-même et à autrui. (*YB*, 402)

> [In reality, speech is vaster than language and it bears within it that which language does not, that is to say, hope for the future, movement toward other states of the relation between the subject speaking to himself or to others.]

Even more importantly, because *parole* is always an act determined at a specific moment by an individual speaker, Bonnefoy attributes to it the capacity to break the bonds of the linguistic system and provide the theoretical opening of language to *présence*. Succinctly, thus, one might say that for Bonnefoy, *parole* is the wedge driven into the heart of all linguistic representation, forcing an opening at the place where language tends naturally to seal itself, and us, off from life.

But concretely, how can *parole*, the ordinary utterance of any person, become *présence*? Naughton sheds some light on the matter when he accurately pinpoints the origin of *présence* as being extra-linguistic, stressing that 'when Bonnefoy speaks of presence, he is evoking what first of all occurs outside the world of language. Poetry does not begin as words, it begins as a relation'.[69] It is difficult to contradict Naughton's position, since it concurs with much of what Bonnefoy himself indicated. This view, nevertheless, has its own shortcomings, since the problem confronting Bonnefoy was not so much acknowledging the inner conviction that 'any element of creation, however simple and "impoverished", may become a presence, may become the lamp that beckons toward unity', but rather the very concrete problem of how to convey not only this conviction, but even more importantly, *présence* itself through language.[70]

Bonnefoy's solution to the problem was simultaneously abstract and practical in the sense that he used *parole* and deixis to counter the deconstructionist challenge to language's capacity to fully express *présence*. Indeed, in response to the famous Hegelian observation that language can apprehend neither 'here' nor 'now' as objective entities, Bonnefoy acknowledges the impact this position had on his thinking: 'ce furent précisément ces pages de la *Phénoménologie de l'Esprit* qui ont été un des ébranlements fondateurs de ma réflexion poétique, ces pages sur l'ici-et-maintenant' [it was precisely those pages on the here-and-now from the *Phenomenology of the Spirit* that shook the foundations of my poetic reflection] (*YB*, 45). The response he brought to bear indicates, however, his visceral opposition to Hegel's analysis, as Christian Berg indicates when he argues that Bonnefoy upends the Hegelian position by anchoring sense-experience — the keystone of Bonnefoy's edifice — not in knowledge, but in absence and death.[71] Berg's point is well taken, for Bonnefoy's opposition to conceptual knowledge is clearly established. More concretely, however, I would argue that Bonnefoy's rejection of the Hegelian model is also materialized in deixis and the affective capacities of poetry. Hegel demonstrates the inadequacy of language by writing, 'To the question: "What is Now?", let us answer, e.g. "Now is Night"'.[72] In many cases, that answer is clearly false. In response, however, Bonnefoy writes in 'La Poétique de Nerval', an essay connecting the poet Nerval and Hegel: 'Oui, le maintenant est la nuit, nous dit aussi l'auteur d'*Aurélia*, et l'ici est la nuit encore. L'approche de l'unité est barrée de monstres, nos fantasmes' [Yes, now is night, the author of *Aurélia* (Nerval) also tells us, and here is night also. The path toward unity is barred by monsters, our chimeras' (*VP*, 63). Bonnefoy suggests that though Hegel's association might have been randomly chosen, the semantic weight of the word 'night' translates an anguish to which poetry is a possible response. Thus Bonnefoy continues, 'Mais il faut avancer dans cette ténèbre. Et si maintenant c'est la nuit, rien ne dit que demain, et grâce à quelques poèmes, un peu de jour ne paraisse' [Yet, we must advance through these shadows. And if now is night, nothing says that tomorrow, thanks to a few poems, a little daylight will not appear] (*VP*, 63). His project is unquestionably ambitious. It is precisely the Saussurian framework that allows him to oppose the Hegelian view of language, for if language itself creates Hegel's inability to express the deictic *hic et nunc*, Bonnefoy's reversal of the Hegelian model uses the tools provided by Saussure to resolve the problem of indicating deixis through language.

In essence, the perception Saussure and Bonnefoy have of linguistic terms appears as though each of them perceived the same image from an inverse perspective. The high value Bonnefoy gives to *parole* does indeed derive from the characteristics that Saussure imputes to it. The latter dismisses *parole* as an inadequate object of study. He defines the manifestations of speech as 'willful', 'individual', and 'momentary' and thus concludes that the study of speech 'must not be confused with linguistics proper, whose sole object is language'.[73] For Bonnefoy, by contrast, it is the very contingency, variability, and momentaneity of *parole* that allows it to reproduce faithfully the nature of reality, which he describes as being eminently anchored in the passage of time and the vicissitudes of the unforeseen, in 'tout ce qu'on peut nommer notre incarnation' (*E*, 62). All of these undeniable aspects of the reality that are experienced by individuals in their embodied, 'incarnated' selves are, for Bonnefoy, encapsulated in the use of *parole*. And it is precisely this double capacity of *parole* to be the expression of the individual speaking being and the accurate reflection of reality that allows it to become a harbour for *présence*. As he writes, 'The difficulty of poetry is that language is a system, while poetry's speech is presence' (*E*, 97).

At the same time, however, Bonnefoy is careful not to put too much faith in the capacity of *parole* alone, saying pointedly that although the contingent nature of *parole* gives it the potential to express *présence*, this capacity does not automatically devolve to all instances of speaking. On the contrary, the relation between *parole* and *présence* is predicated on three factors that oppose it to Hegel and Derrida. In the first instance, the capacity of *parole* to become the path to *présence* is connected with something resembling phenomenological 'intentionality', through what Bonnefoy calls 'the poetic act' ('les mots peuvent être avant tout notre acte', *I*, 127). More specifically, the poetic act implies disengaging the truth of *parole* from the entrapping structures of language:

> Le vrai commencement de la poésie, c'est quand ce n'est plus une langue qui décide de l'écriture, une langue arrêtée, dogmatisée, et qui laisse agir ses structures propres; mais quand s'affirme au travers de celles-ci, relativisées, littéralement démystifiées, une force en nous plus ancienne que toute langue, une force notre origine, que j'aime appeler la parole. (*E*, 34)

> [The real beginning of poetry is when it is no longer language that decides writing, a language that is fixed, dogmatic, and which lets its own structures act; it is when a force, our origin, affirms itself through these structures which are thereby relativized, literally demystified, a force within us that is more ancient than all languages, a force I like to call speech [*la parole*].]

Needless to say, this wholly Bonnefoyian comment linking language, *parole*, and origin is not neutral. On the contrary, it provides a subtle thrust against what Bonnefoy reads as the reductive nature of the deconstructionist position, in which the individual becomes the vassal of a language that acts autonomously and can never be inflected by its users. To oppose this, Bonnefoy will use *parole* as the weapon of predilection against the deconstructionist absence of origin. As he comments to Alain Bosquet, 'What have we wanted since the beginning of humanity if not to be the origin of the meaning that is engendered by language and not simply an aspect of it?' (*E*, 62). The individual's self-conscious production of an 'act of poetry' through the use of *parole* is thus the intentional attempt to disengage poetry from the entrapping system of language. The idea of 'disengaging' brings us to the second aspect of relation between *parole* and *présence*, which is its capacity to 'literally demystify', or 'unhide', and the 'disclosure' or 'unveiling' contained in the expression cannot but recall the importance of the notion for Heidegger. For Bonnefoy, as for Heidegger, language provides access to *présence*. And as critic Jean-Pol Madou suggests, for both writers this access to *présence* must nowadays be read in parallel with the ideas carried by deconstructionism: 'the texts of Bonnefoy, like those of Heidegger, allow us today, beyond the strategies of deconstructionism, to pose again the question of *présence* in its matinal and enigmatic simplicity; [they] invite us to rethink the relationship between language and reality against the post-Hegelian tradition which makes of the word the murderer of the thing'.[74]

And yet, Bonnefoy's position is not simply a direct echo of the Heideggerian vision, for, as we saw earlier, though the latter does give primacy to poetic language, for him *all* language allows human beings to fully enter into the specificity of their humanity. By contrast, it is perhaps Bonnefoy's narrower focus on *parole* rather than on language as a whole that enables him to construct a more viable response to the Hegelian rejection of the deictic 'here' and 'now'. And in this trajectory, Bonnefoy finds in the Saussurian structure the means to modulate Heidegger's position, for as I suggested above, it is through his remotivation of the Saussurian *parole* that Bonnefoy can more 'scientifically' consolidate the potential of language to oppose the Hegelian model. Bonnefoy's 'method' functions by integrating deixis. In what might seem like a paradoxical gesture, his use of *parole* co-opts deixis to resolve the problem of the incompatibility Hegel proposes between language and its grasp of the *hic et nunc*. Indeed, there can be no doubt that at a certain level Bonnefoy accepts Hegel's mistrust of language. 'Yes,' he states, 'c'est vrai, la parole vide l'ici et le maintenant de tout contenu concret, de toute épaisseur d'existence, pour autant qu'elle essaie de les décrire' [it is true that speech empties the here and now of all concrete content, of all depth of existence insofar as it tries to describe them] (*YB*, 45). And yet, he continues, 'il lui reste possible de le *désigner*, cet ici-maintenant, si, précisément, elle rompt avec le dessein de le décrire' [it remains possible for it [*la parole*] to *designate* this here-now, if indeed it breaks with the objective of describing it] (*YB*, 45).

Several key points are connected to this '*designate*' that encapsulates Bonnefoy's opposition to the Hegelian model. Its importance is patently underscored by the italics: through them, indeed, Bonnefoy materializes the etymological function of *désigner*, that is, marking something with a sign in order to draw attention to it. 'To designate' means to point to something, and this, of course, is the very function of deixis, returning us to the object of the Hegelian obloquy. But in opposition to Hegel, Bonnefoy clearly suggests a rehabilitation of language through the double approach contained both in the intentionality materialized in the italicized gesture of pointing, and in the semantics of the word *désigner*. Further, in a strange coincidence, its 'normal' meaning can give rise to a more creative interpretation allowing us to read it as *dé* + *signer*, where the privative prefix literally 'undoes' the sign, thus becoming a pure deictic. More generally, Bonnefoy's argument can appear surprising because of its seeming circularity: the inability of language to indicate the objects of deixis can be undone by deixis itself. However, this position also confirms the double function, simultaneously descriptive and indicative, of language. His *désigner* thus points again toward *parole* as the only agent of language able to undo the system to which it belongs in order to authentically express *présence*. A statement from the essay 'L'Acte et le lieu de la poésie' confirms this suggestion. There, Bonnefoy writes about *parole* that 'elle opère la transmutation de l'abouti en possible' (*I*, 132), Under the agency of *parole*, thus, 'l'abouti' (the finished [poem]) is undone and transformed back into fresh possibility, clearly reversing the more expected, and logical, transformation of possibility into finished object.

Finally, interconnection between *parole* and deixis plays out on a spatial level that is encapsulated in the structuralist *différence* evoked earlier. The relationship between the term and Bonnefoy's writing operates at several levels. The first addresses the notion of a metaphysical space created within the structure of language, while the second is linked to a specific type of differentiation within language that is predicated on imputing positive or negative values to words. Once again, these aspects demonstrate Bonnefoy's construction of his own philosophy of language and meaning, carefully demarcating his position at the very place where it intersects with that of structuralism. The point of connection is the well-known formulation 'l'arbitraire du signe'. Bonnefoy writes, regarding the materiality of language and its strangely arbitrary nature:

> C'est pourquoi les mots ont offert à l'anxiété poétique aussi bien leur opacité matérielle, ces lettres arbitraires et fascinantes que la clarté du concept. Je dis *une fleur*, et le son du mot, sa figure mystérieuse est le rappel de l'énigme. (*I*, 132)

> [This is why words have offered to poetic anxiety both their material opacity, those arbitrary and fascinating letters, and the clarity of the concept. I say *a flower*, and the sound of the word, its mysterious figure is a reminder of the enigma.]

These 'material' and 'conceptual' poles echo the structuralist paradigm and its idea that the fundamental relationship between signs hinges on that which differentiates them, whether at the level of the signifier, or at the level of the signified.[75] Difference, in fact, is so much the essential requirement of a linguistic system that although it is possible to imagine a crude code dividing the world into two categories — food, and non-food, perhaps — and thus using only two terms, say, 'tick' and 'tock', a one-term system could establish no meaningful communication. In other words, if everything were called 'bleem', then because 'bleem' meant everything, it would mean nothing. To take a concrete example, 'chair' for instance, Saussure asserts, in a now-familiar argument, that there is no special 'chairness' that connects the word to the thing it designates. Rather, we derive meaning from the constellations of words which surround it and assign to it a meaningful space within the linguistic system. Thus at the level of the signifier, 'chair' exists in a differential relationship with all other words which phonetically abut on it: 'bear', 'stair', 'beware', etc. A similar distinction exists at the conceptual level, where the signified, 'chair', is surrounded by and differentiated from adjoining notions: 'armchair', 'sofa', 'stool', etc. The net result is that any given term in language derives its meaning solely from its 'spatial' relation with surrounding words. The question of this linguistic space which determines the semantic content of any word finds significant resonance in the metaphoric building blocks that construct Bonnefoy's thinking, as a number of critics have pointed out. Patrick Née devotes an entire monograph, *Poétique du lieu dans l'œuvre d'Yves Bonnefoy*, to Bonnefoy's relation to place. More specifically, Argyros writes concerning *Douve*: 'By far the dominant trope in the poem is that of *place* [...], the poems which comprise *Douve* are repeatedly concerned with the question of a finite location'.[76]

As we saw earlier, Derrida's extension of Saussure's differential relationship between words shows that each word contains not only its own meaning, but also the negative poles of all the spatially related terms that it is *not*, in an endless differing of meaning. This last point marks a crucial aspect of Bonnefoy's rejection of structuralism in the sense that where Saussure perceives the differential relationship of all words in a voluntarily neutral fashion, for Bonnefoy, words are not inert agents of meaning, but are rather invested with a moral imperative derived, inevitably, from his need to show *présence* through language. Thus, when he writes 'what poetic intuition has hoped for in words — in some words at least — is that unity, divinity shine in them, that there be true presence' (*APP*, 124), the important statement buried in the sentence is the almost casual 'in some words at least', which points to a wholly Bonnefoyian differentiation that appears at the semantic level. This notion becomes clearer in his comment on the words 'bread' and 'wine', about which he writes:

> Ce n'est donc pas seulement qu'ils signifient *autre chose* que farine ou verre ou bouteille, disons, mais qu'ils signifient *autrement*. Et les prononcer, les employer sous ce signe, c'est donc faire apparaître au sein de la langue une liaison structurelle, qui n'est pas pour autant simple différenciation de signifiants, mais création d'être. (*E*, p. 21)

> [It is not only that they mean something *other* than, let's say, flour, or glass, or bottle; they mean *differently*. Speaking them, using them under this sign, is showing a structural connection at the core of language that is the creation of being and not just the differentiation of signifiers.]

This statement is perhaps not so surprising, since we saw earlier that 'bread' and 'wine', the symbols of communion, are motivated words for Bonnefoy. But what is perhaps more unusual is that we find Bonnefoy arguing in an extensively developed analysis that 'all words in a language do not lend themselves equally to poetic intention' (*I*, 255). On the contrary, some words are more naturally poetic, that is, more invested with a potential for *présence* than others: 'Ainsi *brique*, déjà, parle à l'esprit de poésie de façon moins évidente que *pierre*, parce que le rappel du procédé de fabrication l'emporte, dans la donnée de ce mot' [Thus brick speaks less obviously to the poetic spirit than stone, because a recollection of the manufacturing process dominates the condition of the word] (*I*, 255). The reason for this, Bonnefoy contends, is that some words encompass entire categories of human activities, while other words remain peripheral because they 'ne font que le décrire, n'ont pour signifié qu'un *aspect*, difficilement perpétuable dans l'intériorisation que la poésie se donne pour tâche d'effectuer' [do no more than describe, and have as their signifier only a single aspect, which is difficult to perpetuate in the interiorisation that is the task of poetry] (*I*, 255). 'To drink', therefore, points toward an essential act, while 'to sip' is merely descriptive, a facet, and not something that *désigner* that can call into *présence*. And while these latter words have their place in poetry, their use renders the poet's task of bringing *présence* into language more difficult.

That said, it is interesting to note that despite the seemingly intransigent quality of the distinction he draws, he also argues that 'de nombreux mots qui semblent dire l'aspect pourront être repris, rachetés par le souci poétique' [poetic attention can redeem many words that seem to voice [only] an aspect] (*I*, 256). The constructions Bonnefoy uses here reconnect the specificity of his vision of language to the philosophical and theological roots of *présence*. 'Redeem' certainly works this way. Additionally, his almost casual qualification that certain words only *'seem* to say' points again to poetry as an act whose function is to reveal that which is hidden, thus harkening back to the notion of phenomenological disclosure we saw earlier. Finally, this view of language gives another level of meaning to the notion of difference, one that is wholly particular to Bonnefoy. Indeed, his difficulty with so-called 'aspectual' words clearly lies in a triumvirate of negative associations he provides: they describe rather than designate; they remain outside, thus do not transform inner reality; and they fragment the unity that *présence* seeks to show. These three elements must be understood as grounding elements, both of Bonnefoy's *imaginaire* and of his intellectual position; they combine not only to consolidate the specificity of Bonnefoy's interpretation of Saussurian *différence*, but they also cast into sharp light Bonnefoy's problem, which is rooted not only in the ephemeral and elusive nature of the *présence* that he is trying to capture, but also in the parallel problem of finding a form of writing adequate to house it. Attempting to reconcile these two imperatives inevitably leads to a form of paradox, as Arnaud Buchs so aptly indicates, when he writes that 'concept must be overcome in order to reach what Bonnefoy calls *présence* — also written Presence, thereby pinpointing the problem more clearly — which is imagined as a way to capture the object as it is outside of language'.[77]

And yet, as Buchs points out, the 'grands vocables' of Bonnefoy's poetics, '*l'Un*', '*la Présence*', '*l'Image*', are themselves none other than concepts being used to denounce the concept, and thus poetry cannot provide the means to escape the circle and find 'a pre-linguistic apprehension of reality'.[78] Buchs pinpoints the problem with precision locating it in the paradoxical duality at the heart of *présence*, particularly with respect to language and its incompatibility with a non-linguistic, 'direct' experience of reality. This duality is to be put into parallel with the pitfalls associated with 'aspectual' language. Poetry, we have seen Bonnefoy arguing in many instances, is the only form of writing that can 'redeem' language and *be* a form of *présence*. Therein lies the problem: simply 'being', it would seem, does not suffice to convey meaning; *présence* is both an experience to absorb and a concept to understand, and like anything that needs to be learnt, readers have to comprehend what they are looking for in order to see it. Bonnefoy's essayistic project is a direct response to the problem of synthesizing concept and experience in order to transmit the duality of *présence*. This becomes possible precisely because of the characteristics of the essay, its theoretical and rhetorical parallels with poetry, its embracing of paradox, and its propinquity with deixis. Indeed, it is no coincidence that the defence of the essay constructed by Georg Lukács in his celebrated 'essay' on the essay is based on his intuition that it can incorporate the 'two types of reality of the soul', 'life' and 'living', and that these, in turn, appear to be no more than different terms describing the duality of *présence*.[79] These diverse indicators combine to show that despite Bonnefoy's disparagement of the essay, its hybridity actually obtains more functional usefulness in conveying *présence* than other forms of writing.

Notes to Chapter 1

1. See Richard Vernier, John Jackson, Jean Starobinski, Gérard Gasarian, John Naughton, or Patrick Née, to name but a few of the critics who have studied the subject.
2. The translation of *sensible*, which is relatively transparent in French ('that which can be apprehended by the senses'), is complex in English, both because of the unusual quality of 'sensate', and because of the interference of another definition of 'sensate' as 'an object or thing that has senses'.
3. Yves Bonnefoy, *L'Improbable* (Paris: Mercure de France, 1959), p. 137.
4. de Lussy and Bonnefoy, *Yves Bonnefoy*, p. 54.
5. Richard Vernier, *Yves Bonnefoy ou les mots comme le ciel* (Tübingen: Gunter Narr, 1985), p. 25.
6. For this aspect of Bonnefoy's writing, the reader can consult his interviews with Bernard Falciola, reprinted in Bonnefoy, *Entretiens sur la poésie*, as well as the work of Jean-Pierre Jossua and Ronald Giguère, among many others.
7. Ronald Gérard Giguère, *Le Concept de la réalité dans la poésie d'Yves Bonnefoy* (Paris: Nizet, 1985), p. 21.
8. Jean-Pierre Jossua, *Pour une histoire religieuse de l'expérience littéraire*, 4 vols (Paris: Beauchesne, 1985), I, 223, n. 7.
9. Cited by Jean-Paul Sartre, *Qu'est-ce que la littérature?* (Paris: Gallimard, 1985), p. 303, n. 6.
10. Leuwers, *Yves Bonnefoy*, p. 13.
11. André Breton, *Nadja* (Paris: Gallimard/Folio, 1965), p. 157.
12. Svein Eirik Fauskevag, 'Yves Bonnefoy et le réalisme poétique', in *Yves Bonnefoy*, ed. by Favre, pp. 455–68 (p. 466).
13. Karl Bühler, *Sprachtheorie* (Jena: Gustav Fischer, 1934), p. 102.
14. Jean-Pierre Richard, *Onze études sur la poésie moderne* (Paris: Seuil, 1981), p. 281–82.
15. Stephen Levinson, 'Deixis', in *The Handbook of Pragmatics*, ed. by Laurence R. Horn & Gregory Ward (Malden, MA: Blackwell, 2006), p. 11.
16. Ibid.
17. Ibid., p. 15.
18. Lev Shestov, *Athènes et Jérusalem*, trans. by Boris de Schloezer (Paris: Aubier, 1993), p. 45.
19. Bernard Martin, 'Lev Shestov: A Russian Jewish Existentialist', *Theology Today*, 23.3 (October 1966), 386–402 (p. 387).
20. Ibid., p. 393.
21. Lev Shestov, *In Job's Balances*, trans by Camilla Coventry and C. A. Macartney [1932], ed. Bernard Martin (Athens: Ohio University Press, 1975), II.26 ('Deus ex machina') <http://shestov.phonoarchive.org/ijb/jb1_5.html> [accessed 25 June 2022].
22. Pinson, Jean-Claude, 'Du Spéculatif au Dialogue: Philosophie et Poésie selon Yves Bonnefoy', *Dalhousie French Studies*, 60 (2002), pp 11-16. David Jasper, 'La Même Voix toujours', in *Translating*

Religious Texts: Transgression and Interpretation, ed. by David Jasper (New York: St Martin's Press, 1993), pp. 106–21 (p. 111).

23. John T. Naughton, 'The Notion of Presence in the Poetics of Yves Bonnefoy', *Studies in Twentieth & Twenty-First Century Literature*, 13.1 (1989), 43–59 (p. 18). Barthes, in *La Chambre claire*, describes the *punctum* as something which 'jabs' one. It is opposed to the coded *studium* apprehended through conscious reflection. Bonnefoy said of this work that it moved him particularly because he saw in it a true movement toward poetry that had not been present in Barthes's prior work.

24. John T. Naughton, *The Poetics of Yves Bonnefoy* (Chicago: University of Chicago Press, 1984), pp. 43–44.

25. Yves Bonnefoy, *The Act and the Place of Poetry*, trans. by John T. Naughton (Chicago: University of Chicago Press, 1989), p. 103 (hereafter referenced in *APP* in the main text).

26. Yves Bonnefoy, *Entretiens sur la poésie* (Neuchâtel: La Baconnière, 1981), p. 91. This essay was not included in the 1990 edition of *Entretiens sur la poésie*.

27. Yves Bonnefoy, *Correspondance*, ed. by Odile Bombarde and Patrick Labarthe (Paris: Belles Lettres 2018), p. 908.

28. Bonnefoy was to destroy this text some years later.

29. Emmanuel Lévinas's French translation of Husserl's *Méditations cartésiennes* appeared in 1931, almost twenty years before the German version, which was published in the first volume of *Husserlaniana* in 1950.

30. Edmund Husserl, *L'Origine de la géométrie*, introduction and trans. by Jacques Derrida (Paris: Presses universitaires de France, 1962), p. 92.

31. As quoted by François Lyotard in *La Phénoménologie*, (Paris: Presses universitaires de France, 1954), p. 19.

32. As quoted by James M. Edie in 'Husserl vs. Derrida', *Human Studies*, 13.2 (1990), 103–18 (p. 106).

33. Lyotard, *La Phénoménologie*, p. 19.

34. Ibid., p. 213.

35. Richard A. Cohen, 'Levinas: Thinking Least about Death — Contra Heidegger', *Self and Other: Essays in Continental Philosophy of Religion*, ed. by Eugene Thomas Long (= special issue of in *The International Journal for the Philosophy of Religion* 60.1–3 (2006) 21–39, p. 24.

36. Beaufret, for many years, was considered as *the* French specialist on Heidegger. He began an unfinished doctoral thesis under the direction of Jean Wahl, who was to become Bonnefoy's director for his thesis on sign and signification.

37. Martin Heidegger, *Lettre sur l'humanisme*, trans. by Roger Munier (Paris: Aubier Montaigne, 1964), p. 109.

38. J. Glenn Gray, 'Heidegger's "Being"', *Journal of Philosophy*, 49.12 (1952), 415–22 (p. 416).

39. Odile Bombarde, 'La Pensée du rêve', in *Yves Bonnefoy: poésie, recherche et savoirs. Actes du colloque de Cerisy-la-Salle*, ed. by Daniel Lançon and Patrick Née (Paris: Herman, 2007), pp. 547–77 (p. 572).

40. Cohen, 'Levinas', p. 23.

41. Ibid., p. 24.

42. Gray, 'Heidegger's "Being"', p. 416.

43. Martin Heidegger, *Poetry, Language, Thought*, trans. by Albert Hofstadter (New York: Harper & Row, 1971), pp. 198–99.

44. Maurice Blanchot, *L'Entretien infini* (Paris: Gallimard, 1967), p. 10.

45. Mario Maurin, 'On Bonnefoy's Poetry', *Yale French Studies*, 21 (1958), 16–22 (p. 21).

46. Argyros, 'The Topography of Presence', p. 247.

47. de Lussy and Bonnefoy, *Yves Bonnefoy*, p. 155.

48. Ibid. The word 'absolutization' is a direct translation of the Bonnefoy neologism 'absolutisation'.

49. George Steiner, *Real Presences* (Chicago: University of Chicago Press, 1989), p. 132.

50. John Sallis, 'Heidegger/Derrida — Presence', *Journal of Philosophy*, 81.10 (October 1984), 594–610 (p. 597).

51. Husserl, *L'Origine de la géometrie*, p. 164.

52. David B. Allison, 'Derrida's Critique of Husserl and the Philosophy of Presence', *Veritas (Porto Alegre)* (2005), 89–99 (p. 90).

53. Ibid., p. 93.
54. Ferdinand de Saussure, *Course in General Linguistics*, trans. by Wade Baskin (New York: McGraw-Hill, 1959), p. 118.
55. Lucie Guillemette and Josiane Cossette, 'Déconstruction et différence', *Signo*, ed. by Louis Hébert, para. 2.2.1 <http://www.signosemio.com/derrida/deconstruction-et-differance.asp> [accessed 25 June 2022].
56. Jacques Derrida, *Of Grammatology*, trans. by Gayatri Chakavorty Spivak (Baltimore, MD: Johns Hopkins University Press, 1976), p. 47.
57. Gayatri Chakavorty Spivak, 'Translator's Preface', in Derrida, *Of Grammatology*, trans. by Chakavorty Spivak, p. xvii.
58. Chung Chin-Yi, 'Deconstruction and the Transformation of Husserlian Phenomenology', *Kritike*, 2.2 (December 2008), 77–94 (p. 80).
59. de Lussy and Bonnefoy, *Yves Bonnefoy*, pp. 161–62.
60. Ibid., p. 156.
61. Saussure, *Course in General Linguistics*, p. 20.
62. It must be noted that Saussure's triad translates incompletely into English, as the distinction between *langage* (the human capacity for language) and *langue* (languages) is erased by the single word 'language' that translates both.
63. Bruno Gelas, 'Figures et fonction de la voix', in *Yves Bonnefoy*, ed. by Favre, pp. 383–97 (p. 388).
64. Saussure, *Course in General Linguistics*, p. 67.
65. de Lussy and Bonnefoy, *Yves Bonnefoy*, pp. 163–64.
66. Ricardo Otheguy, 'Saussurean Anti-nomenclaturism in Grammatical Analysis', in *Signal, Meaning, and Message*, ed. by Wallis Reid, Ricardo Otheguy, and Nancy Stern (Amsterdam: Johns Benjamins 2002), pp. 373–403 (p. 397).
67. Saussure, *Course in General Linguistics*, p. 9.
68. Ibid., p. 13.
69. Naughton, 'The Notion of Presence in the Poetics of Yves Bonnefoy', p. 47.
70. Ibid., p. 46.
71. Christian Berg, 'Le Chemin interdit par la déesse', in *Yves Bonnefoy*, ed. by Favre, pp. 165–93 (p. 170).
72. Georg Friedrich Wilhelm Hegel, *The Phenomenology of the Mind*, trans. by James Black Baillie (New York: Harper Colophon, 1967), p. 60.
73. Saussure, *Course in General Linguistics*, pp. 19–20.
74. Jean-Pol Madou, 'La Poétique d'Yves Bonnefoy: un défi au nihilisme mallarméen', in *Yves Bonnefoy*, ed. by Favre, pp. 27–39 (p. 38).
75. Saussure does not present the notion of the 'arbitrariness of the sign' as new. Many thinkers have been aware that there is no 'natural' relationship between an object and its linguistic representation. Even signifiers that appear to be motivated by their signifieds, onomatopoeias such as 'buzz' or 'hum', are dismissed by Saussure: 'onomatopoeic formations are never organic elements of a language system [and] their number is much smaller than is generally supposed' (*Course in General Linguistics*, p. 69).
76. Argyros, 'The Topography of Presence', p. 253.
77. Arnaud Buchs, *Une pensée en mouvement* (Paris: Galilée, 2008), p. 12.
78. Ibid., p. 13.
79. Lukács, *Soul and Form*, p. 4.

CHAPTER 2

❖

The Hospitable Essay

Présence, as we have seen, has inscribed within its very core a form of duality that Arnaud Buchs underscores when he describes it as *both* an experience and a concept.[1] Considering the pains Bonnefoy took to express his rejection of concept, seen as the very antithesis of a direct experience of *présence*, Buchs's observation presents an unquestionable challenge. Bonnefoy himself is painfully aware of this problematic duality, writing 'nous sommes des êtres doubles, à la fois langage et existence' [we are dual beings, both language and existence] (*E*, 91). The problem, however, lies not only in the duality of *présence*, but also in some of the more practical hurdles that compromise Bonnefoy's stated ambition to convey it through his poetry. In part, as I suggested in the Introduction, a first level of concern addresses the reader's capacity to recognize and embrace the true experience of *présence*: if Bonnefoy's firm commitment to the notion allows him to posit the capacity of poetic language to communicate it, far less certain is the idea that readers not conditioned to recognize it will adequately perceive *présence* in a text. In some senses, then, the reader must be taught to 'see' it. A second, even more pragmatic consideration is the inescapable fact that Westerners live in a society with diminishing numbers of readers of poetry. As a consequence, poetry alone may not touch significant numbers of readers, and may thus not allow enough people to come into contact with the notion of *présence*. These constraints, however, are external, societal; Bonnefoy was also confronted with impediments linked to the genre itself. Using a highly poetic image, he comments to Bernard Falciola about the potential limitations of poetry, remarking that its synthetic dimension, 'si elle place des cimes dans la lumières, laisse aussi des vallées dans l'ombre' [while illuminating the peaks, also leaves the valleys in shadow] (*E*, 49). Unsurprisingly, then, his quest for a solution to this intrinsic duality is inscribed into the very fabric of his writing, finding expression in the essay, whose 'mixture of the cognitive and the aesthetic' Claire de Obaldia defines as 'its greatest resource'.[2] In some highly significant sense, Bonnefoy's essays bear silent witness to his inability to wholly show *présence* through the imagistic capacity of pure poetry. The essay indeed provides the clearest path to resolving his problem of conveying the duality of *présence* inasmuch as it constantly seeks an equilibrium between a mimetic contact with experience and a more discursive expression of idea. Bonnefoy's poetic evocation of the illuminated summits of poetry and the shadowy valleys of the thought process leading to it is helpful and reinforces the idea of the essay's greater potential for transparent communication by showing that it illuminates a path without which the summits of poetry might forever remain inaccessible. As this chapter shows, the essay provides a textual space whose generic characteristics enable Bonnefoy to embrace and give form to both dimensions of *présence*: on the one hand, the essay's constant interaction with fragmentation allows it to mirror the brief, flashing moment of experiential *présence*; on the other hand, that very fragmentation is constantly undercut by forms of unity more consonant with *présence*-as-concept and with certain aspects of that *ce qui est* which so important to him.

These qualities of the genre set us on the path of answering the question posed in the Introduction, namely, why the essay? As it happens, beneath its subdued humility, the essay responds with particular acuity not only to the problem of duality of *présence*, but also to Bonnefoy's complementary problem of how to convey meaningfully all the facets of his profound understanding of the notion. In part, what makes his plethoric use of the essay so fascinating is that the more one examines this low-key, somewhat neglected genre, the more one realizes how keenly its characteristics — both those that garner widespread consensus, as well as those that encounter more opposition — meet and respond to the Bonnefoyian project of bringing readers to a more complete awareness of *présence*. Telling, also, is the fact that with a few notable yet crucial exceptions, many of the essential and formal characteristics of the critical essay — subjectivity, truthfulness, brevity — map directly onto the poem, thus contributing to the essay's ability to parallel, more closely indeed than other genres, the mimetic forms that are the hallmark of contemporary poetry. Meanwhile, those that specifically distinguish the essay, its hybridity and didactic potential, as well as its capacity to provide a common textual space, enable the forms of discourse needed to narrate the path to *présence*.

Heretically, I would argue that more so even than his poetry, it is the essay that is the 'vrai lieu' which is such a recurrent trope in Bonnefoy's work. The essay is indeed so much a tool of predilection for Bonnefoy's project that it almost comes as no surprise to realize its proximity to that very deixis which allows him to create a formidable breach in the edifice of philosophical conceptions and thus anchor the textual possibility of *présence*. Laurent Mailhot echoes a number of other critics when he writes:

> The essay — rather than the essayist — says 'I'; it likewise says *here* and *now*; it shapes its own representation, one which is both current and situated. For it is against itself (and against the world as discourse) that the essay struggles. It drifts, it wanders in order to trace a map of its own questionings: its detours determine its contours.[3]

It is impossible not to be struck by the fact that the *I-here-now* that Mailhot applies to the essay is identical to the deictic triplet used in Bühlerian terminology. In that correlation of essay and deixis, Mailhot, of course, echoes Theodor Adorno, who writes in his well-known article 'The Essay as Form' that 'the essay moves in so close to the *hic et nunc* of the object that the object becomes dissociated into the moments in which it has its life instead of being a mere object'.[4] What we observe in Bonnefoy's work is the very materialization of this essayistic deixis. He writes:

L'objet sensible est *présence*. Il se distingue du conceptuel avant tout par un acte, c'est la présence.

Et par un glissement. Il est ici, il est maintenant. Et son lieu, parce qu'il n'est pas le lieu propre, son temps, parce qu'il n'est qu'un fragment de temps, sont les éléments d'une force étrange, d'un don qu'il fait, sa présence. O présence affermie dans son éclatement déjà de toutes parts! (*I, 26*)

[The sensate object is *presence*. It differs from the conceptual above all by an act: presence.

And by a shift. It is here, it is now. And its place, because it is not the proper place, its time, because it is no more than a fragment of time, are the elements of a strange power, of a gift it gives, its presence. O presence strengthened already by its complete shattering!][5]

In addition to the explicit connection between deixis and *présence*, this complex passage provides a first glimpse of many of the major Bonnefoyian techniques addressed in the subsequent chapters, showing how Bonnefoy visually provides the reader with a textual echo of *présence*. Fragmentation is shown not only as a metaphor within the text ('a fragment of time'), but also as a physical and syntactic aspect of the text. *Présence* gains its meaning and its strength from the paradoxical simultaneity of a fragmentation and unity that are syntactically thematized through the obvious visual rupture of the paragraph break repaired by the 'and' which is patently the continuation of the idea. The second 'and' materializes the shift readers must make, for it breaks syntactically with the first 'and', requiring them to pivot rapidly in order to understand the text.

Returning to Mailhot's description of the essay, equally important for my analysis is his correlation of the essay with the image of wandering, of changing course, a definition that is so frequently evoked as to have become commonplace. Bonnefoy, indeed, spontaneously reproduces this trope frequently, materializing it, for instance, in the title *La Vie errante*, or in a passage in the 'Les Tombeaux de Ravenne', where he brackets a segment of text between blank lines, thereby visually highlighting the physicality of his textual change of direction and writes: 'J'avais tracé le dessin d'une théorie de l'ornement. Je l'ai laissée pour une autre' [I had traced the outline of a theory of the ornament. I have abandoned it for another] (*I, 17*). A second example reinforces the idea that the essay's internal characteristics authentically replicate his thought process. There, he acknowledges the significance of these shifts in orientation, writing, 'Pour tous les linguistes, semble-t-il, ce que le mot *cheval* représente, c'est ce qui est, disons, ni l'âne ni la licorne' [for all linguists, it would seem, the word *horse* represents what is, let's say, neither the donkey, nor the unicorn] (*I, 247*). But 'justement', he continues, in a statement cited in the Introduction, 'poetry is not a "use" of language'. He then gives an example of a word used poetically: 'Que je dise 'le feu' (oui, je change d'exemple, et cela déjà signifie)' [if I say 'fire' (yes, I'm changing my example, and that itself has meaning)] (*I, 248*). Such a radical change of direction — perhaps impossible in scientific discourse — is eminently possible in the essay. Finally, Mailhot's suggestion of 'tracing a map' shows the essay as an itinerant venture producing a form of cartography. This is particularly interesting, for it parallels exactly my analysis of the function of Bonnefoy's collected essays and reinforces my argument that they can be read both as an itinerary and as a proto-map indicating the path to *présence*.

Yet, the prodigious versatility of the essay, its so-called 'protean' form, is inversely proportional to its prestige. In his well-known letter to Leo Popper, reprinted as 'On the Nature and Form of the Essay', Georg Lukács writes, 'Were one to compare the forms of literature with sunlight refracted in a prism, the writings of the essayists would be the ultra-violet rays'.[6] Lukács's poetic image suggests that essays are an almost invisible form of writing whose existence shades off the edges of our perception. Invisibility might seem like a peculiar word to use for a genre seemingly so ubiquitous. Possibly, however, it is its very omnipresent familiarity that makes us feel that attempts at definition are superfluous. Perhaps Bonnefoy's silence on his essayistic production derives simply from the 'self-evident' nature of the essay: just as for the seemingly transparent notion of *présence*, everyone knows what an essay is. This familiarity, however, can be a type of fallacy. In the celebrated preface to *The Phenomenology of the Mind*, Hegel comments on how familiarity can create blind spots:

> What is 'familiarly known' is not properly known, just for the reason that it is 'familiar'. When engaged in the process of knowing, it is the commonest form of self-deception and a deception of other people as well, to assume something to be familiar, and to let it pass on that very account.[7]

Bonnefoy's conversancy with Hegel, through his close work with French Hegelians Jean Hyppolite and Jean Wahl hardly needs to be demonstrated: it is, for example, to Hegel he turns for the epigraph to *Douve*. Thus the use of Hegel's remark intends not to criticize Bonnefoy himself, but rather to introduce the complexity of defining a genre purported not only to be a 'natural' mode of expression allowing the transparent transfer of thought, but also one associated with the most negative connotations of prosaic writing, that is, uninspiring and unable to aspire to the elevated and elevating status of poetry. Indeed, while there can be no doubt that such definitions impinge upon the understanding readers have of the genre, they also orient — perhaps even to a greater extent — essayists themselves. In a talk at the Bibliothèque nationale de France (on 12 May 1998) where he discussed the historical relationship between prose and poetry, Bonnefoy stressed the importance prose has had in maintaining a meaningful intellectual space from within which poetry can emerge. After the talk, and in response to my question, however, he told me that the role of his essayistic prose was essentially ancillary, certainly of less import than his poetry.

This negative perception is not unique to him. Critic Jean Starobinski (incidentally, one of Bonnefoy's close friends) when accepting the 1982 Prix de l'Essai, humorously described the essayist as a 'kindly amateur' and the essay as a 'suspiciously non-scientific' genre in the habit of shifting shapes to become something else, a chat, a pamphlet, an editorial, etc. He concluded ruefully: 'To put it crudely, if someone said that I devote myself to essayism, I would be somewhat hurt, I would take that comment as a reproach'.[8] In many senses, the negative tone of Starobinski's qualification is consonant with general perceptions of the essay, reinforcing the idea that writers are as subject to ambient notions as anyone. Yet, he, like Bonnefoy, relies heavily on the genre. What conditions these seemingly inconsistent positions? Indubitably, the answer lies in the nature of the essay, whose characteristics, as I suggested, interlock perfectly with Bonnefoy's philosophical goals and his quest for a textual space to transmit the notion of *présence*. The essay sets the groundwork for creating that 'good reader' so essential to his project, while providing a unique literary space allowing him to resolve a number of the contradictions inherent in poetic access to *présence*. This, however, is only possible because of the highly specific characteristics of the essay. What the essay can *do* is intimately bound to what the essay *is*: a hybrid genre uniquely able to provide a literary space wherein the contradictions of poetry and prose can be momentarily reconciled as, for example, they are in that fragment of an essay quoted in the Introduction where Bonnefoy metaphorically links poetry and hope: 'je voudrais réunir [...] la poésie et l'espoir'. It is emblematic that the union of poetry and hope takes place in a prose sentence embedded in an essay. It is precisely the characteristics of the latter that allow for such permeability.

Existing critical literature devoted to the essay reveals a strong tendency to circumscribe and define it. This propensity underscores the impression of theoretical uncertainty, even anxiety, that surrounds the genre, leading Pascal Riendeau to suggest that this normative tendency reveals the general perception that existing definitions are inadequate.[9] To address this definitional hiatus, many critics turn instinctively to historical considerations (Montaigne, notably), classifications (essays described as personal, critical, polemical, introspective, etc.), or comparisons (essay and novel; essay and poetry, etc.). The present chapter takes a different tack. Using the Lukácsian trope of visible and invisible forms of writing, it describes the essay first from the perspective of highly consensual 'visible' definitions, which include hybridity, subjectivity, and truthfulness. It then addresses more 'invisible' issues such as style, didacticism, and fragmentation, all of which engender greater critical variance, often showing distinctly opposed positions. This structure was deliberately chosen to bring out the distinction between things everyone supposes they know about the essay and those elements that linger at a more subliminal level and thus may have a greater subconscious influence on why essayists choose to use the genre.

Visible Forms of Definition

Hybridity and formlessness appear as commonly accepted descriptors of the genre. In this, it is a faithful replica of what Paul de Man identifies as a far broader contemporary trend that eschews fiction to focus on forms more closely connected to reality, leading, he writes, to 'emphasis on hybrid texts considered to be partly literary and partly referential'.[10] In this, the essay is particularly of its time. As Pierre Glaudes indicates, it would be difficult to find a canonical model for the essay, which would always lead to the same 'reading pact'.[11] (His 'pacte de lecture' deliberately echoes, of course, Philippe Lejeune's 'pacte autobiographique', consolidating the argument I develop in Chapter Four, that a subliminal autobiographical dimension drives Bonnefoy's structuring of his essays into collections.) In its negative interpretation, this formlessness and hybridity traditionally gave rise to epithets such as 'amorphous', 'evasive', 'trivial', while a more positive interpretation evoked an open form marked by a creative absence of constraints. Intuitively, one can imagine that for some writers, the possibilities offered by such a fluid form might positively condition their decision to write essays. In Bonnefoy's case, an additional element factors in: the hybridity of the essay replicates the theo-philosophical hybridity of *présence* itself. We will return to this point.

Current critical perspectives have moved past the commonly invoked 'difficult to define', and it is now admitted that the essay does, in fact, demonstrate certain criteria that can be agreed upon. Reda Bensmaïa goes even further, suggesting that the essay is no 'mixing of genres', but might rather be seen as an 'Ur-genre', all other genres being only the historically determined actualizations of what has potentially always existed in the essay.[12] Along those lines, it seems important to underline the fact that it is precisely what Bensmaïa and others describe as the formal potential of the essay that makes it such a useful genre for thinkers such as Bonnefoy. This potential is linked first to the almost infinite variety of subjects, both serious and trivial (along with all the intermediate shadings thereof) that can serve as the object of the essay. Second, it is connected to the plethora of styles the essay can adopt, even to the point of having them happily co-exist within a single essay. In parallel with its thematic freedom, the second element of criticism levelled at the essay is oriented along a more technical axis. For along with the freedom that comes from the absence of rhetorical constraints (figures, forms, rhythms, themes), the essay's essential formlessness can also be seen in the variety of discursive patterns it can assume. One of the key indications of this discursive variability is clearly seen at the taxonomic level where the attempt to distinguish between different types of essays gives rise to ever more precise labels as de Obaldia underscores when she cites, for example, the philosophical essay, the polemical essay, the autobiographical essay, the aphoristic essay, and so on.[13] The technical, writerly corollary to the essay's 'formlessness' and taxonomic heterogeneity lies in its capacity to encompass a large variety of writing styles, inserting here a dialogue, there a narrative episode, an autobiographical fragment of memory, or a few lines of poetry. This stylistic malleability reflects the multifarious character of a form that has the potential to shift across many different generic boundaries, reinforcing its usefulness for Bonnefoy, in his quest to express the plurality of *présence*.

Critical theorizations of the essay clearly point to its kinship with other genres. Indeed, a fruitful approach for the study of Bonnefoy's essays lies in the theoretical debate opposing Lukács and Adorno.[14] Though their positions on the finality of the essay are radically opposed, their congruence on the historical links between essay and poetry lays the groundwork for thinking about Bonnefoy's essays. Lukács writes, and Adorno reiterates, that 'the essay form has not yet, today, travelled the road to independence which its sister, poetry, covered long ago — the road of development from a primitive, undifferentiated unity with science, ethics and art'.[15] The essay's supposed lack of demarcation from other genres proves vital to readers' (and writers') perception of it as a hospitable writerly space open to infiltration from all sides. Moreover, Lukács's suggestion of an archaic relation between essay and poetry shows more clearly the connection between Bonnefoy the poet and Bonnefoy the essayist, and suggests that the distance is perhaps not so great. As the subsequent sections of the chapter show, the complex interactivity of the essay with poetry reveals an oscillation between real proximity and substantive differentiation that meshes perfectly with Bonnefoy's goal to bring readers to *présence*. That goal is also served by the internal dynamics of the essay, which deliberately adopts what de Obaldia describes as a 'spontaneous', 'natural', and 'artless' style mimicking 'the informality of speech'.[16] Clearly, Bonnefoy capitalizes on this intrinsic characteristic of the essay and magnifies it, for a number of texts he published as essays were originally talks, giving readers the impression that his voice, his presence as a singular individual, is almost materially carried through by the genre.

The significant locus of interpretation for the above hypotheses lies in the central position of the writing subject and its desire to carve out a space for its subjectivity. We need, however, to tread carefully here. Earlier, I evoked the essay's embrace of paradox, which I associate with its capacity to maintain simultaneously positions that appear (and indeed are) contradictory. This is so much the case that I would propose the term 'subjective objectivity' to define the essay's relation to the speaking subject. The subject/object couplet is highlighted by Jean-Marcel Paquette in his cogent definition of the essay as reflexive discourse produced by a 1) non-metaphorical 'I' 2) that generates an enthymematic discourse 3) of a lyrical nature 4) whose object originates in a cultural corpus.[17] Bracketing for the moment the other descriptors, the key element in Paquette's definition concerns his evocation of a non-metaphorical 'I', that is, the impression given by the essay that a real person stands behind the text. That there is, in other words, a decisive co-incidence between the author of the essay and the subject using that literary space to present his or her real thoughts about the cultural object that serves as the essay's starting point. It is this ostensible transparency that most dominates our mental construction of the essay and colours our definitions of it.

It can, of course, be argued that any text has a ground level of subjectivity that is present even when masked or deliberately suppressed, as, for example, in a scientific article or a philosophical work. Certain rhetorical devices, such as the use of citations, expressly contribute to engendering the illusion of objectivity. Paul Woolridge, for example, refers to the 'scholarly ventriloquism' that academics commonly use to downplay their subjectivity, while validating their claim to knowledge and authority. He writes that 'the "as [so and so] puts it" construction [is] a mode of depersonalization that mediates any direct contact the reader could have with the writer's personal voice'.[18] These distancing mechanisms appear antithetical to the goals pursued by the critical or personal essay, which, on the contrary, works to foreground the voice of the subject. The rhetorical strategies that accomplish this are very apparent in Bonnefoy's essays, notably through his use of typography and of italics, that, very much in the manner of deixis, insistently point to an element of the discourse. Thus, though one finds few instances of direct quotations in his essays, italics abound. Sometimes, as is customary in English, they signify an accent stressing a word or phrase ('*voir* la mort', *I*, 86), but they are also the markers of a deeply internalized conceptual borrowing. *Parole* is frequently used so, as are other expressions we have encountered, such as, *ce qui est*, which can be traced back to Kierkegaard, or *théologie négative*, taken from Plotinus. In the case of poetic phrases ('*le vent s'est tu* écrit Dante' [*the wind became silent* writes Dante], *I*, 72), the italics show the 'normal' borrowing we engage in when we memorize poems that speak to us and recite them to underscore a point. The fact that such forms of borrowing should remain vague is part of the understated aesthetic of the essay, as de Obaldia shows when she says that since Montaigne, 'no one will deny the essayist the right to quote from the original without being required to provide the corresponding references or footnotes, for example, or indeed to quote at all accurately'.[19]

Bonnefoy's references to Mallarmé provide an instructive example of the manner in which he capitalizes on that very dimension of the essay and its attendant claim to convey the authentic voice of a real person. In the essay 'Paul Valéry', Bonnefoy uses inverted commas to cite Mallarmé, writing: 'he, too, equated word and Idea, the flower with that which is "absent from any bouquet"' (*APP*, 97). In a fascinating 1982 article, Gerhard Butters points out Bonnefoy's misquotation of the original Mallarmean text, which reads, of course, 'absente de tous bouquets' [absent from all bouquets].[20] The mistake is minor, but the multiple printings of the text ('Paul Valéry' is itself a reprinting of a 1958 *Lettres nouvelles* article entitled 'Paul Valéry, l'apostat') reinforce the essay's accommodation of error, patching it into its etymological connection with the central essayistic trope of *errance*, and making of it thereby the ostensible mark of an unfiltered authenticity.[21] By contrast with the italics Bonnefoy uses to quote Mallarmé a few paragraphs later ('*la presque disparition vibratoire*'), the inverted commas of the earlier 'bouquet' quote creates a textual distance allowing us to see better the process taking place: his material texturing of writing through italics is consonant with his philosophical goal of circumventing the conceptualization of language. In a technique that works in a very essayistic manner to reinforce the subjectivity and authenticity of the relationship between the speaking 'I' and the reader, the italicized quotations represent words and knowledge that he has internalized to the point of being able to cite them spontaneously. The italics represent visually the change in tone that might be used in ordinary speech to indicate to listeners the conscious quoting that is happening. Bonnefoy's choice to make a single sign, italics, take on multiple roles blurs the difference between the words he intends to emphasize and the words whose exterior origin he wants to indicate. By contiguity, both appear to mimic the physical voice of the writer, thus focusing the reader's attention on the speaking subject and reinforcing its centrality in the essay. This is even more so the case for the poetic phrases, where the italics allow the reader to 'see' the mental content Bonnefoy has chosen to acquire.

Yet, in the paradoxical approach that is its forte, the essay, though embracing this focalization, simultaneously undercuts the subject by pointing insistently to the ostensible object of the essay. It is this 'object taken from a cultural corpus', this real, identifiable object that upholds the essay's implicit 'it's not about me' statement, thereby consolidating in readers' minds the objectivity and 'scientificity' of the essay. As it turns out, examining reader perceptions turns out to be productive, particularly in the French context, for it brings up a pervasive resistance to certain attitudes that perceive the scientific method as the only means of procuring an accurate understanding of reality. Tendrils of this position are frequently present in Bonnefoy's work. He recalls in 'Entretien avec John Jackson', his discomfiture with the then-recent discoveries of processes in physics and biology that cut through the real objects that actually *are* for us, in order to address their atomic existence. Modern science, he says, does not even see these real things that shape our reality, whereas 'l'ancienne science' was able to retain everything and give it meaning in a network of correspondences (*E*, 114). In what seems a clear echo of Shestov's positions, Bonnefoy relates the glaring inadequacy in scientific method to its incapacity, or unwillingness, to perceive the world at a human level. His use of the term *correspondance* evokes, of course, Baudelaire's celebrated poem and suggests a way of perceiving the world that is particularly germane to Bonnefoy's own thinking, especially when one remembers that for him, Baudelaire's poetics created 'the truly decisive moment' of modern poetry (*I*, 122). The idea that all meaning, perhaps all truth, derives from the relationships found in a 'network of correspondences' is a point that Jean-Pierre Maulpoix also makes, connecting Baudelaire and the difficulty of apprehending Bonnefoy's poetry, which 'blurs its own contours in an ambiguous discourse which erases boundaries, which refuses to over-circumscribe its objects, which undoes the separation between things in order to re-establish a body of *correspondences*'.[22] This characteristic is echoed in Bonnefoy's essays, where the notion of *correspondance* informs not only the content, but also the structure of the texts, and opposes them to a scientific reduction of knowledge that reduces the world into parts we can no longer recognize as belonging to our own reality. More globally, the idea of *correspondence* plays a key role, as we will see, in the organization of Bonnefoy's essays into integrated collections.

Marielle Macé's reflections on perceptions of scientific thought and their relationship to the essay are exceedingly helpful in thinking about the indisputable importance that the genre acquired over the course of twentieth-century France. Taking as her starting point the putative non-existence of the essay in the nineteenth century (she quotes the 1912 edition of the *Catalogue de la librairie française* where under the heading 'Essai', the reference reads: 'Essais. Voyez Romans' [Essays. See Novels]), she analyses the reasons for its development into a dominant literary genre. Macé's fascinating hypothesis suggests that the current omnipresence of the essay is related to the development of what is called in France 'les sciences humaines'. This new discipline, she argues, was from the outset convinced of the validity of applying an empirical scientific approach — that is, non-subjective, verifiable, and reproducible — to all domains of thought. It thus forced a change in the way writing, and particularly literary writing, could deal with reality. From that point onward, the novel, which had long been perceived as a window into a true understanding of human nature, lost its central literary position. More broadly, science and representation, knowledge and fiction, essay and novel exchanged places at the beginning of the twentieth century. From that time onward, the essay, because of its closer relationship with the perceived neutrality of scientific writing, and because of reader perceptions that it eschews fictional universes, seemed better suited to address reality. It therefore moved to fill the vacuum left by the displaced realistic or naturalistic novel of the nineteenth century.[23] Yet, as Macé points out, despite the kinship people perceive between the essay and scientific truth, the essay is crucially distinct from a scientific article because it can marginalize the discourse of science to favour constructions that are more literary. For her, the essay reflects a subliminal attempt for literature to maintain a position both in the construction of knowledge and in providing a valid interpretation for an ever more complex understanding of reality. Through this very process, the essay also works against the marginalization of literature in what is increasingly perceived by the literary community as a world that places value solely on the knowledge obtained through scientific methodology.

As we saw in the previous chapter, this reservation is very present in what Bonnefoy seems to take from Shestov's thought. What is questioned by both writers and, more generally, by the literary community is not, of course, scientific progress, but rather its claim to universality through its assertion that scientific experiments alone produce true knowledge because they can be infinitely iterated, producing identical results at each repetition. By contrast, the essay, despite its veneer of accuracy, can create a literary space that embodies the rejection of the scientific method and its reproducible experiments. Indeed, knowledge produced in an essay can never be iterable, because it is conditioned by its central dynamic, to wit, the world filtered through the subjectivity of the essayist. The value of the essay lies precisely in the fact that the information it transmits remains unique. As Lukács points out, the essay is distinct from 'critical writings which, like a hypothesis in natural science, like a design for a machine part, lose all their value at the precise moment when a new and better one becomes available'. As proof, he reminds us that people continue to find satisfaction in reading the critical essays of past essayists even though other essayists have since sustained points of view that modify or even contradict the older essays. These comments serve as a springboard toward his central postulate that the essay is an art form: 'Science affects us by its contents, art by its forms; science offers us facts and the relationship between facts, but art offers us souls and destinies'.[24]

In thinking more closely about Lukács's 'souls and destinies', it difficult not to avoid drawing some parallels with other genres, most notably autobiography. Indeed, it is precisely the presence of the non-metaphorical 'I' engaged in non-fictional discourse that gives the impression that there are fewer textual barriers between reader and writer in the essay than in other genres. Nonetheless, could the seeming transparency of the essay not also be an instance of the Hegelian blindness we saw earlier? Riendeau points out that though the subjectivity of the essay is frequently evoked, its autobiographical dimension is much less often discussed.[25] Yet, the parallel is suggested by the fact that both genres conflate author, narrator, and character. The essay, de Obaldia writes, foregrounds a privileged relationship between imagination and writing, between the real flesh-and-blood essayist, and the way that same person is created out of words. Yet, she is also aware that a breach is also possible in the apparently transparent 'contract' the essay establishes between writer and reader because, she suggests, just as in fiction, there is no formal requirement for the author to be identical to the essayistic 'I' who, for the purpose of the essay, assumes a point of view, recalls an event, or describes a painting.[26] Other critics reject the autobiographical nature of the essay on less formal criteria. Some return to the original meaning of the word *essai*, seeing in the tentative quality of the essay a rejection of the self-aggrandisement of autobiography. Glaudes, for example, argues that the omnipresence of the essayist's 'I' exists more as the authentication of a personal and limited truth than as a desire for autobiography or autoportrait.[27] As we will see in Chapter Four, the ambivalent status of the essay's autobiographical potential has a vital role in Bonnefoy's work inasmuch as this subliminal possibility lays the groundwork for his deliberate organization of his essays into structured collections whose underlying goal is creating the good reader through the didactic possibilities of autobiography.

Glaudes suggests that the real subject standing behind each essay, overtly taking on responsibility for the discourse, legitimates the essay's claim to truth.[28] Generally speaking, these notions of 'truth', reality, and non-fiction are pervasive descriptors, leading to the feeling that the essay speaks of an authentic encounter and eschews the fictional constructs that would lead us away from the truth of the experience it presents. These ideas are spontaneously articulated by non-specialists, who perceive the essay as having some sort of prerogative in expressing *a*, or perhaps even *the* truth. Literary critics, using more technical terminology, say essentially the same thing, with, for instance, Francine Belle-Isle Létourneau arguing that the literary essay starts from a point in reality and seeks to prove the legitimacy of its signified through the strength of its signifier.[29] It is noteworthy that her use of structuralist vocabulary parallels Bonnefoy's roughly contemporaneous co-opting of that very terminology, suggesting thereby its generalization in the critical thought of the time.

Indeed, the essay's connection with reality and truth is one of the vital points that might have led Bonnefoy — both from pragmatic and philosophical considerations — to rely so heavily on it. However, contrary to critical agreement on the subjectivity and formal hybridity of the essay, its truthfulness gives rise to more dissenting interpretations. In that, it prefigures the more conflictual essayistic descriptors characterized later in this chapter, namely shared textual space, didactic potential, and fragmentary discourse. The multiplicity of valid interpretations reflects the plurality of the genre. Thus, while Glaudes suggests that the so-called 'situated' nature of the essay seems to guarantee that the essayist can hardly do other than present the truth as he or she perceives it, critic Jean Sarocchi states bluntly that the essay's relationship to truth is problematic, comparing it with Blanchot's notion of an 'unattainable centre'.[30] This larger philosophical context serves also to demonstrate the affinity between essay and poetry, whose similar focus lies in the attempt to regain a centre perceived to be the place of primordial origin.

(Bonnefoy's readers will remember that both the notion of place and that of origin are frequent themes in his work.) More broadly, the notion of 'centre' as organizing principle reinforces the idea that the critical or personal essay has a much closer kinship with poetry than other forms of writing that are more inextricably bound to the linear sequences, whether these be logical, as in a philosophical text, or chronological, as in conventional forms of the novel. Adorno goes even further and suggests that the essay has a unique relationship with this originating centre. The essay, he writes, 'owes its freedom in the choice of its objects, its sovereignty in the face of all priorities of fact or theory, to the fact that for it all objects are in a certain sense equally close to the centre'.[31] His statement indicates that the perception of truth which emanates from the essay is — perhaps to an even higher degree than for other more recognizably artistic forms of creation — independent of some exterior standard that validates the 'suitability' of object to form. A banal example can illustrate the point and show that other forms of discourse might have to work much harder than the essay to address subjects that are perceived as lying outside their natural sphere: taking shoelaces or flypaper as an object of study might be virtually impossible in a philosophical analysis, difficult to manage in certain forms of literature, but far more easily conceivable in an essay or in a poem. The reason for this is that like poetry, the essay can build on a seemingly insignificant element whose 'truth' becomes the foundation for deeper reflection. Indeed, for Adorno, the equidistance of the essay from a possible centre is linked to the fact that the real object of the essay resides not in the ostensible object of its study, but elsewhere. He himself equates that 'elsewhere' with 'the relationship of nature and culture' and suggests that the essay is always reflecting on the fact that cultural objects are no less apt than 'natural' objects to provide access to truth. The essay's claim to truth is thus intrinsic, and is both generated within the essay and then constructed by it. Paradoxically, this allows the truth to be everywhere: 'the untruth in which the essay knowingly entangles itself,' Adorno adds, speaking about the essay's ostensible object of reflection, 'is the element in which its truth resides'.[32] Consequently, the very approach of the essay makes some form of truth accessible to the reader inasmuch as it explicitly acknowledges the 'truth potential' of any subject.

Yet one of the reasons underpinning our conviction that essays reflect the truth lies perhaps not in the essay itself, but in contemporary shifts in the perception of truth. Indeed, it has become almost commonplace to state that the truth is inherently subjective and unstable, indissociable from its instantiation, a point which is not the sole province of scholars: contemporary novels that have enjoyed broad readership such as Yann Martel's *Life of Pi*, deal with the same problem of narration and the fluidity of truth. As it happens, the very nature of the essay embraces this shift. Paul Heilker, for instance, defines the essay as 'an epistemologically sceptical quest for new visions of truth in an uncertain universe and world in flux'.[33] More succinctly, Marie-Catherine Huet-Brichard writes that the essayist does not hold *the* truth, he holds *his* truth.[34] Glaudes alludes to this when he explains the relationship of the essay to truth to be contained in the essentially localized quality inherent to the genre: 'Essayistic discourse is always situated. Within the essay, the quest for truth is continually linked to a specific existence and its experience within the contingency of time'.[35] In some highly significant sense, these positions are reassuring because they suggest possible responses to a modern anxiety that concerns both the absence of any absolute truth, and the vigilance needed to resist the imposing of any external truth. If essayists circumscribe their ambitions within something that is clearly conditioned by their own particular existence, then we readers are reassured that no exterior authority seeks to impose its dictates upon us. The essay thus brings a measure of security to readers, and paradoxically, even leads them to accept a delimited form of truth as long as it does not come into conflict with the scepticism they might feel regarding larger constructions of truth.

A second point is that the essay also allows writers to grapple with the central problem of contemporary writing, namely, the pervasive fear that language may not be an adequate tool to express reality. Inevitably, Bonnefoy's work is suffused with this anxiety, as is shown by his frequently hostile interaction with the work of Nietzsche, Saussure, or Derrida, all of whom question the capacity of language transparently to bear meaning. His essays testify not only to this struggle, but demonstrate also an actual *mise en œuvre*, via the plasticity of the genre, of his conviction that language can overcome its arbitrariness and express reality. Thus, though he does not often explicitly evoke Nietzsche, Bonnefoy was a close reader, ultimately rejecting the German philosopher's vision of metaphor in favour of the metonymy that provided an impetus for his own reflections on how to counteract the disjunction between language and truth. Nietzsche, like many other thinkers, points to the arbitrary nature of the relationship between words and the things they designate, questioning the value of language through the apparently rhetorical question 'what is truth?' He answers with a highly poetic text criticizing the falsehood inherent in any truth expressed through language. Truth, he writes in a well-known passage from 'Über Wahrheit und Lüge im außermoralischen Sinne' [On Truth and Lies in an Extra-moral Sense], is:

> A mobile army of metaphors, metonyms, and anthropomorphisms [...] illusions about which one has forgotten that this is what they are; metaphors which are worn out and without sensuous power; coins which have lost their pictures and now matter only as metal, no longer as coins.[36]

Our very senses contribute to the lie in which we live since the exterior world is only accessible to us via the sensory images transmitted by our nerve impressions. Language lies further yet along the chain of dissimulation, for the words we ascribe to these sensory images are even more distanced from the exterior world. Connecting the appropriate word with the image associated with it, saying for example, 'sky', while pointing upward, means 'using the customary metaphors — in moral terms: [it means lying] according to fixed convention'.[37]

Yet, the way of avoiding falsehood lies in remembering that man is himself 'an *artistically creating* subject'.[38] Practically, then, wresting some measure of truth back into language lies in generating new metaphors to describe reality, in using poetic language as he does in his own philosophical texts. The essay, as it happens, has an even greater degree of writing latitude because of its inherent polymorphism.

Indeed, a convincing link between the essay and the use of metaphoric language to express truth is provided by Adorno, who argues that the essay can take on a function similar to that of metaphor in undoing the arbitrariness of language: '[The essay] wants to heal thought of its arbitrary character by incorporating arbitrariness reflectively into its own approach rather than disguising it as immediacy'.[39]

The truthfulness inherent to language that is explicitly poetic correlates well with the experience readers have of Bonnefoy's essays, for one of their more arresting characteristics is their highly poetic quality, a quality that is so pronounced that it has been amply commented on, both by casual readers, and by theorists reading Bonnefoy critically. This characteristic forces us to rethink the function of style in the essay, bringing into sharp focus the specificity of Bonnefoy's essays and the symbiosis we see there with his poetry. Certainly, the physical characteristics — acoustic and visual — of language, and its latent potential for interaction at a sensory level derive from a network of antecedents which have traditionally provided ways of thinking about verse. For poetry, these material qualities naturally include the audible dimension of the poetic text, its alliterations, rhymes, and rhythms; but they may also include the visual appearance of the poetic text, the physically structuring of the words on the page, a prominent example being, for instance, poetic calligrams. Similar types of structuring process are present in Bonnefoy's poetry, particularly in the long sequences of ellipses he uses so insistently in *Dans le leurre du seuil* to simultaneously segment the poetic verse and suggest a textual absence that necessarily orients the reading of the poem. More commonplace tools such as the visual division of longer poems into sections marked either by some distinguishing symbol (numeral, asterisk, etc.) or simply by blank spaces are also regularly found in Bonnefoy's work, as Jean-Michel Gouvard has noted in analysis of *Hier régnant désert*.[40] Though typography and layout are common tools in analysing poetry, it is important to note that physical composition and the division of the text by typographical means play a crucial role in the analysis of Bonnefoy's essays as well. Many instances within them show that the typographical layout bears semantic weight that works either to counteract or to underscore the meaning carried in the text. Indeed, based on Nietzsche's observations, introducing such poetic techniques into the critical and the philosophical essay is no mere aesthetic choice, but a means of grounding and enhancing its so-called 'truth-value'. Still, allowing that the poetic potential of the essay grants it a privileged access to the truth inevitably brings up the corollary question of purpose: why adopt a poetic discourse in a text that, whether obliquely or explicitly, seems to aim exclusively at expressing the truth? For if metaphors provide the greater goal of expressing truth then, perforce, they have some rhetorical function going beyond the merely aesthetic. As the analysis of Bonnefoy's prose shows, clearly this function can be connected to the goal of bringing readers to an enhanced understanding of *présence*.

Metaphors, however (and through them, style) are but one part of the picture. The second half of this chapter concentrates on characterizations of the essay that engender more disagreement, though they clearly must be factored into reflection on Bonnefoy's need for the essay. Succinctly, these issues concern the essay as a sort of mental common ground; the didactic potential of the essay; and, finally, the more technical question of the essay as a literary space wherein the lines between unity and fragmentation are drawn. Interwoven through these definitions is the complex issue of the poetic possibilities inherent in essayistic discourse. As the analysis of specific segments of Bonnefoy's work in subsequent chapters shows, all these elements condition the role the essay plays in his work.

Invisible Forms of Definition

Earlier, we saw Glaudes highlighting the essayist's modest acknowledgment of the limited nature of his or her 'own truth' which, for Glaudes, tended to abrogate any tendency toward self-aggrandisement.[41] Indeed, combining the essay's essential subjectivity with the truthfulness and modesty that are also its descriptors invites us to perceive it as a textual space whose focus is *not* on the 'I', but points insistently instead to the 'true' subject of the text, which, suggests critic Michael L. Hall, provides the grounds for a genuine interaction between writer and reader: 'the experience of author and reader is central to the genre's rhetorical appeal'.[42] For this authentic exchange to occur, however, the text must afford a stable place for reader and writer to occupy concurrently. The essay is perceived as particularly well-suited do this because, as Guy Larroux says of it, 'it is an opening into the present moment that enunciator and co-enunciator inhabit together, as contemporaries'.[43]

Indeed, a number of critics have noted the essay's potential to create a space which knits together a community of readers and conjoins it with the essayist, these critics at times going so far as to suggest that it is one of the rare examples of literary work explicitly to carve out a place for the reader. Jean-Pierre Zubiate describes the essay as one of the very few discursive forms that show esteem for readers by including them in its own questionings and highlighting its own relativity.[44] Kuisma Korhonen, whose dense analysis is devoted to the topos of friendship as the federating element of essays takes the trope even further. He stresses the importance of the common ground that the genre strives to create, writing that neither the aesthetics nor the epistemology of the essay can be understood 'without first considering the ethics of writing, assuming that the ethics of writing are understood as a reflection on the conditions that make the encounter with the Other through written texts possible'.[45] The idea of a textual common ground thus appears clear. Less obvious, however, are the rhetorical strategies that would allow a writer to create such a space.

Paquette's description of the essay as an enthymematic discourse is a first indication of how the essay builds this shared place. Though quite technical, his terminology is apt, inasmuch as the Aristotelian definition of the enthymeme describes it as a type of syllogism that is grounded not in explicit premises, but in the suppositions that writer and reader are imagined to share. A commonly given example is Descartes's 'cogito, ergo sum', where the tacit premise that all human beings are able to think undergirds the conclusion. The listeners are key, as Thomas Sloane stresses: 'It is the audience in its particularity to which the rhetor must have recourse in constructing persuasive enthymemes, for these draw their premises from the common beliefs of the specific audience to be persuaded'.[46] Taken as enthymematic discourse, then, the essay actively undercuts the value of deductive logic in favour of something that relates to a desire to convince. The same can be said about its relationship to the inductive reasoning of scientific experimentation wherein all facts are derived from repeatable observation. And if we recall Macé's thesis of the essay as a literary space that seeks to reclaim the intellectual terrain in danger of being taken over by scientific discourse, we can see that even beyond counteracting the isolation of the individual, the essay can preserve a writerly 'zone of free circulation'. Indeed, Mailhot suggests something of this nature when he writes that 'the essay is not an agent or a mediating genre, but rather the passage (the common ground) from one kind of narrative or one type of lyricism to another'.[47]

Along similar lines, Glaudes describes the essay as a genre that targets the entire community and prevents individuals from isolating themselves within their private spaces.[48] This capacity to break open hermetic zones suggests an explanation for why poets such as Bonnefoy might be attracted to the genre. Briefly, it can be argued that over time, poetry has undergone a shift in the perception the reading community has of it. This observation runs parallel to Macé's analysis of the change in the status of the novel, and follows the idea that at discrete time periods, specific literary genres are perceived to be in resonance with or, on the contrary, a barrier to a directly obtainable understanding of the writer's inner world. In the sixteenth century, for example, the English Metaphysical poets or the Pléiade poets of France gave readers the impression that poetry was a form of writing that allowed direct access to the thoughts and feelings of the writer. Today, this vision has much more difficulty gaining currency. On the contrary, in the literary landscape that has dominated since the middle of the twentieth century poetry is viewed as a particularly hermetic and self-referential genre. Poetry is too often experienced as a form written by specialists for specialists, no longer a space for mutual encounters.

Indeed, Bonnefoy's problem is clearly linked to the so-called 'intransitivity' of poetry that Roland Barthes evokes in his well-known dichotomy between *écrivains*, for whom language is a material to be fashioned, and *écrivants*, who are 'transitive people', using language as a tool to communicate.[49] This notion of transitivity conditions Bonnefoy's choice of genre, and he cannot avoid expressing his own anxiety in Barthesian terms, indicating in *Le Nuage rouge* that 'writing transposes intention, undoes the transitive voice' (*NR*, 268). His difficulty lies in the fact that poetry has remained, or even become the most intransitive of genres, as he himself recognizes when he writes that:

> Le poète dit désormais *autre chose* que ceux qui cependant sont restés ses proches. Et il le dit d'une façon qui ne peut que leur demeurer obscure, puisque [il utilise] [...] cette langue qui n'est qu'à lui, cet idiome comme privé. (*E*, 208)

> [Henceforth, the poet speaks of things *removed* from the circle of people around him. And he says things in a way that can but remain obscure to them because he uses [...] a language that is his alone, almost a private idiom.]

Obviously, the risk engendered is the disaffection of readers for the genre, producing in turn a loss in the communicative capacity of poetry. And when Bonnefoy said in 1984 that what struck him the most in contemporary poetry was not the weakening of its creative vigour, but its 'capacity, its need, its will to *communicate* with the reader' (*E*, 204), one senses that he is really speaking about his own passionate desire to communicate. This desire, he laments, no longer encounters the people naturally able to receive it, for we have lost a common language that poet and people share: 'la poésie, en somme, fut longtemps le dire commun simplement porté à son intensité la plus grande' [poetry long was the common speech of everyone, simply taken to its highest intensity] (*E*, 205).

But if this 'common speech' no longer abides in poetry, it can more easily be found in the essay, which, by constructing something resembling a common ground that both writer and reader can inhabit, presents a greater capacity for communication. It is thus now perceived as the literary genre that appears to provide the clearest direct contact between writer and reader, gathering, as Glaudes suggests, the whole of the reading community under the spread of its wings.[50] The only real challenge to the idea of the essay as a common ground, comes, surprisingly perhaps, from its kinship with poetry, with de Obaldia arguing that in both genres, the reader seems to 'overhear' the private meditations of the writer.[51] Her analysis suggests that closure marks the essay, for while the reader does indeed seem to observe another mind at work, that mind feigns to ignore the act of reading that comes upon the heels of the writing. Although de Obaldia's comment muddies the waters a bit, the construction of this 'unexpected encounter' can also be seen as belonging to the range of techniques that the author possesses to produce the enthymematic common ground upon which writer and reader can meet. The first of these is external, and concerns the use of citations. The second, by contrast, is located at an internally rhetorical level and addresses the flexibility of the essay to shift from an 'I' to a 'we' intended to include the reader.

As concerns the use of citations, Woolridge, quoted earlier, referred to them as a distancing mechanism allowing the speaking 'I' to give the illusion of disappearing from the text. However, Woolridge himself recognizes that quotations also implicitly insert the essayist into a larger community. The author of the scholarly essay, Woolridge writes, 'gets his point heard by using the words of another, by placing himself discursively in relation to the many voices within this discourse community'. In a keen observation, Woolridge continues with the comment that 'in general, the psychology of this fact [the adhesion of the author to a community] often passes unnoticed in our everyday thinking on citation in academic discourse'.[52] The critical essay would seem to have the same function: its object — text, painting, sculpture, etc. — provides the implicit recognition of a community comprising the observers of that cultural object. Some elements of this process are clearly present in Bonnefoy's absorption and use of terms such as 'presence', 'salvation', 'original sin', 'negative theology', or even, as we saw earlier, Saussurian vocabulary, all of which serve also as a common lexicon for a community of readers.

The second 'technical' aspect in the analysis of the essay as common ground lies in its flexibility to shift from a solitary 'I' toward an inclusive sort of plurality that seems explicitly to enfold the reader, inviting him or her to not only share, but actually partake in the experience of the writer. Larroux, for instance, considers the 'we-potential' of the essay to be one of its defining characteristics. It allows the essay to create a literary space within which the subject moves from a singular perception of the world toward a plural relation with others.[53] This is plainly also one of Bonnefoy's goals. A critical comment highlights the specificity of subjective relation he wants to create. 'Maurice Blanchot,' he says, 'mentioned somewhere that literary creation was the shift from an *I* to a *he*'. In response to this half-remembered quote, he stresses that for him, the issue centres rather on the shift from an 'I' to a 'you' (*YB*, 330).

In spite of this unifying potential, however, the possibility for failure remains, and Larroux is no naive reader. He recognizes that the 'we' can serve to reinforce the vertical relation between he or she who knows and those who know not, or know less'.[54] Bühler, from a linguistic point of view, confirms the double function of the deictic pronoun 'we', which allows the speaker to choose between including or excluding the interlocutor.[55] In sum, then, the essayist's 'we' harbours the potential for alienation and manipulation. Though it can obviously serve to unite writer and reader, it can almost as easily distance the latter if it evokes the particularity of a 'we' with which he or she cannot identify. Along those lines, Larroux cites Valéry's impossible beginning to *La Crise de l'Esprit*, 'nous autres, civilisations, savons que nous sommes mortelles...' [We, civilized ones, know that we are mortal]. The apposition of 'civilisations' to the pronoun serves, for our contemporary perceptions, as the archetype of an essayistic 'we' to repudiate. More broadly, the transition away from an 'I' can also be interpreted as an artificial construction through which the author manipulates the reader into sharing his or her point of view. Isabelle Serça provides a keen analysis of how the essay resembles the way Proust uses the *je/nous/ on* pronouns to draw the reader into accepting his own perceptions as markers for universal notions. It is the fact that the narrative begins by recounting the emotions of the 'I', she argues, that legitimates its shift to a 'we' determined by the emotion now shared between writer and reader, and this, in turn, allows the emergence of the third person pronoun 'one', which then takes on the burden of enunciating a general truth.[56] The point resonates for the reader of Bonnefoy's essays for, indeed, he often uses the technique of providing a personal experience in the first person singular, and then shifting pronouns to suggest the inclusion of the reader into the experience described. This approach is particularly evident in, for example, the 'salamander episode' analysed more closely in the following chapter, where the narrative shifts from an 'I' ('j'imaginerai' [I will imagine]) to a 'we' ('disons' [let's say]) to a 'one' that is directive, almost prescriptive ('dans l'espérance de la présence, on ne "signifie" pas' [in hoping for presence, one does not 'signify']).

Finally, the technique of using pronoun shifts has another notable function: Korhonen draws a connection between the creation of a virtual common space and the reader's acceptance of the truth contained in the essay. He writes:

> The author wants us to believe that the hermeneutic movement is governed by
> the will to truth and understanding, and that this common will that both the

author and the reader share is more powerful than any single claim to power that the author makes.[57]

Thus, the creation, through the essay, of a textual meeting ground demonstrates the genre's capacity for providing an interaction between writer and reader that simply cannot be obtained as efficiently in other forms of writing. Are these essayistic strategies manipulative? Latent behind these writing tactics is the question of purpose. Korhonen, we saw, suggests that goal to be friendship. A more negative vision speaks to the idea of a didactic spin to the essay, a potential which does indeed seem dependent on a prior textual common ground, since such a didactic function can only work if the reader, consciously or not, colludes with the essayist.

The didactic thrust of the essay is one on which the lack of consensus is particularly striking. Time and again critics return to the widespread notion that essayists themselves seek knowledge and that they have no particular desire to impose a particular opinion or ethos on the reader. Freedom is the hallmark of the genre, as Alfred Kazin indicates when he says that the essay aims to express 'the individual's wholly undetermined and freely discovered point of view'.[58] Even the highly structured Paquette resoundingly rejects the idea of essayistic didacticism, arguing that the essay is characterized by its attachment to the lyrical mode, which itself involves the expression of an inner world rather than the imposition of this particular vision on others.[59] In the end, the dominant position is perhaps best expressed by Montaigne himself: 'je n'enseigne poinct, je raconte' [I do not teach, I tell].[60] Yet, as I have already suggested, these received ideas are at variance with the notion with which I would like to engage in the next section: whether the writer chooses to highlight it or not, the essay can, de facto, be a natural receptacle for containing a didactic axis.

★   ★   ★   ★   ★

It is, of course, in its presumptive didactic potential that the essay differs most sharply from contemporary poetry. A number of critics have drawn attention to the fact that despite its close association with tentative modes of thought, the essay can be a literary space open to infiltration by both poetic and didactic ambitions, as indeed Spanish critic and essayist Eduardo Gómez de Baquero explicitly suggests when he writes that the essay 'está en la frontera de dos reinos: el de la didáctica y el de la poesía y hace excursiones del uno al otro' [is located at the boundary between didactics and poetry, and conducts expeditions from one to the other].[61] The suggestion of a contiguous relationship between poetry, didacticism, and the essay, coupled with the latter's potential for very naturally integrating highly poetic language into its own discourse plays a significant role in the way Bonnefoy's greater project capitalizes on the theoretical capacities of the essay. This attention to language, conjoined with the question of the lyrical subject that both poetry and essay are said to contain serves as a starting point for analysing the didactic capacity of the essay. Other more rhetorical, but no less significant, factors include its argumentative and performative capacities, which dovetail with another important — though often overlooked — element driving the didactic impulse, namely an underlying moral imperative felt by the essayist to share some form of knowledge that he or she has acquired. Finally, paradox also forms a significant substratum of the rhetorical techniques that enable Bonnefoy more easily to present the specificity of his ideas.

The historically close relationship between essay and poetry evoked by Lukács and Adorno is reinforced by Zubiate's convincing demonstration of how their proximity allows the essay to compensate for the perceived shortcomings of contemporary poetry. He suggests that in the twentieth century, the two genres went from being mutually contradictory means of understanding the world, as they were in the nineteenth century, to becoming aware that they mutually sustain each other, and that 'a common ideal of intellectualisation through language makes them converge toward a type of writing which blurs the differences between their similar lyricism and mediation'. Zubiate furthers this analysis by suggesting that the essay, relying on the supposed objectivity of its mediating function, can be seen as a means of recuperating and redeeming the lyric 'I' from the discredit into which it had fallen by the end of the nineteenth century.[62] But what are the characteristics of this 'lyricism' that has, as Zubiate suggests, devolved from poetry to the essay? And in what sense is this postulated lyricism a potential function of the didacticism that might also inhabit the essay? These questions are far from trivial, for definitions of the lyrical form parallel a significant number of the characteristics that the essay has developed over the past century. Understanding lyrical forms thus can help us to identify similar or even identical forms in the essay, consolidating Paquette's suggestion that one of the defining features of the essay lies in the lyrical nature of the prose it contains. Certainly, the question of lyricism is rendered complex by its double polarity: purely musical on the one hand, or the site of intense subjective emotion on the other. As it happens, these definitions of the lyrical text resonate particularly strongly with Bonnefoy's positions. He writes concerning the sound of words, their musicality:

> If one becomes attached to the sound of the word, if one decides to embody it in a music of verse, then the concept — its knowledge, its structures, its logic — will, in this new use of words, no longer have control over discourse, at least at those moments when the music asserts itself with particular force and sudden immediacy.[63]

This theoretical position is concretely materialized in a number of his essays whose language suddenly develops poetic resonance, most notably in the passage from 'Les Tombeaux de Ravenna' analysed in Chapter Three and in the 'Dédicace' analysed in Chapter Four.

The subjective dimension of the 'lyrical I' also correlates with Bonnefoy's positions, as is seen in the terminology Philippe Hamon uses when he equates the lyrical text with an individual voice that is 'an authentically physical mark which says both "I am here" and "it is I"', thus grounding 'a place of speech ("*parole*") which is simultaneously *place*, *centre*, *presence*, and *identity*'.[64] The problem, however, as Zubiate points out, is not so much in the pertinence of definitions, but in the historically determined problem of the so-called 'crisis of the lyrical subject', which he evokes to buttress his claim that the essay has taken up the mantle of lyricism that poetry was forced to abandon over the course of the twentieth century. He imputes this 'crise du sujet lyrique' to the problem of language and representation, to the oft-cited incapacity of a language used by all to express truly the deeply individual feelings of the lyrical subject.[65] Along the same lines, as we saw in the discussion on deconstructionist ideas, the suggestion that language itself is not merely a barrier, but an actual distortion of the expression of the self, further compromises the ability of the subject to reveal itself authentically through the medium of language. A last factor concerning the disfavour into which the lyric voice has been plunged concerns the negative view of its intensely personal quality which makes of it, as H. L. Tracy suggests, 'essentially an individual [voice], since the world of the lyric poet is himself first of all' expressing emotions that are highly personal: 'the true lyric must be like a cry of joy or pain, and give the impression that it arises immediately from an experience'.[66] The counterpoint to these qualities lies in the latent danger of narcissism, a point Zubiate deems crucial to the essay's recuperation of the lyrical space formerly held by poetry. He writes:

> After the crisis of the lyrical subject, the essay has effectively become the other (l'autre) of poetry because it can integrate that [very] subject from which poetry seeks to take distance. However, insofar as this integration is precisely that which separates the essay from differing genres, a common ground emerges between its goals and that of contemporary poetics: in both, an identical subject seeks to define itself negatively, as non-narcissistic.[67]

The rejection of the siren-call of narcissistic self-absorption plays a crucial role in the essay's capacity to highlight its difference from poetry and to develop its didactic potential. Indeed, in order to successfully demarcate itself, the essay must take its inspiration from sources other than the highly personal ones used by poetry, thus leading, suggests Zubiate, to the essay's attachment to the things of the real world, its close concern with the 'a broadly defined cultural corpus' evoked by Paquette. However, once the scission between the essayist and the potential narcissism of the lyric voice has been made, the value of using explicitly poetic language changes: no longer perceived as a handicap for the essayist, on the contrary it becomes one of the means by which he or she might engage the reader by, as we saw, the Nietzschian 'truthfulness of metaphor'. For, if language is the problem, it is also one of the possible solutions. Indeed this is without a doubt the conclusion at which Bonnefoy himself arrived, using the power of words — their intensely material qualities, their physical shape, the sounds they represent — to oppose the structuralist and deconstructionist critiques of language and its capacity to entrap writer and reader. The essay has similar capacities, as Korhonen shows by using Blanchot's notion of the 'double négativité' of poetic language, where:

> The reader is forced to move incessantly between sensuality and ideality. This movement [...] defines both poetic and essayistic writing. Just like poetry, essayistic writing has confronted, from Montaigne onwards, the following dilemma: how can it name and define the world and its object, and still maintain its contact with the sensuality and materiality of the living experience?[68]

Korhonen's comment explicitly highlights the parallel quest, in both essay and poetry, for a language able to reveal the truth.

Though this 'material' conjunction between poetry and essay provides the rhetorical grounding for the didactic possibilities of the essay, that didactic sub-stratum is not a notion that is easily admitted by critics. Riendeau explicitly refers to the essay's 'absence d'intention didactique'; Zubiate even goes further and suggests that if the reader can discern a demonstrable didactic element in the text, then it can no longer be considered an essay, becoming instead a manifesto or a diatribe.[69] Nonetheless, the suggestion that there might indeed be such an didactic intention factors importantly into thinking about the specific characteristics of Bonnefoy's essays, as does his abundant use of the genre, a use that can be tied to the urgent need to transmit some form of knowledge he himself arrived at. One of the clearest indicators of this urgency is seen in the themes treated in various forms of writing, moving from narrative to poetry to essay, seeking, it would seem, a more broadly understandable expression. Strikingly, two of Bonnefoy's most memorable essayistic attempts to define *présence* (analysed in Chapter Three) show this characteristic. This literal quest for a 'true' place sought through the different forms of writing is revelatory, consolidating my argument that it encapsulates both the anxiety of contemporary poetry regarding the possible inadequacy of the mimetic functions it proposes and the corresponding discursive value the essay has relative to poetry.

It must, however, be said that the clear separation between the genres is fragile, even untenable, and the essay once again plays on its capacity to sustain paradox and duality. The very possibility that a didactic axis might exist there presupposes the idea that the essay's multifaceted characteristics serve to further a teleological goal that might even function the better by remaining subliminal. Consequently, positing the possibility of a didactic ambition present in the essay allows us to rethink the dominant models that govern it. In other words, though the normative definition of the essay describes it as a tentative genre, several of its inherent characteristics — notably, its argumentative axis and its so-called performative qualities — allow us to question the validity of this prevailing position.

As concerns its argumentative potential, even critics who reject the essay's didactic ambitions (Riendeau, for example) stress the fact that the essay typically contains an argument whose acceptance it seeks to obtain by means of rhetoric.[70] Thus form becomes function in the essay, for it serves to impel an underlying objective. A logical expansion of this notion suggests the natural possibility for the essay to integrate poetic language into its own discourse in order to further a goal that may not necessarily be itself poetic in nature. Returning briefly to Paquette's definition of the essay as a prime example of an enthymematic type of discourse reminds us that the force of the enthymeme's argument lies more in persuading from a position of shared understanding than in logical demonstration. The clear invocation of a shared cultural corpus is certainly a strategy more frequently encountered in Bonnefoy's essays than his poetry. A good example is found in *L'Improbable*, where he writes:

Nous sommes des Occidentaux et cela ne se renie pas. Nous avons mangé de l'arbre de la science, et cela ne se renie pas. Et loin de rêver d'une guérison de ce que nous sommes, c'est dans notre intellectualité définitive qu'il faut réinventer la présence, qui est salut. (*I*, 42)

[We are Westerners, and that cannot be disavowed. We have eaten from the tree of knowledge, and that cannot be disavowed. And rather than dream of a cure to what we are, it is in our irrevocable intellectuality that we must reinvent presence, our salvation.]

His concatenation of image and idea furnishes a vivid illustration of the enthymematic potential of essays, which can so easily provide an image to serve as common coin for writer and reader. In Bonnefoy's telling, above, our inextricable involvement with science is couched in the religious imagery that subtends the theological dimension of *présence*. The freedom of the essay allows him to condense both the Old and New Testament; the 'tree of knowledge' ('arbre de la science') is a clear evocation of the Genesis myth while the repetition of the connoted verb 'deny' evokes Peter, who, in all four Gospels denies Christ three times. The use of the word 'salvation' is, of course, transparent.

From the perspective of the function of the essay, however, the manner in which Bonnefoy constructs his argument parallels many of the thematic and literary concerns that are germane to the essay as genre. Globally speaking, his ambivalence regarding scientific discourse reproduces one of the central paradigms of the essay: grittily maintaining a place against the onslaught of scientific discourse. This is precisely what we see in Bonnefoy's biblical extract. First, his use of biblical imagery to talk about knowledge provides an enthymematic connection with the reader, demonstrating both the essay's hospitality to a cultural and literary past, and reinforcing thereby the value of such a past in constructing contemporary knowledge. Second, Bonnefoy's concession that we must accept our 'irrevocable intellectuality' indirectly recognises that poetic experience might not be enough to account for our interaction with the world. The potential inadequacy of poetic experience points again to the dual nature of *présence*, suggesting once more the fact that the essay is perhaps the only form of writing that can account for this duality. As Lukács points out concerning the need for the essay, 'There are experiences, then, which cannot be expressed by any gesture and which yet long for expression [...] I mean intellectuality, conceptuality as sensed experience, as immediate reality, as spontaneous principle of existence'.[71] Plainly, the conceptuality rooted at the heart of *présence* must also find expression.

This point allows us to reflect on the didactic ambition that subtends the enthymematic discourse: if the aim of such a discourse is to persuade, then it follows that there must also be something of which the writer wishes to persuade. This notion returns us to a more focused consideration of the writer, who becomes the key actor in this desire to convince the reader of the validity of a point of view. One might even advance the hypothesis that the stronger the writer's feeling is, the more the essay will tend to use rhetorical devices to bring the reader to accepting the essayist's position. Hence, we see Baudelaire writing in 'Salon de 1846' essay from *Curiosités esthétiques*: 'In order to be accurate, that is, in order to have its reason for being, criticism must be subjective, impassioned, and political'.[72] Yet, subjecting Baudelaire's argument to the cold light of analysis reveals that the passion he exhorts critics to feel could also be no more than another type of rhetorical device. Indeed, as Korhonen suggests, essays are constructed on rhetorical devices. The fact that these devices may be perceived as artificial does not suppress their use, but tends instead only to modify their appearance. He writes, 'The essay has, by necessity, a certain rhetorical and persuasive level, and the attempts to overcome rhetoric tend to create new forms of rhetoric instead of just getting rid of the old'.[73]

The combination of the author as actor and the use of argument as a vector for persuasion evokes the second important point in the didactic axis of the essay: its 'performative' function, to which Larroux refers when he writes that the essay almost always accomplishes something, or seeks to do so: explaining, correcting, diagnosing, warning, rehabilitating, defending, foretelling, and so on.[74] Larroux's reading of the essay's potential to do things is particularly germane to what J. L. Austin describes as 'perlocutionary acts', and has an impact both on general definitions of the essay, and in thinking about how Bonnefoy positions his own essays with respect to an unspoken didactic agenda. Austin's linguistics are indeed a particularly useful tool with which to analyse Bonnefoy's writing because Austin's careful attention to the notion of 'act' lies at the heart of Bonnefoy's thought as well. In the distinction Austin makes between different types of speech-act he gives a particularly telling example, saying that 'we can distinguish the locutionary act "he said that..." from the illocutionary act "he argued that..." and the perlocutionary act "he convinced me that..."'.[75] Austin's typology corroborates Larroux's intuition that the essay frequently contains a performative aspect, making clear that despite its ostensibly tentative nature, the essay can harbour the solid ambition of transmitting a position. Yet, Larroux's terms (explaining, correcting, diagnosing, etc.) concern the illocutionary aspect of speech acts. They thus engage the behaviour of the writer, who performs an act by writing them, but not the transformation of the reader. In point of fact though, the nature and structure of the essay allow it also to embrace the perlocutionary speech acts (obtaining agreement, convincing, persuading, etc.) which strive to effect a change in the reader. As we saw earlier, through the poetic language it integrates, the essay can assume this possibility of becoming 'actantial' (to co-opt a Greimassian term that effectively conveys the function of different elements of a text). Multiple instances of this language shift constellate Bonnefoy's essays, interlocking particularly effectively with the idea of the essay as a site for performance, and a place — perhaps even on an equal footing with poetry — for the 'act' that Bonnefoy's equates with poetry.

Robert Crawshaw provides an interesting approach to the problem of the essay as performance, pinpointing several elements that are particularly relevant for Bonnefoy's essays, most notably the fact that a substantial number of them were originally lectures addressed to audiences, thus, materially, performances.[76] For Crawshaw, it is the transfer from spoken to written text that is of interest. He argues that the 'relationship between "essay" and "performance" is complex, yet not as contradictory as might appear', for the very idea of transforming into a printed essay a voiced talk whose only persistence lies in the memories of the few who heard it strongly suggests the need felt by the essayist to transmit to a broader community some form of knowledge that he or she has acquired.[77] This process, in Bonnefoy's work, connects directly to a strong sense of moral obligation deriving from the overwhelming importance he gives to the notion of *présence*. At an enthymematic level, this moral obligation to adequately convey *présence* doubtless factors heavily into his repeated recourse to the Western theological vocabulary that might most easily speak to his readers. As John Naughton shows, however, Bonnefoy's *présence* finds echo in the Zen philosophy of the East as well; though these religious connections cannot, as concerns Bonnefoy, be taken in the primary sense of material adhesion to a religion, their common denominator lies in the moral gravity they impart to the message and the knowledge he seeks to transmit.

In *The Poetics of Yves Bonnefoy*, Naughton was among the first critics to draw attention to the parallel between Bonnefoy's positions and Zen transmission of knowledge.[78] Regarding *présence*, he compared Bonnefoy's description of it to the Zen experience of *satori* wherein the narrow boundaries of the individual self-dissolve into the plenitude of a total experience of the surrounding world.[79] Taking this further, I would argue that just as important as the experience of *satori* is the question of moral obligation that devolves to all those who have attained some form of enlightenment. Anja Pearre builds on Naughton's premises and highlights the complementarities between Bonnefoy and seventeenth-century Japanese poet Bashō. She links Bonnefoy's fascination with Bashō's haikus directly with Zen modes of transmitting knowledge. Because *kōans* are celebrated for the paradoxical nature of the teaching they provide, she describes the haiku as Bonnefoy's own personal *kōan*.[80]

Meditation on the *kōan* is perceived as a dynamic activity that aims to be transformative: its very performance should have the function of changing the subject.[81] A very similar process at work in Korhonen's description of the essay as 'the progression of some conceptual ideas in the consciousness of the essayist [...], the actions then being the changes in his (and maybe the reader's) conceptual field'.[82] The change in the 'reader's conceptual field' suggests that text is transformative; the reader is convinced, persuaded, swayed, etc., reinforcing the essay's didactic capacity through its integration of Austin's perlocutionary functions. However, as Zubiate suggests, the power of this underlying didactic function can only be well served if it remains latent, never really appearing as an overt goal. Several techniques allow the essay to tamp down to a subliminal level any didactic ambitions it might harbour, among which are Korhonen's 'trustworthy *ethos*' of friendship created by the 'consensual' descriptors we saw earlier, namely the essay's subjective objectivity, its truthfulness, and the common ground it establishes.[83] Once this rapport of confidence has been established, it is far easier for the essayist to diverge from the language of pure reason and use that divergence itself to impart additional meaning to the text through, for example, poetic language and paradox.

Paradox is vital to Bonnefoy's approach. A case in point is the word *improbable*, which is equated directly to *ce qui est* in the dedication to *L'Improbable*. The apparent paradox created truly functions as a *kōan*, for closer study reveals the association to be less a paradox than an authentic means of seeing the world. As the antonym of *le probable*, which deals with things that are likely but do not, in fact, exist, *l'improbable* speaks to a category of experience whose fundamental quality lies in the fact that it *is* and, against all odds, persists. This, of course, is the quintessence of the type of experience Bonnefoy's work seeks to show. In similar fashion, the plural levels of meaning he retains for the single word *présence*, can be seen as analogous to the function of paradox, for in the same manner as the *kōan*, it allows him to activate several ideas, maintaining each one simultaneously present in the mind of the reader. These examples raise an odd question: can there be a didactics of paradox? I believe there can, for the notion of paradox that lies at the heart of Zen teaching, and is expressed as an intellectual opposition to either/or binary processes, is completely consonant with the underlying objectives of Bonnefoy's writing. It is that very rejection of a universal binary that appears so paradoxical to Western frames of philosophical reference, where obtaining cognitive understanding means establishing a clear distinction between a positively valued 'concept' and a negatively valued 'thing'. As his poem 'Anti-Platon' clearly demonstrates, Bonnefoy resoundingly rejects the primacy of concept in favour of 'l'acte de la poésie'.

It is from this perspective of act and action that paradox can assume a didactic function within a text. Indeed, paradox can be a linguistic tool whose function dovetails perfectly not only with themes that circulate through Bonnefoy's writing but also with the generic characteristics of the essay itself. Paradox (*para*, 'against', and *doxa*, 'opinion') goes against received ideas and thus speaks to the essay's quest to express the truth and resist the domination of scientific language. Cleanth Brooks notes in *The Well-wrought Urn* that 'paradox is a device for contrasting the conventional views of a situation, or the limited and special views of it such as those taken by scientific discourse, with a more inclusive view'. He specifies that the rejection of scientific knowledge emerges not out of a need to confer aesthetic value, but because paradox is indeed the only way of expressing a certain type of truth. Scientific language, Brooks writes, disdains paradox because 'it is the scientist whose truth requires a language purged of every trace of paradox; [...] the truth which the poet utters can be approached only in terms of paradox'.[84] In Bonnefoy's practice, what we see is that paradox can almost literally be materialized in language, with the text itself becoming a paradox. Resolving the paradox of *l'improbable* is an act whose necessary corollary is that this act can itself serve to effect a change in the reader's behaviour. It is in this sense that the essayist (or Zen teacher's) active use of paradox has the didactic function of imparting knowledge to the reader (or student). Moreover, beyond the intellectual action of seeking its solution, the paradox can also be seen from a more poetic point of view that is not dissimilar to the surrealist notion of a verbal shock revealing what Breton called 'le réel absolu'. Paradox is arresting and engages readers through its surprise value. It forces them to consider language for itself while engaging with its semantic content. Grappling with textual paradox becomes an act completely consonant with the poetic reading that Bonnefoy's essays require. Finally, the question of paradox is related to the essay's uneasy accommodation of both fragmentation and its opposite, unity. Though the essay assumes the burden of fragmentation through its formal characteristics, it would appear that the yin of fragmentation cannot be treated without simultaneously evoking the yang of unity. Thus, Adorno writes of the essay that 'it thinks in fragments, just as reality is fragmentary, and finds its unity in and through the breaks and not by glossing them over'.[85] Whether by conscious choice or not, his comment reproduces the inseparability of the two terms, foreshadowing an issue that lies at the core of Bonnefoy's philosophical ambivalence.

*   *   *   *   *

This last section of the chapter deals with one of the more conspicuous formal characteristics of the critical essay, namely its predilection for the moral value of fragmentary forms. Glaudes writes of the essay that 'its ethical orientation naturally has an effect on the writing [...], which refuses both the linearity of traditional persuasive discourse and the closure of dialectic structures in favour of an aesthetics of fragmentation'.[86] Yet, it seems far too neat a solution to say that it is the nature of the essay to be fragmentary because fragmentation is its most appropriate form of expression. Indeed, the whole structure can appear so tautological that one is tempted to ask, what does it mean to be fragmentary? It is fascinating for the Bonnefoy reader to see that the multiple theoretical and philosophical ramifications of fragmentation are strikingly germane to the writerly task he seems to set himself. As his essayistic definitions of *présence* (analysed in Chapter Three) show, the use of fragmentation clashes with an overwhelming desire for unity. This marked characteristic of his work appears most clearly in his essays precisely because the genre's formal and moral connection with the notion of fragmentation echoes the plurality of a *présence* that exists, much like the fragment, suspended between multiple possibilities. Thus, Philip Beitchman writes, 'A fragment is the kind of statement that is neither an affirmation nor a negation'.[87] Because it is neither, it can be both, just as Bonnefoy's *présence* is neither a philosophical concept nor a religious term, and yet encompasses both those terms.

In her analysis of the literary fragment, Françoise Susini-Anastopoulos notes that its form coalesces the crises that modernity continues to struggle with, notably, the very possibility of closure or completion, and the perception that totality is somehow monstrous. Interesting, then, with respect to the essay, is her suggestion that the fragment is a response to what she calls the modern 'crisis of genre', which created a breach in the value of traditional genres, allowing fragmentary writing to assume the value it currently holds.[88] Certain aspects of Susini-Anastopoulos's analysis, particularly the notion of generic instability, are particularly apposite to the essay. Indeed, the essayist's choice of form can almost be perceived along a negative axis: the decision to write an essay might more accurately be interpreted as the decision not to use another, more clearly defined form of writing. In similar fashion, the fragment is predominantly defined along negative, 'not-this' lines rather than positive formulations. The etymology of the word furnishes a useful grounding point inasmuch as 'fragment' is derived from the past participle of the Latin *frangere,* to break. The word *fragment* can thus be seen as the metalepsis of the whole. It exists in metonymic relation to a broader action, 'to break', but this action itself can only function, as Blanchot reminds us, because of the mental priority we give to the notion of the whole, whether it be an anterior whole, now broken, or a future whole built upon the current fragment.[89]

The crisis in the very possibility of totalizing visions of the world is linked to a second problem, that of language and its ability to express reality. These collective perceptions connect to several major issues that continuously resurface in reflections on the essay. If we follow the arc linking the contemporary world back to the Romantics, who first theorized the fragment, the truly modern feeling discernible is the loss of faith in social institutions whose function it is to guarantee transmission of ideas and provide an overarching sense of meaning. The attraction for the fragment reflects the contemporary perception that its very form corresponds to some of the anxieties latent in modern consciousness. Further, it is felt that the fragment might even provide a means of reconciling some of the greater contradictions felt by modern writers regarding language. Hence, regarding Blanchot's use of the fragment, Beitchman writes, 'the power of the fragment is thus founded on its ability to express certain profound incompatibilities in the nature of things [...] between man and his power to communicate (his inability to express himself)'.[90]

Moreover, fragmentary writing can also be seen as a response to a problem that is both political and moral. The great cataclysms of the twentieth century produced a feeling that any form of totalization is dangerous because it tends toward ideological systems that purport to provide an explanation for the totality of the world. The more typically discursive forms of writing, such as novels or philosophy, have traditionally attempted to describe entire structures. In their traditional forms, they therefore have difficulty in abstracting themselves from giving what now appear as prescriptive systems. The contemporary disaffection for poetry, on the other hand, stems from a different problem: it appears as the most visible form of the literary disengagement with political reality. As Benoît Denis argues in his study of 'la littérature engagée', poetry's focus on form makes of it the antithesis of writing that engages with the political and existential condition of society. Poetry, he writes, is 'an autonomous and closed form; it is its own principle and its own end [...] As the summum of intransitive forms, poetry resists [political] engagement with its entire "being"'.[91] As a result, a more 'politically responsible' position asks whether we can even consider aesthetic matters after the barbarism of the twentieth century and the more crucial global problems of the present century. There is thus a sense in which fiction and poetry are perceived as objects that distract — in the Pascalian moral sense of *distraire* — from more important matters which should be the real focus of our concern. It is in this vein that Sousini-Anastopoulos sees the increasing legitimization of fragmentary forms of writing like the essay as a bulwark against the inauthenticity of the long fictional text and the increasing difficulty of traditional poetic forms.[92] The fragment thus represents a morally responsible and perhaps even psychologically safe solution not only to the problem of representing reality, but also to the trauma of that reality itself. The corollary to this perception emerges in a new understanding of the nature of reality, of which the fragment becomes the very figure. In a position that is very consonant with that of Bonnefoy, Blanchot argues that rather than being the signs of our misunderstanding of the world, the discontinuity and 'finitude' that are the marks of our human condition are instead indications of the true nature of reality.[93] The fragment, thus, would have the salutary function of forcing us to confront the truth that our understanding of reality can only be partial.

The essay engages in many of the same reflections and expresses similar discomfort with more discursive textual lengths that tend toward prescription and systematization. Adorno highlights the sense of rupture it provokes, reflecting on the way it confronts problems associated with the notions of modernity evoked by Sousini-Andropoulos: questions of identity, of totality, of fragmentation. For him, the essay's attachment to these issues separates it decisively from other forms of writing. In a statement whose gist recalls Bonnefoy's use of paradox to maintain opposing ideas in suspension, he writes, 'The essay allows for the consciousness of non-identity, without expressing it directly; it is radical in its non-radicalism, in refraining from any reduction to a principle, in its accentuation of the partial against the total, in its fragmentary form'.[94] At the same time, however, the essay is not a fragment in the same way as are, for example, Barthes's *Fragments d'un discours amoureux*. How then does fragmentation enter the essay? From a formal perspective, it is brevity and the lack of exhaustiveness that most characterize the fragmentary aesthetic of the essay. In the Anglo-American critical sphere (less so in France where, for example, Bonnefoy's 200-odd page *Rimbaud par lui-même* is also *un essai*), this brevity is a strong descriptor of the essay. Arguably, however, while brevity taken for itself is not a very useful defining characteristic, seeing it as a figure introduces a more incisive approach. Crawshaw suggests that because the essay exists 'on a relatively small scale, it exemplifies discontinuity and thereby accommodates an exteriorized, fragmented identity on the part of its author that is expressed through its character as "event" ("*événement*") rather than necessarily being part of a wider narrative structure or series'.[95] His reference to the idea of 'event' — understood as a singular moment differentiated from a larger temporal or structural framework — works also to consolidate the parallels between essay and poetry as mimetic forms whose structure replicates their meaning. Crawshaw's broader definition describes the essay as a discontinuous form, an autonomous piece of writing that begins and ends with itself, a characterization that reinforces its proximity to poetry through the parallel thematic freedom in their choice of objects 'appropriate' to their discourse. Indeed, as I suggested earlier, the brevity and discontinuity of the essay allows it, like poetry, to benefit from the nebulous feeling that all matters are pertinent to it, an impression that is perhaps less often granted to the novel or to the philosophical text. Similarly, both essay and poem can exist as independent units disconnected from a larger framework. Both, of course, can have this connection; indeed, it is precisely the relationship between individual essays contained in the various collections that is one of the focal points of Chapter Four. But in contradistinction to a chapter from a novel, or a section of a philosophical text, which cannot easily exist as free-standing units, neither the essay nor a poem needs this connection in order to be. Finally, the essay can also use the notion of 'event' as a catalyst, thus amplifying what Crawshaw sees as the singularity that demarcates the essay from other forms of writing and links it to poetry. Indeed, latent in Crawshaw's attention to brevity and discontinuity is the suggestion that because the essay has no obligation to be integrated into larger structures, its relation to event can allow it to focus on that which is minute, or particular. Like poetry, which is also viscerally attached to giving an account of the particular, the essay has a greater capacity to take a small, isolated incident (or, in the case of critical essays, a specific painting, novel, poem, etc.) as its impetus.

Its robust parallels with poetry allow us a better understanding of how the essay integrates fragmentation. Indeed, certain forms of poetry have no difficulty in incorporating both the idea of fragmentation and, more tellingly yet, fragmentation itself. Emmanuel Hocquard describes the two contrasting visions of poetic fragmentation, first, the figure of a lost unity shown by the sorrowful classic elegiac poet, who gathers up the fragments of a shattered past to salvage them, for they represent all that remains of a vanished original state that their existence constantly recalls. Simultaneously, however, Hocquard says, the very same fragments fascinate not because of 'their causal link with the events of a past life, but rather the fact that they are so alive', their vitality giving them current meaning.[96] Consonant with Bonnefoy's paradoxical tactics, both values engage with the mental structures that govern his poetry and essays. His double allegiance points to a tension that is omnipresent in his work, appearing both in his poetry and in the interstices of a number of his essays. A good poetic example is found in the collection *Dans le leurre du seuil*, where the long sequences of dots that break the poems up explicitly thematize the notion of fragmentation. By contrast, certain essays foreground structural separations whose divisions are constantly undercut by a discourse that 'mends' the breaks, reproducing what Hamon describes as a double movement of the 'centripetal and centrifugal oscillation of the lyrical voice, which plays out in descriptions and extended metaphors that unify a text, suturing the divisions created by logic and causality'.[97] The essay 'Les Tombeaux de Ravenne' contains several instances that are particularly striking because they are so visual. The following quotation shows the exact text layout:

> Or le défini est incorruptible, il assure malgré la mort et pourvu qu'on oublie les apparences brutales une étrange immortalité.
>
> Provisoire immortalité, mais suffisante.
>
> Elle se prend comme un opium. Qu'on pressente par cette image quelle sorte de critique, avant tout morale, je veux opposer au concept. (*I*, 14)

> [But that which is defined is incorruptible; in spite of death, and provided we forget the brutal appearance of things, it ensures a strange immortality.
>
> A provisional, but sufficient immortality.
>
> It is taken like opium. Let readers understand through this image the kind of criticism, above all moral, I want to oppose to the concept.]

Like the example given at the beginning of the chapter ('The sensate object is *presence*') the logical links between the sentences are immediately perceptible to the reader, yet the structuring clearly functions deictically, using layout to provide additional semantic information. The fragmenting of the text visually highlights the central sentence, underscoring its importance. At the same time, the sentences form a semantic unit that undercuts the fragmentation, the whole section thereby revealing a high level of authorial intent that seems to run counter to the tentative, meandering nature the essay projects.

Part of the unassuming strength of the essay, indeed, is that it can both allow such strong control over form and meaning and downplay it through its explicit claim to limitation and lack of exhaustiveness: the essay presents itself from the outset as a fragment of knowledge excised from a larger perspective that lies beyond its scope. The choice is deliberate. As Lukács suggests, these notions are materialized by the fact that 'the title of every essay is preceded in invisible letters by the words 'Thoughts occasioned by...'".[98] Hence, Adorno writes:

> The essay reflects what is loved and hated [...]. Luck and play are essential to it. It starts not with Adam and Eve but with what it wants to talk about; it says what occurs to it in that context and stops when it feels finished rather than when there is nothing to say.[99]

Adorno's very interesting anthropomorphizing of the essay (a tactic that would merit its own study) hints, through its reference to luck and play, at what might almost appear as the random, piecemeal quality of the genre. In the end, however, he will argue that the fragmentariness of the essay corresponds to a conscious engagement with reality and truth: its apparent randomness is a calculated strategy designed, as we saw, to reinforce the proposition that all subjects are equidistant from a central notion of truth. The essay's rejection of exhaustiveness allows it to materialize another truth, namely the idea that we cannot know everything about a subject. The fragmentation of the essay, its propensity to end whenever the essayist chooses, is thus the marker of this position, allowing it to integrate the same philosophical claims made for the fragment, notably with respect to conceptual models.

Along similar lines, Blanchot's defence of the fragment suggests that in contra-distinction to the longstanding tradition of Western dialectics, knowledge cannot be constructed by synthesizing oppositions: 'the break, or rupture, demanded by fragmentary writing, implies a separation from traditional thought — the major defect of which [is] its tendency to be frozen into systems that give us the illusion of understanding and dominating existence'.[100] Blanchot's position dovetails perfectly with Bonnefoy's own violent denunciation of the chimera of understanding provided by conceptual systems of thought. Through its openness to fragmentation, the essay can be seen as fundamentally anti-conceptual, a point which Adorno explicitly highlights when he writes, using terminology that is familiar to the readers of Bonnefoy:

> Because the unbroken order of concepts is not equivalent to what exists, the essay does not aim at a closed deductive or inductive structure. In particular, it rebels against the doctrine, deeply rooted since Plato, that what is transient and ephemeral is unworthy of philosophy — that old justice done to the transitory, whereby it is condemned again in the concept.[101]

Still, using fragmentation can never be a complete panacea, because to a greater degree than poetry or the novel, the essay deals with ideas. Indeed, Adorno states emphatically that 'the essay is distinguished from art by its medium, concepts'.[102] In that, it marks its difference from other genres. Typically characterized by an absence of the diegetic structures fundamental to the novel, the essay differs also from poetry in that it need not employ with the same high density the rhetorical and formal figures that typify poetry. These features, combined with the external subject that serves as its ostensible catalyst, make of the essay the pure expression of thought. This is but a variant of general perceptions which see it as the genre that allows for the most direct transfer of ideas from writer to reader. The conundrum is clear: the essay can reject conceptualization through its incorporation of fragmentation, but at the same time, the medium it works with is the thinking process itself, a process whose weakness Blanchot denounces because 'it tends to unify whatever it touches'.[103]

As the following chapters show, the tension between a text presented as fragmentary, but which reintroduces unity through subterranean means is particularly germane to the reading of Bonnefoy's essays. Indeed, considerations on the fragment must ineluctably take into account its Janus-like opposite, unity, because the two terms are conceptually inseparable. The essay's connection to unity can be confirmed by opposing it to other genres. Lukács was perhaps the first to suggest that the difference between poetry and essay lies precisely in an ancient model of an undifferentiated unity that the essay was unable to discard. The unity he sees in the essay lies thus in the connections it maintains with other fields of knowledge and expression. Adorno, we know, reads Lukács's comment as deriding the essay for its lack of independence. Is this criticism valid? Splintering knowledge into different fields is, according to Lukács, artificial and unrepresentative of reality, for in spite of the plethora of subjects open to the critical essay, its ostensible subject is, in some sense, immaterial. Each essay has the same transversal object, an object which Lukács calls 'life-problems', for the essayist is 'always speaking about the ultimate problems of life, but in a tone which implies that he is only discussing pictures and books, only the inessential and pretty ornaments of real life'.[104] Lukács's insight may not have pertinence for all critical essays, but it does have great resonance for those of Bonnefoy, particularly in the manner in which the subjects he chooses consistently aim to transmit a particular vision of the world.

Lukács's perception of the versatility of the essay shows that incorporating highly diverse subjects allows us to return to the hybridity and subjectivity of the essay, which also contribute to the sense of unity it can project. Glaudes provides a solution to Bonnefoy's discomfort with the scientific reduction of reality to its atomic or molecular level by showing that the ductile form of the essay allows it to incorporate into a broad hermeneutic arc the different disciplines that academic discourse generally fragments.[105] And on the question of the essay's subjectivity, Crawshaw's suggestion that the brevity and discontinuity of the critical essay fragments the identity of the author over its multiple objects of study can be collated with Lukács's analysis to show that the multifarious subjects that the essay can address are, in the end, no more than pretexts for far less variable underlying considerations, and that unity, far from being fragmented into the different subjects addressed, is, on the contrary, projected through the author. Rather obviously, this sense of unity derives from the fact that despite the plethora of subjects, there is but a single intelligence collecting the information, organizing it, structuring it. Even in those essays that seem to rely most heavily on juxtaposition to propel their subject, the selection of which elements to juxtapose is not, of course, random, but the result of deliberate authorial choices. The matter is particularly pertinent to Bonnefoy's essays because of the multiple levels of determination that characterize them. As the reader will remember, they are collected into volumes that themselves comprise a larger unit. The high degree of authorial organization they demonstrate suggests that the structure of his individual essays can, and even must, be read 'architecturally', as fragments of a larger unifying structure predicated on the drive to transmit an ontology of *présence*. As the following chapter shows, they are the 'vrai lieu' of which Bonnefoy so often speaks, the place which can house all dimensions of *présence*.

Notes to Chapter 2

1. Buchs, *Une pensée en mouvement*, pp. 12–13.
2. Claire de Obaldia, *The Essayistic Spirit* (Oxford: Clarendon Press; New York: Oxford University Press, 1995), p. 115.
3. Laurent Mailhot, 'The Writing of the Essay', trans. by Jay Ludtz, *Yale French Studies*, 65 (1983), 74–89 (p. 76).
4. Theodor Adorno, 'The Essay as Form', in *Notes to Literature*, trans. by Shierry Weber Nicholsen, 2 vols (New York: Columbia University Press, 1991–92), I, 1–23 (p. 14).
5. For 'sensate', see Chapter One, n. 2.
6. Lukács, *Soul and Form*, p. 7.
7. Hegel, *The Phenomenology of the Mind*, p. 17.
8. Jean Starobinski, 'Peut-on définir l'*essai* ?', in *Approches de l'essai*, ed. by François Dumont (Quebec: Nota Bene, 2003), pp. 165–82 (p. 169).
9. Pascal Riendeau, 'La Rencontre du savoir et du soi dans l'essai', *Etudes littéraires*, 37.1 (2005), 91–103 (p. 92).
10. Paul de Man, *Allegories of Reading* (New Haven, CT: Yale University Press, 1979), p. 3.
11. Pierre Glaudes, 'Introduction', in *L'Essai: métamorphoses d'un genre*, ed. by Pierre Glaudes (Toulouse: Presses universitaires du Mirail, 2002), pp. i–xxvi (p. i).
12. Reda Bensmaïa, *Barthes à l'essai* (Tübingen: Gunter Narr, 1981), p. 124.
13. de Obaldia, *The Essayistic Spirit*, pp. 6, 13.
14. This opposition has obviously struck other critics: Obaldia's *The Essayistic Spirit* relies substantively on it.
15. Lukács, *Soul and Form*, p. 13.
16. de Obaldia, *The Essayistic Spirit*, p. 18.
17. Jean-Marcel Paquette, 'De l'essai dans le récit au récit dans l'essai chez Jacques Ferron', in *L'Essai et la prose d'idées au Québec*, ed. by Paul Wyczynski, François Gallays, and Sylvain Simard (Montreal: Fides, 1985), pp. 621–42 (p. 623).
18. Paul Woolridge, 'Activist Essayism' (2007), p. 3 <https://www.ucl.ac.uk/opticon1826/archive/issue3/RfP_Art_A_H_Paul_Essay.pdf> [accessed 11 November 2021].
19. de Obaldia, *The Essayistic Spirit*, p. 10.
20. Gerhard Butters, '"L'absente d'aucun bouquet": Stéphane Mallarmé repris par Yves Bonnefoy', *Studia Neophilologica*, 54 (1982), 141–50.
21. It is this original title, 'Paul Valéry, l'apostat', that provides an explanation for that apologetic Bonnefoyian note ('have I been too critical of Valéry'?) quoted in the Introduction.

22. Jean-Pierre Maulpoix, 'Introduction à la lecture de l'œuvre d'Yves Bonnefoy' (2005) <http://www.maulpoix.net/Oeuvre%20de%20Bonnefoy.htm> [accessed 11 November 2021].
23. Marielle Macé, *Le Temps de l'essai* (Paris: Belin, 2006), p. 6.
24. Lukács, *Soul and Form*, pp. 2, 3.
25. Riendeau, 'La Rencontre du savoir et du soi dans l'essai', p. 95.
26. de Obaldia, *The Essayistic Spirit*, pp. 15, 16.
27. Glaudes, 'Introduction', in *L'Essai*, p. x.
28. Ibid., p. xx.
29. Francine Belle-Isle Létourneau, 'L'Essai littéraire: un inconnu à plusieurs visages', *Études littéraires*, 5.1 (April 1972), 47–55 (p. 49).
30. Jean Sarocchi, 'L'Essai, un drôle de genre', in *L'Essai*, ed. by Glaudes, pp. 17–28 (p. 24).
31. Adorno, 'The Essay as Form', p. 19.
32. Ibid.
33. Paul Heilker, 'Rehabilitating the Essay', cited by Glaudes, 'Introduction', in *L'Essai*, p. v.
34. Marie-Catherine Huet-Brichard, 'L'Avant-texte de l'essai (XIXe-XXe siècles)', in *L'Essai*, ed. by Glaudes, pp. 29–46 (p. 37, my emphasis).
35. Glaudes, 'Introduction', in *L'Essai*, p. vi.
36. Friedrich Nietzsche, 'On Truth and Lies in an Extra-moral Sense', in *The Portable Nietzsche*, trans. by Walter Kaufman (New York: Viking, 1977), p. 50.
37. Ibid.
38. Ibid.
39. Adorno, 'The Essay as Form', p. 19.
40. Jean-Michel Gouvard, 'Métrique et variations dans *Hier régnant désert* d'Yves Bonnefoy', *Semen*, 24 (2007), 2–20 (p. 2).
41. Glaudes, 'Introduction', in *L'Essai*, p. xi.
42. Michael L. Hall, 'The Essay and Discovery', in *Essays on the Essay: Redefining the Genre*, ed. by Alexander Butrym (Athens: University of Georgia Press, 1989), pp. 73–91 (p. 82).
43. Guy Larroux, 'L'Essai aujourd'hui', in *L'Essai*, ed. by Glaudes, pp. 459–72 (p. 467).
44. Jean-Pierre Zubiate, 'Essai et poésie au XXe siècle', in *L'Essai*, ed. by Glaudes, pp. 381–416 (p. 395).
45. Kuisma Korhonen, *Essaying Friendship: Friendship as a Figure for the Author-reader Relationship in Essayistic Textuality from Plato to Derrida* (Helsinki: Yliopistopaino, 1998), p. 276.
46. Thomas Sloane, *Encyclopaedia of Rhetoric* (Oxford & New York: Oxford University Press, 2001), p. 248.
47. Mailhot, 'The Writing of the Essay', p. 79.
48. Glaudes, 'Introduction', in *L'Essai*, p. x.
49. Roland Barthes, *Essai critiques* (Paris: Seuil, 1991), p. 148.
50. Glaude, 'Introduction', in *L'Essai*, p. x.
51. Obaldia, *The Essayistic Spirit*, p. 3.
52. Woolridge, 'Activist Essayism', p. 3.
53. Larroux, 'L'Essai aujourd'hui', p. 469.
54. Ibid.
55. Bühler, *Sprachtheorie*, p. 251.
56. Isabelle Serça, 'Roman/essai: le cas Proust', in *L'Essai*, ed. by Glaudes, pp. 83–106 (p. 94).
57. Korhonen, *Essaying Friendship*, p. 20.
58. Alfred Kazin, *The Open Form: Essays for Our Time* (New York: Harcourt Brace, 1970), p. x.
59. Jean-Marcel Paquette, 'Prolégomènes à une théorie de l'essai', *Kwartalnik Neophilologiczny*, 33.4 (1986), 451–54 (p. 453).
60. Michel de Montaigne, *Œuvres complètes* (Paris: Seuil, 1967), p. 327 (III, 2).
61. Eduardo Gómez de Baquero, *El Renacimiento de la novela española en el siglo XIX* (Madrid: Mundo Latino, 1924), pp. 140–01.
62. Zubiate, 'Essai et poésie au XXe siècle', pp. 382, 386.
63. Yves Bonnefoy, *The Lure and the Truth of Painting*, trans. by Richard Stamelman (Chicago: University of Chicago Press, 1995), p. xv.

64. Philippe Hamon, 'Le Sujet lyrique et l'ironie', in *Le Sujet lyrique en question*, ed. by Dominique Rabaté, Joëlle de Sermet, and Yves Vadé (Bordeaux: Presses universitaires de Bordeaux, 1995), pp. 19–25 (p. 21, my emphasis).

65. Zubiate, 'Essai et poésie au XXe siècle', p. 388.

66. H. L. Tracy, 'The Lyric Poet's Repertoire', *Classical Journal*, 61.1 (October 1965), 22–26 (p. 23).

67. Zubiate, 'Essai et poésie au XXe siècle', p. 388.

68. Korhonen, *Essaying Friendship*, p. 239.

69. Riendeau, 'La Rencontre du savoir et du soi dans l'essai', p. 100; Zubiate, 'Essai et poésie au XXe siècle', p. 394.

70. Riendeau, 'La Rencontre du savoir et du soi dans l'essai', p. 92.

71. Lukács, *Soul and Form*, p. 7.

72. Charles Baudelaire, *Œuvres complètes de Charles Baudelaire, tome 2* (Paris: Michel Lévy frères, 1868), p. 82 <http://catalogue.bnf.fr/ark:/12148/cb30066456s> [accessed 16 July 2022]

73. Korhonen, *Essaying Friendship*, p. 51.

74. Larroux, 'L'Essai aujourd'hui', p. 468.

75. J. L. Austin, *How to Do Things with Words*, ed. by J. O. Urmson and Marina Sbisà, 2nd edn (Cambridge, MA: Harvard, 1975), p. 102.

76. Robert Crawshaw, 'The Essay as Performance: Michel Foucault's *Ordre du Discours*', in *The Modern Essay in French*, ed. by Charles Forsdick and Andy Stafford (Bern: Peter Lang, 2005), pp. 219–32 (p. 222).

77. Ibid.

78. See also on this subject, Vernier, *Yves Bonnefoy, ou les mots comme le ciel*, pp. 29–34.

79. Naughton, *The Poetics of Yves Bonnnefoy*, p. 165.

80. Anja Pearre, 'Le Bouddhisme et la poésie contemporaine: Yves Bonnefoy', *Dalhousie French Studies*, 46 (1999), 167–77 (pp. 171, 174). *Kōans* are the aphorisms and commentary used by the Zen teacher to guide students to enlightenment by means of meditation on the paradox contained in the *kōan*. Well-known in the Western world is the *kōan* that asks what the sound of one hand clapping is.

81. Victor Sogen Hori, 'Translating the Zen Phrase Book', *Bulletin of the Nanzan Institute for Religion and Culture*, 23 (1999), 44–58 (p. 50).

82. Korhonen, *Essaying Friendship*, p. 75.

83. Ibid., p. 68.

84. Cleanth Brooks, *The Well-wrought Urn* (New York: Harcourt Brace, 1947), pp. 257, 3.

85. Adorno, 'The Essay as Form', p. 16.

86. Glaudes, 'Introduction', in *L'Essai*, p. xviii.

87. Philip Beitchman, 'The Fragmentary Word', *SubStance*, 12.2 (1983), 58–74 (p. 62).

88. François Susini-Anastopoulos, *L'Écriture fragmentaire* (Paris: Presses universitaires de France, 1997), p. 2.

89. Blanchot, *L'Entretien infini*, p. 451.

90. Beitchman, 'The Fragmentary Word', p. 62.

91. Denis, *Littérature et engagement*, pp. 19, 71.

92. Susini-Anastopoulos, *L'Écriture fragmentaire*, p. 23.

93. Blanchot, *L'Entretien infini*, p. 11.

94. Adorno, 'The Essay as Form', p. 9.

95. Crawshaw, 'The Essay as Performance', p. 224.

96. Emmanuel Hocquard, 'Cette histoire est la mienne (Petit Dictionnaire autobiographique de l'élégie)', in *Le Sujet lyrique en question*, ed. by Rabaté, Sermet, and Vadé, pp. 273–86 (p. 281).

97. Hamon, 'Le Sujet lyrique et l'ironie', p. 22.

98. Lukács, *Soul and Form*, p. 15.

99. Adorno, 'The Essay as Form', p. 4.

100. Beitchman, 'The Fragmentary Word', p. 61.

101. Adorno, 'The Essay as Form', p. 10.

102. Ibid., p. 5.

103. Beitchman, 'The Fragmentary Word', p. 63.

104. Ibid., p. 9.
105. Glaudes, 'Introduction', in *L'Essai*, p. x.

CHAPTER 3

❖

By the Grace of Words:
Essayistic Image as the 'vrai lieu'

To return to the central question raised at the end of the previous chapter, might the essay not *also* — or even more so? — be the 'vrai lieu' that Bonnefoy wills poetry to be? At the beginning of *L'Improbable*, he tells us, as we saw, that 'le vrai lieu est toujours un ici' [The true place is always a here] (*I*, 22). In the last essay of that volume, he proposes a path by which to reach that deictic true place. The descriptors he chooses connect directly to the essay and its characteristic itinerancy: 'Je prétends que rien n'est plus vrai, et plus raisonnable ainsi, que l'errance, car — est-il besoin de le dire — il n'est pas de méthode pour revenir au vrai lieu' [I claim that nothing is truer, thus more reasonable, than to wander for — need it be said? — no method exists to return to the true place' (*I*, 130). One of the images he conjures to talk about the 'true place' which the deictic 'ici' is pointing to, is an imagined *patrie*, a mental homeland where nothing would feel foreign. Metaphorically, the example points to the problem of a contemporary poetry that feels alien, subliminally contrasting it with a welcoming, familiar place, the very trope Korhonen uses to describe the essay. That 'ici' essay's close parallel with the poem, 'Hic est locus patriae', from *Douve*, introduces a pattern that is omnipresent in Bonnefoy's work: the significant number of similar, indeed identical, images that navigate from poetry to essay. The shift is unidirectional and is made possible by the essay's proximity to poetry, by its capacity to parallel the mimetic discourse of the latter through a similar use of language and images.

A first axis of my analysis concerns the question of form in the essay. Certainly, one of the significant characteristics of Bonnefoy's essays is their appropriation of a dense, often highly poetic language. Doubtless such language is fundamentally natural for him, but based on the essay's generic characteristics, that appropriation contributes to one of the genre's more covert rhetorical functions, namely its persuasive ambitions. Bonnefoy's integration of poeticity into his essays must also be viewed through the lens of the difference he draws between poem and poetry. Expanding on the surprising negative evaluation in *Le Nuage rouge* of a poem that does not speak, but merely *is* (*NR*, 271), he describes in a later interview the ambiguity of publishing poems, saying that this ambiguity exists 'parce que des poèmes, ce n'est pas pour autant la poésie, celle-ci étant l'épiphanie d'une réalité immédiate que ne peuvent donc que voiler nos représentations' [because poems are not the same as poetry; the latter is an epiphany of the immediacy of reality that all representation veils].[1] From the perspective of his essays, the effect of his surprising dissociating of poem and poetry breaks open the term 'poetry', allowing it to inhabit other forms of writing. This in turn suggests that the 'poeticization' of language is one of the primary methods for the essay to approach the notion of *présence*. And yet, *présence*, as we have seen, is as much concept as experience. In this, of course, it parallels the essay, which also deals in both, and in which form becomes more important than in other kinds of 'factual' writing. Thus, Adorno writes that 'the essay takes presentation more seriously than do modes of proceeding that separate method and object and are indifferent to the presentation of their objectified contents'.[2] Form thus allows the essay to remain true to an authentic representation of its subjects, as is shown later in this chapter through the paradoxical example of Bonnefoy's 'allegorisation'.

There is indeed a direct connection between Bonnefoy's construction of his essays and his poetry. About the latter, Alex Gordon writes, 'Rhythmically, Bonnefoy's poetry bespeaks [an] authoritative hand. Any opening in the form is a calculated effect, a variant on the high manner of tradition. Bonnefoy looks even to visual effects, as in the beautifully arranged epitaphs of *Pierre Ecrite*'.[3] The same 'authoritative hand' is clearly at work in the internal arrangement of the essays. Even from a purely visual perspective, they tend to parallel his poetic work. Cavallini, for instance, analysing the typography of Bonnefoy's essays, suggests that their visually dense quality mirrors the Renaissance essay.[4] Her reasoning certainly accounts for the compact appearance of individual paragraphs, but her overall evaluation must be nuanced, for what one observes systematically in Bonnefoy's essays is that his visual subdivision of the text through obvious rhetorical means (blank spaces, Roman or Arabic numerals, etc.) is frequently undermined by the semantic construction of a message which flows unchecked through the breaks. This purely formal characteristic of the essay resembles the poetic technique of enjambment, itself a means of intensifying the semantic depth of the poem by creating breaks that construct meaning and provide connections not otherwise possible in the text. This indeed demonstrates exactly what critic Korhonen suggests more generally:

> The poetic essay can, of course, be poetic in several different ways. It may use language that comes near to poetry with its different figural expressions and strong presence of sensual experience; it may use the textual space in ways that are common to verse-poetry (making for example, the empty space between the lines meaningful).[5]

All of these techniques are present in Bonnefoy's essays, complementing and reinforcing his arresting use of images to describe *présence*.

Of course, much critical literature already exists on the question of Bonnefoy's highly ambivalent relation to images.[6] Certainly, his poetry demonstrates at times a detachment from and even mistrust of images, as when he writes in *Douve*:

> La mer intérieure éclairée d'aigles tournants,
> Ceci est une image
> Je te détiens froide à une profondeur où les images ne prennent plus.

[The inner seas lighted by turning eagles,
This is an image.
I hold you cold at a depth where images will not take.] (*P*, 57; *D*, 58)

By revealing the mechanism of its own function, his poetic discourse here hints at a solution that would lie beyond representation, suggesting thereby the potential inadequacy even of *parole* to adequately describe *présence*. This point is reinforced by the fact that the four volumes of poetry collected in *Poèmes* contain only one instance — in *Douve* — which tries to say what *présence* is: 'La plus pure présence est un sang répandu'. [The purest presence is blood which is shed] (*P*, 74; *D*, 78). In every other instance, *présence* is found in a grammatical context that disallows description because it is the subject or the object of a verbal structure (for example, 'Présence ressaisie [...] je te découvre morte', [Presence seized again [...] I find you dead', (*P*, 53, *D*, 54).

Globally, thus, the reader is faced with the following conundrum: a poetics of *présence* comprised of poetry that is virtually devoid of descriptions of *présence* and a series of 'subaltern' essayistic texts that, as it happens, do define and give image to what this *présence* might be. There is, of course, a certain logic to this: poetic *présence*, Bonnefoy seems to suggest, cannot be shown as an image. It is an act and thus must, through the technical agency of *parole*, be directly experienced in order to have an impact on the reader. But this position masks or deliberately ignores the whole reality of *présence* and what Buchs described as its double nature, both visceral experience and abstract idea.[7] And although Bonnefoy insists on the primacy of poetic *parole* in giving an experience of *présence* without the mediation of images, the parallel existence of his essays and their dense interaction with the images found in his poetry suggests that they might, in fact, be responding to the potential limitations of poetic *parole*. Perhaps, as I suggested earlier, we simply cannot experience *présence* in the poem if we do not beforehand know what it is. And in order to know it, and thus feel it in a poem, it must first be shown to us, described by means of images, explained through example and text. This is precisely what is given in *L'Improbable*, where several striking and memorable images — the 'leaf' image from 'Les Tombeaux de Ravenne' and the 'salamander' one found in 'La Poésie française et le principe d'identité' — explicitly seek to provide the reader with a holistic impression of *présence* through very different perspectives.

Though the two descriptions seem to stand at polar opposites, inasmuch as the former describes *présence* through the image of fragmentation, while the latter shows unity to be the grounding condition of *présence,* those very tropes precisely reproduce the point of equilibrium between *présence* and *ce qui est*. Another vital similitude concerns their imagistic displacement from other places in Bonnefoy's work; this chapter deals with the textual origins of the salamander image, while Chapter Four shows the migration of the leaf. Generally speaking, the nomadic images we observe in the essays of *L'Improbable* originate in more imaginative genres (novel, poetry). In each case, they describe a trajectory whose final place is the essay, subliminally suggesting that relative to Bonnefoy's broader goals, the essay may actually be a superior mode of expression, allowing him to add to the value of those older images by proposing a didactic interpretation for them. The chapter thus focuses on the images that Bonnefoy displaces from genre to genre, showing that if this transposition is rendered possible by the close parallels between poetry and essay, it is also rendered necessary by the imperative to convey a functional form of *présence*. Finally, the chapter shows that interpreting the 'allegorical' dimensions contained in both the leaf and the salamander descriptions of *présence* provides the key to one of the main goals of the present work, namely that of reading Bonnefoy's collected essays.

★   ★   ★   ★   ★

The previous chapter challenged the naive perspective that places essay and poetry at polar opposites of the literary spectrum and suggested that poetry presents greater kinship with the essay than with many other forms of writing. In that diffuse, empathetic way, described in that chapter, the essay may 'feel' like poetry, producing perhaps its strong appeal for Bonnefoy. More tangibly, a number of the criteria defining the essay can easily be transposed to poetry, notably the essay's foregrounding of the seemingly unfiltered voice of a subject speaking directly to the reader, and its ability to attain immediacy by integrating tools such as deixis into the density of a language that can be highly poetic. Even the relative brevity commonly correlated with both poem and essay connects them with that morally viable defence of fragmentation we saw in the previous chapter. All of these more 'concrete' issues are linked to a cardinal point of contemporary struggle, namely the question of whether truth can really be expressed in language. This question is arguably the *terminus ad quem* of Bonnefoy's work. Consequently, it is hardly coincidental that the notion of truth finds substantive echo in his writing: 'vrai lieu' is of course the expression of a deictic place, but it is also the place of truth, as is another recurrent expression, 'vérité de parole'. Both are leitmotivs of his work, appearing repeatedly in the early poetry and essays, and subsequently taking a more central position by their transformation into titles: the last section of *Douve* is called 'Vrai lieu' as are a number of poems it contains; *Vérité de parole* is the title of the third volume of the collected essays. This focus on truth explains why the images he uses to describe *présence* play such a major role in his struggle to represent reality: these images point to an authentic moment of reality and the very nature of the essay (and poetry) almost automatically inflects them with broader significance and truth.

Their common concern with truth also conditions the relationship between essay and poetry, starting with their common attitude toward the problem of converting experience into writing, precisely the point Adorno makes when he writes, 'the essay [...] does not try to seek the eternal in the transient and distill it out; it tries to render the transient eternal'.[8] His comment is equally applicable to poetry: it is precisely in the mental gesture of going from the minute to the universal that the essay most resembles poetry. Bonnefoy himself is clearly aware of this quality, connecting it particularly to poetry in English. He remarks in his essay 'La Poésie française et le principe d'identité' that 'la poésie anglaise s'engage dans le monde du relatif, de la signification, de la trivialité (le mot est intraduisible), de l'existence de tous les jours, d'une façon presque impensable en français' [English poetry penetrates into the world of the relative, of meaning, of mundane detail, of triviality (the word is untranslatable) of everyday life in a way almost unthinkable in French poetry] (*I*, 259). Indeed, Naughton draws attention to Bonnefoy's awareness of 'the Platonic aspect of his own idiom, its tendency to transform the rich diversity of the world into manageable intellectual categories' (*APP*, xx). This, of course, is the omnipresent temptation toward conceptualization Bonnefoy so painfully acknowledges. It is therefore all the more telling that when he explains how the particular leads to *présence*, his very description drifts toward the conceptual. In that same essay from *L'Improbable*, he continues: 's'attacher à l'anecdote, cette vision "extérieure" du fait humain [...] c'est découvrir — ironie secrète de la Présence — que c'est dans notre réaction à l'inessentielle que notre essence se manifeste' [focusing on anecdote, that 'exterior' vision of human existence [...] is discovering — thus is the secret irony of Presence — that our essence is revealed in our reaction to the inessential] (*I*, 259). Here, his capitalization, 'Présence', transforms the experience of *présence* into the idea, showing thereby the overwhelming propensity of concept to assert itself, despite all attempts to keep it at bay.

One solution to this problem lies in that Nietzschean suggestion to deliberately renew language through poetic forms whose more authentic truth would counter the positivist idea of the complete separation between form and content. As we saw, Bonnefoy intellectually grounds the proposition that form can be set as equal to content through his theorization of the *parole* that he co-opts from Saussurean linguistics. Yet, even that linguistic tool cannot provide a complete panacea to the difficulty of binding *présence* to poetry. The poetic act can miscarry; instead of providing a transparent access to *présence*, the poem can fail to speak, and merely 'be', as Bonnefoy says in *Le Nuage rouge* confirming that distinction we earlier saw him making between poem and poetry (*NR*, 271). The problem remains of why Bonnefoy's carefully constructed linguistic justification for textual *présence* can go awry. The answer returns us to the idea of reader response and the need to educate readers to see *présence*. Indeed, Bonnefoy's reiterated use of the expression 'act of poetry', leads us to believe that poetic *présence* is the result of the dynamic act through which the poet produces the poem. I would argue, however, that another interpretation is necessary: it involves readers' ability to read phenomenologically. More specifically, it involves their capacity to engage with the poetic text through intentionality, making themselves receptive, not to the poem as a finished object, but to the initial conditions that allowed its existence, so as to replicate the path and relive the experience. In poetry, Bonnefoy writes, the reader must:

> Revivre le JE dans son mouvement même vers l'Autre, vers celui ou celle qui est désigné par le TU. Un autre est interpellé dans le poème alors que lui, le lecteur, a précisément, par rapport à l'auteur, cette nature de l'autre. Et pourtant tout l'appelle à prendre la place, non de cet autre du texte, mais du JE qui s'y est tourné vers le TU de son expérience propre. (*YB*, 331)

> [Re-experience the *I* in its movement toward Other, toward the *he* or *she* designated by the *you*. The poem addresses an 'other'; the reader has precisely that relationship of 'other' to the author. And yet everything calls on him to

take the place not of that textual 'other', but of the poem's *I* turned toward the *you* of its own experience.]

This receptivity is stimulated, and perhaps even rendered possible, by the essay's ability to shadow poetic expression. Certainly, the essay's so-called 'protean', or hybrid form allows it greater latitude to incorporate — even within the same text — a variety of different tones, styles, and types of language, up to and including poetic discourse itself. And Bonnefoy himself, as we saw, places poetry and essay in a single continuum, associating the latter with an attempt to fill in the gaps left by poetic language. The essays, he seems to suggest, are almost a private means of understanding the more obscure corners of his own poetry. Given this position, it would seem that the essays should naturally demonstrate a form of intellectual clarity that would eschew poetic language. Yet, what one observes is a sort of blurring of the frontiers between poetry and essay, which, in certain key instances, extends to the increasing poetization of the language, as is particularly apparent in some of his essay titles. The original title of 'Un rêve fait à Mantoue' was, for example, the far more pedestrian 'Le Voyage de Grèce'. Similarly, the title of the third volume of essays, *Le Nuage Rouge*, derives from an essay entitled simply 'Quelques notes sur Mondrian'. These overt instances are complemented by more subtle but far more frequent interweaving between poetic image and intellectual idea that the hybridity and plurality of the essay so easily enables. As the examples that follow in this chapter show, these instances provoke, even force, a poetic reading of his essays.

★   ★   ★   ★   ★

As Bonnefoy's readers well know, it is the poetic and densely resistant quality of the essays that tends to first impinge on the reader's consciousness. At the micro-level, there are many instances — the 'poetic' phrase from the 'Dédicace', for instance — where his prose veers toward rhythms that lend themselves to a poetic reading. Jean-Michel Gouvard, in his 'Eléments pour une grammaire de la poésie moderne', suggests that although poetry analysis continues to rely on tools developed for classical forms, modern verse should be analysed through more flexible devices that look beyond single lines or stanzas to larger patterns and echoes based on a 'principle of repetition formalised in the pattern "A_1, A_2, A_3 ...A_n"'.[9] This approach lends itself particularly well to Bonnefoy's work, and Gouvard's 'principle of repetition' can be extended, in fact, to serve as a sort of guiding principle allowing a better understanding both of the poetic images that cross generic boundaries to recur over larger structures, and of the duplication of identical syntactic patterns over different sections of individual essays. These repetitions provoke a 'de-linear' reading that is arguably one of the more important latent functions of Bonnefoy's essays. Indeed, the essays can provide a holistic access to *présence* through their embrace of image and idea. However, the vital purpose of that access is meant to supersede the essays and return us to the pure *présence* contained in a poetry we are henceforth primed to read poetically. These reading patterns thus encourage, even oblige, the reader to circulate back and forth through different texts. A comparison of the short 'Dédicace' text and the poem 'Dévotion' that serve as parerga framing the 1959

L'Improbable confirms this method: both texts identically use the multiple repetition of the dedicatory preposition 'to' (*à*) as a highly visible structuring device; the echo they create confirms and consolidates the unitary nature of the structure to which they both belong. Similarly, and as Argyros brilliantly shows, the penultimate line of the *Douve* poem 'Hic est locus patriae' ('Ainsi le jour baissait sur le lieudit Aux Arbres [Thus the day was dimming on the place called *The Trees*]) requires the reader to read back to the poem 'Les Arbres', found in an earlier section of the poem cycle, and then rethink the interpretation of that poem in the light of 'Hic ist locus patriae'. In keeping with his main argument, Argyros reads this strategy as the creation of spatiality in Bonnefoy's work, for the poem has literally become a place to travel to. As we saw in the Introduction, this producing of textual space parallels the actions seen in the 'Dédicace' to *L'Improbable*, suggesting strongly that this form of circular reading is a process consciously put into place by Bonnefoy to guide the reader, contributing thereby to that crucial 'training' of the better reader.

These examples, however, striking though they are, remain centred around formal issues that show poetic connections. What is far more immediately striking for the reader of Bonnefoy's work are the internal dynamics that literally connect poetry with prose. Globally speaking, we have seen that the essay can, perhaps more easily than other types of prose, integrate a genuinely poetic discourse by calling upon poetic images to uphold and even intensify its contents. There are innumerable examples of essayists whose images lift their essays above the more pedestrian level of lesser texts; Borges's comparison of the good reader with 'rare and singular birds' provides a good example. The specificity of Bonnefoy's essays is different; it lies in the absolutely identical images that navigate back and forth between his poetry and his prose.

A first short passage on the spatial image of the orangery taken from the essay 'L'Acte et le lieu de la poésie', serves here as a methodological tool for the more developed analysis given later in the chapter of the two main examples of *présence* given in *L'Improbable*: the leaf image and that of the salamander. The image of the orangery and its explicit association with death is intriguing, for it introduces a method that is particularly characteristic of Bonnefoy: the recycling of anterior work. In this case, it, reaches back through the poetry of *Douve* to an even older text, *L'Ordalie*, a novel Bonnefoy wrote in the late forties, and subsequently destroyed, except for the last two chapters, which were subsequently published in three different editions: first in *L'Ephémère* (1966), then another edition published by Maeght in 1975, and finally in the 1987 *Récits en rêve*. Consequently, the rather unusual relationship connecting death, being and the architectural structure of the orangery seen in the essay is based on an underlying metonymic relationship that connects novel, poetry, and essay through that image of the *orangerie*. In the novel, a substantial part of the action takes place in an orangery where one of the main characters, Jean-Basilide, having been shot almost ritually by Anne, goes to die. Anne, in turn, is killed there by Cassandre. Numerous lexical equivalences demonstrate the parallels between the poem and the novel: we find in both, for instance, the proper name 'Cassandre'; the description of the space of the orangery; the image of a key; the sound made by the footsteps, etc. These parallels substantiate Vernier's suggestion that the distance separating *Douve* and *L'Ordalie* is simultaneously 'insuperable' because Bonnefoy had recourse to another genre, but also a space occupied by correspondences, images, and characters that bridge the void.[10]

Doubtless, the parallels between the prose of *L'Ordalie* and the poems in the 'Orangerie' section of *Douve* are more easily legitimated by the fact that both novel and poetry are imaginative structures. However, the images that echo between the poetry and the later essay come as a far greater surprise because they transcend the familiar rough divisions generally made between fiction and non-fiction. In *Douve*, the first (untitled) poem evokes the death that readers of the novel know to be the endpoint of the scene: '"Regarde, diras-tu, cette pierre : | Elle porte la présence de la mort"' ['Look, you will say, at this stone: | It bears the presence of death'] (*P*, 93, my translation). The third poem describes the physical place:

> Le lieu était désert, le sol sonore et vacant,
> La clé, facile dans la porte. [...]
> L'orangerie,
> Nécessaire repos qu'il rejoignait,
> Parut, un peu de pierre dans les branches.
>
> [The place was deserted, the ground ringing and empty
> The key, easy in the door [...]
> The orangery
> Necessary resting place where he returned
> Came into view, a bit of stone between branches.] (*P*, 95; *D*, 123)

Encountering the prose text of the essay after the poem, the reader cannot help but make the textual connections through the identical images there present:

> From within the world of essences, death is imagined as the unseen, as absence. That, I assume, is how in that supposedly sunlit century, passing over the rustling sand, one drew near to the closed orangeries. For I consider these the emblematic key to the period, its latent conscience; their great windows under admirable semicircular arches let in the daylight of being; they have no dark areas, and housing as they do choice specimens of plant and flower, they prefigure Mallarmé's garden of the future — yet night, or the memory of night, fills them with a faint odor of sacrificial blood, as though some deeply significant act had once taken place there. The French orangery is the index of darkness. (*APP*, 105–06)

In a characteristic frequently repeated in Bonnefoy's writing, the three texts exist in a continuum that allows the transfer of images from one to the other. But what does this shift show us? What does the essay do for Bonnefoy that the earlier texts may have failed to do? The repetition clearly responds to a form of fascination, as Bonnefoy himself suggests a few lines later when he equates the orangery with the classical French poetry that would 'exercise an irreducible fascination on later poetry' (*APP*, 106). Gérard Gasarian parallels that with 'Blanchot's "fascination" [inasmuch as] the phenomenon described by Bonnefoy consists also in "re-living the event in the form of an image"'.[11] Gasarian's parallel certainly is amply justified by the great number of itinerant images that reveal this fascination — here the orangery, but elsewhere the ivy leaf, the salamander, the character of Phaedra, and others. It is noteworthy, however, that these shifts through genre are not merely repetitions of the images, but are accompanied by qualitative changes that recapitulate the differing focuses of each genre. Thus if the shift from novel to poetry narrows the images to their essence, the move to the essay intellectualizes them. Hence, Bonnefoy's fascination with the orangery resides in the fact that it represents for him an architectural space whose transparency allows it to be filled by the light of pure ideas or, conversely, by the night of the 'significant act' experienced there. Metaphorically, this capacity for idea and experience is familiar, as it recapitulates the 'conceptuality as a sensed experience' description that Lukács gives of the essay.[12] His intuition about the generic function of the essay is completely apposite to what we observe in Bonnefoy's work, where, indeed, we see that only in the essay does the image acquire this double vocation of imaged conceptuality. In L'Ordalie two keys are used to enter physical spaces. The garden door key resists; Anne must use all her strength. By contrast, the second key, to the orangery, slides easily into the lock.[13] The Douve poem, in keeping with the less narrative characteristics of poetry, collapses the two images into a single one; nonetheless, 'the key easy in the door' seems identical to the second Ordalie key. The essay, as is clear, maintains the identical images, but further condenses them, radically changing their function. In what is a clear metaphorization, the orangery becomes an emblem, and the key shifts from physical object (the key in my hand) to mental concept (the key to this idea). This absorption into an idea is reinforced by Bonnefoy's arresting, and very poetic, 'L'orangerie française est l'index de nuit' [the French orangery is the index of darkness], whose metaphor, through the word 'index', literalizes the function of deixis, thus enabling him to deliver doubly his message of the orangery as a mediating place. Indeed, while the orangery points to the 'latent conscience' of French classic poetry, it is also, and maybe even more so, the dark place the 'deeply significant act' indicates. Finally, the 'placeness' which is so profoundly characteristic of Bonnefoy's imaginaire is also reinforced here by reading literally — poetically, that is — that banal construction avoir lieu, or 'to take place', common both to English and French. The 'deeply significant act' is thus doubly localized, semantically by the orangery as place, and grammatically by a quirk of language. Perhaps, however, it is not just a quirk. Perhaps indeed the strange literal meaning of the expression 'to take place' lies in the fact that for an event, an act, or an action to 'take place', or 'happen', it must be, and the very deictic gesture of localizing 'being' contributes to Bonnefoy's philosophical fascination with place. It is this 'placeness' of the orangery that we see shifting from genre to genre.

By providing the hypotext to the image, L'Ordalie has a role in explaining Bonnefoy's work. Clearly, however, Bonnefoy was dissatisfied with the novel: the partial destruction of the text can hardly be interpreted otherwise. Equally clearly, the fact that Bonnefoy allowed three re-printings of the extant chapters is indicative not only of the importance of the images that emerged in the novel, but even more interestingly, of Bonnefoy's desire to render explicitly visible the origin of certain images. Critic Franck Merger postulates that Bonnefoy found the form of the text too polished.[14] Comments by Bonnefoy himself suggest that the destruction of *L'Ordalie* was predicated at least in part on its recategorization into poetry. He writes :

> À peine *L'Ordalie* eut-elle été déchirée, certains passages achevèrent, par la grâce des mots continuant à chercher leur sens, et leur lieu, de se reclasser dans l'autre livre — *Du Mouvement et de l'immobilité de Douve,* surtout dans sa quatrième partie, *L'Orangerie.*[15]

> [Hardly had *L'Ordalie* been torn up than certain passages managed, through the grace of words that continued to seek their meaning and their place, to fit themselves into another book, *Du mouvement et de l'immobilité de Douve,* especially in the fourth section, 'L'Orangerie'.]

Bonnefoy's description of 'tearing up the text' and the idea of words 'searching for their place' provide a valuable means to understanding the migration of images from one genre to another.

In a brilliant analysis, Steven Winspur uses a line from *Douve,* 'Exact presence whom no flame can ever again hold back [...] living, by that blood which springs and flourishes there where the poem is torn' (*D*, 63), to connect the action of tearing, or ripping a text with the very modern anxiety that poetry might not provide sufficient access to *présence.* Winspur cites Roland Barthes's assessment (in *Mythologies*) of modern poetry as an 'objective poetry', concerned with reaching transcendence by recapturing an 'infrasignification, a presemiological state of language'. Given this position Winspur asks the very valid question, 'how does the poem's linguistic structure create the appearance of being its exact opposite — an ideal, or Kantian, object uncontaminated by language?'. In other words, how can a poem, which perforce must deal with language, erase that very language to reveal the referent of the word, that is, the thing itself? Winspur's point is that Bonnefoy's poetry uses a specific form of indirection as well as the notion of 'rending', or 'tearing', language to reveal *présence* by creating 'not poems that show us things, but rather poems *about* utopian poems that would ideally reveal things'.[16] The reader understands that the means of getting past language would be to use language itself and make it indicate the place of authentic access, exactly the point Argyros was making when he showed the spatialization of the poetic goal. Precisely the same analysis can be applied to Bonnefoy's essays, for the image of tearing the text to reveal a more authentic form is the focal image of the anecdote he relates to explain why the publication of *L'Arrière-pays* was delayed:

> J'avais écrit un tout petit livre, plutôt alors un essai, et j'allais l'envoyer à l'éditeur, je lui annonçai même qu'il allait le recevoir avant peu de jours, il ne me restait qu'à le dactylographier. Et je m'assis devant la machine, mais un mot me déplut à la seconde phrase, je le changeai. Hélas, toute la troisième était du coup à refaire; et de proche en proche, et si large bientôt que beaucoup du premier texte se dissipa, zigzagua *l'éclair d'une déchirure* [my emphasis], au sein de quoi j'aperçus les linéaments de l'écriture nouvelle non conceptuelle cette fois.[17] (*NR*, 274)

> [I had written a little book, almost more an essay, and I was about to send it to the editor [...] I needed only to type it up. I sat down in front of the typewriter,

but a word in the second sentence dissatisfied me; I changed it. Because of that, sadly, the third sentence needed to be redone, and so on and on; a lightning bolt tore so broadly through the text that much of it dissolved, leaving me to see at heart of the tear the outlines of a new, non-conceptual writing.]

The image Bonnefoy gives here intersects perfectly with Winspur's idea of indirection, that is, of an ostensible text that hides the 'real' text. Not only does this idea connect directly to the Heideggerian idea of 'unveiling', but it is also one of the substantive theoretical constructs of the essay, as Lukács indicates when he says that the essayist is 'always speaking about the ultimate problems of life, but in a tone that implies that he is only discussing pictures and books'.[18] Winspur's second comment about 'utopian' poems echoes the trope of 'true place' that is an omnipresent aspect of Bonnefoy's writing and brings us back to his idea of words 'searching for their *place*', and not finding it in a particular form of writing, so needing to shift to another form. This textual shift is also, materially, a spatial shift, reinforcing yet again the notion of 'place'.

Still, if the orangery seems to acquire its full potential — both idea and place — in the essay, its connection there with *présence* is tenuous, diffuse. That is not at all the case of two other images that Bonnefoy lengthily develops as explicit examples of *présence* and reality. The first occurs in 'Les Tombeaux de Ravenne', the very first essay from the 1953 *L'Improbable*, while the second comes from the essay 'La Poésie française et le principe d'identité' in the 1965 essay collection *Un rêve fait à Mantoue*. Both essays appear in the 1980 version of *L'Improbable*, which conjoined the formerly separate collections. Juxtaposed in the present analysis, they provide a material example of the larger structuring principle governing Bonnefoy's work, namely the paradoxical simultaneity of fragmentation and unity as the appropriate descriptors of reality.

Chapter Two showed the theoretical legitimacy of the fragment, which engages with truth, authenticity, and spontaneity, thereby providing a tool to connect writing more directly with reality, largely because this reality itself has increasingly appeared to be fragmentary rather than unified. This correlates of course with the rejection of totalization evoked by Adorno and other thinkers, and, as the following sections show, evokes Bonnefoy's own literary practice in the passage from 'Les Tombeaux de Ravenne'. The trope of fragmentation is given there as emblematic of a true access to *présence*: the over-determined fragmentation of the twice-broken leaf is shown to provide an authentic image of *présence* while the hypothetical whole leaf is shown in profoundly negative terms to be the equivalent of the concept. Bonnefoy's focus on the fragment thus provides him with a rhetorical tool to counter our natural tendency to assimilate ideas by conceptualizing them. He seems so forthright in this stance that it is almost disconcerting to see that in the other description of *présence*, the celebrated salamander episode, he seems deliberately to eschew the notion of fragmentation in favour of a positive notion of unity described as a moment of apotheosis revealing the profound unity that connects everything. I suggested earlier that a means to resolve this apparent paradox is to look more closely at Bonnefoy's palpable distinction between the word *présence*, and the expression *ce qui est*. This distinction is far from banal, for it represents a form of contradiction that can really only be resolved by viewing the terms through a phenomenological prism. For if *ce qui est* represents Bonnefoy's shorthand for the incontrovertible, unified existence of the world that lies beyond the observing subject, that existence can only be accessed through the subject's dynamic gesture, the intentional act which is so crucial to the notion of *présence*. Additionally, in a vital demonstration of how the generic qualities of the essay mesh with Bonnefoy's philosophical goals, both descriptions of *présence* clearly mobilize a number of elements of the essayistic paradigm: the centrality of the subjective 'I', the incorporation of a cultural corpus that enthymematically suggests a common ground, and, of course, that underlying question of the paradoxical simultaneity of fragmentation and unity so profoundly thematized by Bonnefoy's use of the essay. de Obaldia writes that 'the marginality and indeterminacy of the essay is perceived as combining both the form's inner fragmentariness and its quality as fragment'.[19] Philosophically, however, Bonnefoy is doing something far more complex, for he capitalizes on the intellectual honesty of the essay's fragmentariness while incorporating ways to undermine it, in order to suggest thereby the possibility of unity. And as the last sections of this chapter show, these 'tools' of fragmentation and unity, far from being an aesthetic means to describe *présence*, have their own finality in the didactic impulse that guides Bonnefoy's moral need to communicate its importance. Finally, and more technically, given the eight to ten years separating the essays of *L'Improbable* from those of *Un rêve fait à Mantoue*, the shift in focus from fragmentation to unity can also be linked to Bonnefoy's incorporation of the tools derived from structuralist linguistics and his increasing faith in the capacity of language to express *présence*. It is indeed useful to remember that it was in the 1960s that Bonnefoy saw the possibility of creating through words an 'archaeology' that would reveal 'the supporting arches' of *présence* (E, 91), and it is also in 'La Poésie française et le principe d'identité' that he described words that can be 'saved' from their conceptual use (I, 255).

As we know, descriptions of *présence* appear almost exclusively in Bonnefoy's essays, and even there, infrequently. Concerning the placing of the 'Les Tombeaux de Ravenne', it is important to recall that Bonnefoy's essays were all written individually for different publications, and were later collected by him into the various volumes of *L'Improbable*. His re-ordering of extant pieces into a specifically determined structure is, I suggested, fundamental to his overall project, and represents the central axis of Chapter Four. 'Les Tombeaux de Ravenne' first appeared singly in the review *Lettres Nouvelles* in 1953 before being collected in *L'Improbable* in 1959, making its gestation roughly contemporaneous with 'Anti-Platon' and *Douve*, Bonnefoy's earliest poems. Clearly, its liminal position in *L'Improbable* is meaningful, for it is this essay that provides the initial call to action and consolidates his early poetry's criticism of the Platonic ideal and of conceptualization. To replace those ideas, 'Les Tombeaux de Ravenne' establishes his own philosophical position, introducing the notion of *présence* to pit against the concept. The leaf passage from the essay is particularly valuable because it presents in condensed form the principal axes of Bonnefoy's struggle to transform *présence* into textual experience. This is seen first through the notion of *présence* as act; then through the images used to call it into the text; and finally through the patent tension between the fragmentation that is semantically foregrounded as morally desirable, and the deep structuring mechanism of the unity that rhetorically consolidates the passage, inevitably recalling Blanchot's warning that the very process of thinking tends to unify whatever it touches.[20]

Visually, the leaf passage attracts the eye. Blank spaces set it off from the text that precedes it, a formal structure showing again the high degree of textual structuring Bonnefoy uses, both in poetry and in essay. The control he exercises over his writing extends to all levels. Hence, though 'Les Tombeaux de Ravenne' is a part of *L'Improbable*, itself part of a larger collection of essays, the single essay is itself divided into multiple sections, each indicated by a Roman numeral. Moreover, like the 'provisional immortality' example given in Chapter Two, certain sections are also further fragmented into units that are visibly demarcated by blank textual spaces setting them off from the surrounding text. These blank spaces are non-trivial: Richard Stamelman points out in his 'Syntax of the Ephemeral' that Bonnefoy's poetic work uses the syntactic interaction between words and white space to semantic intent. 'Syntax and the *mise-en-page*,' Stamelman writes, 'constitute a new kind of writing [...]. Syntax connects and disconnects; it both establishes and undermines relations between signs'. Its ultimate function, he suggests, is to provide 'a mimesis of contradiction and of *rupture*', showing syntax as 'an instrument of dialectical contradiction: orderly arrangements of words following rules of syntactical combination are contested by passages where traditional grammatical and syntactical operations have been suspended'.[21] This is precisely what the 'leaf' passage shows, for the reader quickly realizes that the second paragraph, though rhetorically separate, has no grammatical independence from the first: it literally cannot be read without returning to the first paragraph. The syntactic disposition of the two paragraphs thus demonstrates the transposition into prose of a process that absolutely requires the reader to engage in that circular poetic reading we saw earlier. The passage reads as follows:

> L'acte de la présence est en chaque instant la tragédie du monde et son dénouement. C'est la voix apaisée de Phèdre du dernier acte, quand elle enseigne et se rompt.
> Je dirai par allégorie: c'est le fragment de l'arbre sombre, cette feuille cassée du lierre. La feuille entière, bâtissant son essence immuable de toutes ses nervures, serait déjà le concept. Mais cette feuille brisée, verte et noire, salie, cette feuille qui montre dans sa blessure toute la profondeur de ce qui est, cette feuille infinie est présence pure, et par conséquent mon salut. (*I, 26*)

> [The act of presence is, within each moment the tragedy of the world and its resolution [*dénouement*]. It is the appeased voice of Phaedra in the last act, when she teaches and breaks down.
> I will say allegorically: it is the fragment of the dark tree, this leaf broken from the ivy. The whole leaf, using all its veins to construct its unchanging essence, would already be the concept. But this blackening green leaf, broken

and sullied, this leaf which shows in its wound the whole depth of that which
is [*ce qui est*], this infinite leaf is pure presence, and consequently my salvation.]

The first sentence of the passage eschews 'ordinary' rhetorical devices of comparison
('like', 'as', etc.) and begins with seemingly uncompromising assertions about the
act of *présence*: it *is* 'the tragedy of the world' as well as its 'denouement'; it *is*
'the voice of Phaedra'. In spite of these strong affirmations, however, the passage
continues, as though those examples were somehow not enough to transmit truly
the nature of *présence* and needed a more direct example. That striking image of
the broken leaf, presented as it is through the prism of allegory, is so unusual that
it very naturally compels the reader's attention — to a higher degree perhaps than
the reference to Phaedra, despite its grammatical subordination to the first image.
For when one begins to analyse the second paragraph, 'I will say by allegory: it is
the fragment of the dark tree', one becomes aware that the antecedent of 'it' (in
French, the deictic demonstrative *ce* — *c'est ce fragment*) is 'missing', requiring the
reader to circle back to the preceding paragraph, where 'the act of presence' assigns
a grammatical subject to the pronoun. Nevertheless, though rhetorically tied to
the 'Phaedra' paragraph, the leaf paragraph is not the direct, logical continuation
of its antecedent. Rather, the relationship is much more complex, the paragraphs
functioning together as a concentrated embodiment of the methods and objectives
informing much of Bonnefoy's essayistic work. Indeed, the two paragraphs are
thematically very different, the first one dealing with a clearly identified element
of artistic production, while the second addresses what might be appropriately
termed the 'natural' or 'real' dimension of *présence* as seen through the emblematic
dying leaf. Clearly, Bonnefoy's emphasis is on the leaf: the word itself appears no
less than four times in that single paragraph. Readers of the poem 'Anti-Platon'
will immediately identify a Bonnefoyian method in the repetition of a deictically
identified subject (the twice-repeated '*this* object' ('il s'agit bien de cet object') found
in that early poem) and connect it to his use of deixis in the multiple repetitions of
'*this* leaf' in the essay.

   This lexical focus on the leaf seems, however, to be subverted by structure,
for while Bonnefoy frequently argues for the primacy of the natural world to
connect us to reality, here, the thematic predominance of the leaf is undermined
by its grammatical subordination to the paragraph that speaks of Phaedra. That
subjugation ineluctably gives rise to speculation. Indeed, if, as the text suggests,
the wholly natural leaf and its slow destruction at the hands of time are the true
indicators of *présence*, why has Bonnefoy given rhetorical precedence to the artifice
of a constructed work of art? Bonnefoy's strategy is profoundly essayistic and echoes
Adorno's intuition that the essay is always reflecting on the fact that cultural objects
are just as able as 'natural' objects to provide readers with truth.[22] Indeed, the
seemingly arbitrary division between the paragraphs is 'artificial' in the primary
sense of the term, that is, something of conscious human construction. In a point
that is particularly pertinent to its essayistic matrix, this suggestion is reinforced by
the fact that the transition between the two paragraphs pivots around the speaking
'I', whose function as copula between two radically different domains, the natural

and the artistic, is precisely what Bonnefoy underscores through the particular division of the text. In this passage, it is only after the voice of Phaedra, described as having 'broken down', falls silent (and indeed we know that it is Phaedra's death at the end of the play that resolves the tragedy) that the 'non-metaphorical *I*' identified by Paquette appears.[23] Arguably also, it is the very manner in which this 'I' speaks, allegorically, that allows the integration of the natural world into the artifice of the text, for Bonnefoy's use of the term foregrounds that giving of voice to a natural world that would otherwise remain dumb.

This sequence is by no means unique to the passage; it provides a microcosm of the Bonnefoyian process describing *présence*. Indeed, the position of art preceding nature and the self is consonant with much of Bonnefoy's essayistic writing. More broadly, it demonstrates his intuitive integration of the codes of the critical essay through his summoning in this instance of the figure of Phaedra, which works enthymematically to create a common ground based on a cultural corpus that would be familiar to a number of his readers. More generally, his tendency to assign great value to art when his stated interest seems to lie in the realm of the natural world has been widely noted. In *Entretiens sur la poésie*, John Jackson asks for clarification on that very point: 'you explicitly present your work as a quest for the *présence* in the sensate. Yet you often engage in this quest by means of other art work. Is there not some form of contradiction there?' (*E*, 57). In essence, Jackson identifies the problem as lying in the mediated nature of a work of art. Because *présence*, as Bonnefoy defines it, confers immediacy on the relationship between subject and world, it would seem that using other works as a starting point for his own work would transform and perhaps even adulterate the nature of the quest. Bonnefoy's response expands the quest for *présence* beyond his own work, defining it as vitally important and universal, concerning everyone to some degree. The artists who interest him are those he feels to be co-engaged with him in his own struggle with finitude and indifference, with what he calls 'la mauvaise présence' ['evil/ wrong/ bad presence'] (*E*, 57). This position combines with the passage's articulation around the 'I' to reiterate the grounds for Bonnefoy's reliance on the essay. Indeed, the ideas he expresses, the mutual engagement of writer and reader in a common project, a cultural object as impetus for thought recapitulates some of the more fundamental characteristics of the genre. And though the grammatical dependency of the second paragraph does imply a certain circularity in the reading, at the same time, the rhetorical argument of the two paragraphs follows a specific, sequential development that is very essayistic, showing first artistic representation (the 'cultural corpus'), followed by the interposition of the speaking 'I', whose reflection connects that corpus to the natural world which is the focus of the passage.

In the leaf passage, Phaedra is not simply a name, nor even an abstract literary figure. She is very specifically 'Phaedra in the last act', meaning that if the leaf in the second paragraph is unequivocally fragmentary, the same condition of fragmentariness applies to Phaedra, for not only is her entire character reduced to the fragment which is her voice, but this voice is in turn winnowed down to the calm voice of the last act. This point is important because as a dramatic work,

Phèdre is inherently dual: on the one hand, it is a more or less immutable codex; but on the other hand, this fixed text serves as the basis for a physical production which, of necessity, is a representation, and is thus variable, stamped with individual choice. Bonnefoy's awareness of this duality is omnipresent; it translates throughout his work into that Blanchottian fascination evoked earlier, and is materialized in the multiple recurrences of the figure of Phaedra, a figure whom he qualifies as 'decisive for him' in an essay tellingly entitled 'Quelques livres qui ont compté' [Some Books that Mattered] (*E*, 340). And in a short narrative piece entitled 'Une représentation de *Phèdre*', Bonnefoy describes the physical anguish he felt when the actors playing Phaedra and her nurse inserted what seemed an interminably long pause at the hemistich in the first line of their exchange: 'We have gone far enough. [*very long pause*] Stay, dear Oenone'.[24] Bonnefoy associates his strong emotion with the realization that his reaction had been consciously constructed by that representation of *Phèdre* through the break it had created in the smooth pattern of the alexandrine. In essence, it thus allowed the specificity of an individual representation to redetermine the fixed text, suggesting that his fascination with the image of Phaedra is perhaps linked to the duality of the theatrical codex precisely because it mirrors his rationalization of the interconnection between language and reality. 'Les Tombeaux de Ravenne' dates from 1953; it is uncertain that Bonnefoy's references there to *parole* would by this date have acquired their Saussurian dimension. However, if we look more closely at the codex/ representation duality, it becomes clear that the 'fragmentary', time-bound Phaedra of the last act. is the very enactment of what would become that Bonnefoyian *parole*. Indeed, codex is to language as representation is to *parole*, a willed, particular embodiment that bears the authentic mark of the individual and the moment. It seems thus an early avatar of *parole* inasmuch as in the leaf passage, the 'act of presence' does indeed produce something resembling speech, as is immediately materialized in the first words of the second paragraph: 'I will say', and reinforced by the fact that the leaf 'speaks' after the end of the passage quoted, and it is indeed its 'inlassable voix' [unflagging voice] that produces the rhetorical question 'Qu'est-ce que la présence?'

Still, despite the focus on that 'act of presence' that gave rise to the 'non-metaphorical I', when Bonnefoy finally approaches the discussion of *présence* in the natural context of the leaf, his first statement 'I will say allegorically' is immediately problematic, both from the perspective of the moment of speech (when?) and from its manner (how?). Indeed, the future tense and the allegorical filter immediately and effectively remove the leaf from the sphere of a real encounter with a natural object. The leaf is not 'itself' in any sense of the word. Rather, it is a figure, an allegorical representation of something else, just as its blackened, dying skeleton is a figure for another sort of passing. Inevitably, this has an impact on the nature of the *présence* being described, as Gasarian points out when he writes that 'if the entire discourse emanates from a figure [allegory], the presence which is its object appears as a *representation*: the allegorical "act" for which the leaf is a *character*'.[25] Like Phaedra, then, this 'broken, blackening leaf' is a character in an artistic creation, in this case, the production of the allegory that Bonnefoy is explicitly engaged in at the moment of the enunciation. And despite the undoubted importance of the image of Phaedra, it is indisputably the 'allegorical' image of the leaf that is by far the more notable element.

Given Bonnefoy's insistence on the value of that which is particular and ephemeral, his use of the idea of allegory (explicitly here; indirectly, as we will see, in the salamander episode) can appear as nothing short of astounding. Our astonishment is fed, of course, by the popular conception that equates allegory and abstraction. C. S. Lewis, for instance, in his analysis of medieval allegory, follows a well-beaten path when he defines it as a universal principle of the mind, saying that 'it belongs not to medieval man, but to man, or even to mind, in general. It is the very nature of thought and language to represent what is immaterial in picturable terms'. Yet, as Lewis himself recognizes, allegory is more than just an image; it is an image that originates in an idea. In allegory, he writes, 'you can start with an immaterial fact, such as the passions which you actually experience, and can then invent *visibilia* to express them'.[26] Lewis's objective was to rehabilitate a genre that had, with Coleridge, Goethe, and the Romantic period, become highly criticized, if not unconditionally despised because of the stereotyped nature of those *visibilia*. What particularly interests me is that it is almost a general trope to evoke two oppositions: the first between allegory and symbol; and the second between allegory and allegoresis. These oppositions are central to my reflection both on how Bonnefoy uses the essay to convey the dual dimensions of *présence* and also on how allegory becomes a subtextual element of his didactic objectives, engaging readers to look structurally at his work and to seek out the meanings that can really only be obtained by reading through allegoresis.

Bracketing for the moment its allegorical dimension, it is noteworthy that in direct contrast to the incisive assertion about the act of *présence* in the Phaedra paragraph, we are struck in the leaf paragraph by the paradox of the future tense, 'je dirai' [I will say], that, along with the rhetorical filter of allegory, transforms what is nonetheless perceived as an absolute truth about the relationship between *présence* and reality.[27] The reader's attention is caught by this atypical syntax that uses the future rather than the more expected conditional tense (*je dirais que*).[28] That structure, 'I will say', multiplies the voice of Bonnefoy, for his use of the future tense induces a unsettling duplication of the subject through a temporal split that might be paraphrased as 'I am now saying that I will say later'. Two factors render this possible: the semantics of the verb 'say', and the emergence of an essayistic 'I'. Clearly, this effect could not be obtained if the verb were 'to run': 'I will run' would be a simple future statement. Nor would it be possible if the subject were 'they': 'they will say' is similarly a statement of the future. Here, Bonnefoy's writing strategy clearly seems to mesh with the generic prerogatives of the essay to 'accomplish something, or seek to do so', and it is the combination of the Austinian performative force of 'say' and the essay's unshakeable grounding in the 'I' that enables the act of speech to be enacted literally.[29]

Bonnefoy's use of the future tense clearly connotes a rhetorical strategy, for it is particularly striking that he makes marked use of it again in the salamander episode, the other key image of *présence* he gives in *L'Improbable*. There, Gasarian says, Bonnefoy's use of the future tense acts not only to destabilize the reading, but crucially also undermines the 'reality' of the event by revealing it to be an image. Gasarian argues that reading it, 'we realise that the salamander episode is an event "experienced" through image and not in reality' because Bonnefoy uses the future tense to shift the event into 'the imaginary of the present' thereby underscoring 'the duplicity of images'.[30] Gasarian's analysis of 'event "experienced" through image' is certainly valuable. I would suggest, however, that opposing *présence* and reality is hardly congruent with Bonnefoy's position, and that reading the leaf and the salamander images of *présence* in parallel suggests on the contrary that they are not 'duplicitous', but are, as I show later, predicated on real events: both of these images are grounded in older Bonnefoyian texts, where their structuring implies that they are narrations of real incidents.

In yet another example of the circular type of reading Bonnefoy demands, the future tense of the leaf passage is carefully constructed earlier in the essay. The leaf passage occurs in section IV of 'Les Tombeaux de Ravenne'. A brief comment on Bonnefoy's intertitles is in order here. Gérard Genette signals the difference between 'thematic' (discursive) and 'rhematic' intertitles (simple numerals showing position). He indicates that the latter correspond to a style that 'initially betokened classical dignity, then realistic seriousness'.[31] This, of course, corresponds well to the general message conveyed by Bonnefoy's sober, Roman-numbered intertitles, which paratextually reinforce the message borne in the essays, that is, the importance and gravity of *présence*. Moving back to the text itself, section IV, in which Bonnefoy describes walking through the town of Ravenna, opens with the deictic statement 'Voici ce monde sensible' [Behold this sensate world] (*I*, 24). This sentence is the increasing 'deictisation' of a sentence found at the end of section III: 'Voici *le* monde sensible' [Behold *the* sensate world] (*I*, 23, my emphasis). The shift from *le* to *ce* provides a salient example of Bonnefoy's strategic use of deixis and serves as a harbinger of its striking use in the leaf passage. The not-quite identical duplication of the 'Voici' sentence forces readers to focus on language and its deictic message, while priming them for the importance of repetition. This careful preparing of the reader is found also in the double use of that very expression, 'je dirai' [I will say] (*I*, 24), which will prove so crucial two pages later in the leaf passage. Both sets of repetitions evoke Gouvard's 'principle of repetition' and confirm Bonnefoy's poeticization of his essayistic prose.[32] Indeed, in section III, Bonnefoy suggests that *la parole* must act upon that deictic showing ('Voici') of the sensate world by speaking and naming the things of that world (*I*, 23). The reader will remember that the naming of the things of the world passing in the Grail procession is the very task Bonnefoy assigns to poetry (*I*, 126). This naming is precisely what he provides in the leaf paragraph through his multi-level use of deixis.

In the first sentence of the second paragraph, 'Je dirai par allégorie : c'est ce fragment de l'arbre sombre, cette feuille cassée du lierre', the colon works as a first deictic indicator visually demarcating the future enunciation 'je dirai' from the present tense used for the description of the leaf. The graphic separation of two different moments characterized by two different verb tenses allows us to understand the sequence of actions. In the present moment, there is the event of the dying ivy leaf. To allow that leaf to become functionally present and so provide salvation, it must be experienced wholly, directly. Therefore, in order for the 'I' to be fully present to that event, its narration (as well as its allegorization) can only take place at a later time, as indeed the future tense tells us. The colon also prepares the way for and heightens the impact of the true deictics that follow, and plays a role in the artistic construction of the sentence. Indeed, unconsciously perhaps, Bonnefoy has graced this phrase with a subtle poetic rhythm. The sentence is grammatically structured into three separate parts, each delimited by an obvious grammatical marker (colon for the first and comma for the second), and each of these sections scans into an octo-syllabic rhythm, inevitably reinforcing the artistic aspect of Bonnefoy's opening reference to allegory. Indeed, the regularity of the 'metre' in this first line, implying, as it does, a poetic dimension, is congruent with the allegorical intent of the sentence.

Moreover, the colon's typographical function has a semantic value. As with Bonnefoy's use of italics, it organizes the focus, pointing to the fundamental object of his engagement: *this* leaf which is showing us that the reality of the human experience involves interaction with the things of this world and their passage through time. This understanding is developed through the trope of fragmentation and in the emblematic image of a leaf doubly broken, both because it is a 'fragment of the dark tree' and because it is *not* the negatively connoted 'whole leaf'. And over the course of the single paragraph, in a form of litany that directly impacts on the reader, the deictic expression 'this leaf' is relentlessly repeated, becoming the very figure of the pointing index, insistently calling our attention to the object, naming it in what would appear to be the apotheosis of the poetic gesture. At that point, having rhetorically guided us to see this leaf really, Bonnefoy can give us its 'meaning'. His experience is a description of *présence*, but the all-important task that *présence* accomplishes is greater, as is underscored by the theological lexicon he mobilizes at this juncture: it is no less than salvation. This is important, for as the *telos* of *présence*, the notion of salvation forms one of the substantive bridges linking the leaf description of *présence* with that of the salamander.

★ ★ ★ ★ ★

Although Bonnefoy's second, salamander description of *présence* may not appear as overtly allegorical as the leaf description, both, we will see, are permeated with the figure of allegory. The essay 'La Poésie française et le principe d'identité', like 'Les Tombeaux de Ravenne', first appeared in a journal, the July-December 1965 issue of the *Revue d'Esthétique,* before being collected in *Un rêve fait à Mantoue* in 1967. Both texts work to give a definition of *présence* through images but from very different perspectives. Indeed, just as 'Les Tombeaux de Ravenne' constructed the opposition between *présence* and concept, 'La Poésie française et le principe d'identité' works to define the interaction between *présence* and language by showing the arc of a thinking process. A sense of urgency emanates from the essay, and it becomes rapidly clear that its contents are intended to strike a blow against Saussurian theories of language. As Bonnefoy writes, 'Saussure and his followers [...] assign to the word the unchanging task of merely signifying, and the very richness of their discoveries has become a danger for a meditation on poetry' (*APP*, 119). His reading of the effects of Saussurian linguistics — as distinct, of course, from his own use of the tools of Saussure's nomenclature — is extremely negative. He attributes to it a trivializing of the role of language that is dangerous for society as a whole, his anxiety stemming from what he sees as the human capacity to retreat from an active engagement with the world into the comfort of ready-made signs (*APP*, 119). As the salamander encounter shows, his criticism targets systems that work to remove or stifle individual agency. In point of fact, it is precisely in 'La Poésie française et le principe d'identité' that Bonnefoy develops the idea of the distinct levels of poetry that are inherent in certain words, with 'brick' and 'sip' having less poetic potential, he argues, than 'stone' or 'drink' (*I*, 255–56). Still, even this potential capacity of language comes with a caveat: it is not simply a question of choosing the right words and poetic expression will automatically follow. On the contrary, what is really required is the phenomenological gesture of intention that allows the speaker or writer to actively convert language to individual purpose. This phenomenological gesture lies at the heart of the central moment of the essay, which is Bonnefoy's description of his chance encounter with a salamander.

He initiates the description as a means to obviate any obscurity in what he is trying to express: 'Mais je crains d'être obscur, et je vais prendre un exemple' [But I fear I'm being unclear; I will use an example] (*I*, 248). The whole episode is thus placed under the aegis of the need to communicate transparently. As we will see, the displacement of the salamander image through Bonnefoy's work shows that the essay provides a response, becoming indeed the exemplum of a form that might dissipate the fear of inadequate communication. More broadly, the importance of the episode can hardly be overstated: like the earlier leaf description, the salamander episode can almost be read as a distillation of the relationship between *présence*, poetry, and essay that I have been developing. Not only does the whole episode encapsulate a number of the techniques that Bonnefoy uses to give immaterial ideas a corporeal form within language, but it also demonstrates his careful delineation of the different approaches within language that allow or disallow access to *présence*. Clearly, his objective is not simply to transmit the emotion that he felt at the moment of the interaction. Rather, his intent is to show the *prise de conscience* associated with the episode. His method, in sum, is inherently pedagogical, taking the reader through all the possibilities that were available at that instant of consciousness. Ultimately, however, the larger aim is didactic and seeks to show the reader not only that such an experience is within the reach of any person, but also, more prescriptively, show the 'correct' choice to make.

His text begins thus:

> Et j'imaginerai, ou me rappellerai — on verra [...] que les deux notions

s'équivalent — que j'entre un jour d'été dans une maison en ruine et vois soudain, sur le mur, une salamandre. Elle a été surprise, elle s'est effrayée et s'immobilise. Et moi aussi, arraché à ma rêverie, je suis prêt à me laisser retenir. Je regarde la salamandre, je reconnais ses traits distinctifs, comme l'on dit, — je vois aussi ce cou étroit, cette face grise, ce cœur qui bat doucement. (*I*, 248)

[And I will imagine or will remember — we shall perhaps see later that the two ideas are equivalent — that one summer's day I enter the ruins of a house and suddenly see a salamander on the wall. Taken by surprise, it is frightened, and freezes. And shaken out of my reverie, I, too, am ready to be held captive. I look at the salamander, I recognize those parts we call its distinctive features; I also see that narrow neck, that grey face, that softly beating heart.]

Primed by our reading of the leaf text, Bonnefoy's use of the future tense here confirms the idea that this is a conscious rhetorical strategy and no mere accident of the pen.[33] Equally important here, however, is Bonnefoy's equating of imagination and remembrance in an explicit parallel that is strongly reminiscent of the paradoxical, destabilizing effect he creates by identifying the word *l'improbable* with the expression *ce qui est*. In both the leaf and the salamander episodes, Bonnefoy follows an initiating future tense with the present, which, as we saw, consolidates the immediacy of the event deictically experienced in the *nunc* dimension. Moreover, both describe an act of observation leading to a conscious analysis of the intellectual and emotional possibilities afforded. The salamander episode, however, takes the 'usable' aspect of the experience further, for Bonnefoy describes the several paths that stem from the initial moment of physical perception. The first consists in remaining at the surface of the interaction by simply registering the information and using scientific knowledge to categorize it 'comme ferait le mot de la prose, et me dire: "*Une* salamandre", puis poursuivre ma promenade, toujours distrait, demeuré comme à la surface de la rencontre' [as the prose word would, saying to myself, '*a* salamander', and then walk on, still abstracted, having remained, as it were, only at the surface of the encounter' (*I*, 248). Bonnefoy's italicizing of the indefinite article, '*a*', coupled with his disparaging 'as the prose word would', demonstrates both rhetorically and grammatically the negative value he gives to this option.

The second possibility intensifies the act of classification by focusing more intently on the actions that engendered the initially spurious act of identifying the salamander as '*a* salamander'. This possibility, with its increasingly developed scientific and linguistic analysis, seems at first to be positive because it is clearly associated with a more profound action on the part of the speaker/ observer:

Je puis garder les yeux sur la salamandre, m'attacher aux détails qui m'avaient suffi pour la reconnaître, croire continuer l'analyse qui en fait de plus en plus *une* salamandre, c'est-à-dire un objet de science, une réalité structurée par ma raison et pénétrée de langage. (*I*, 248)

[I can keep my eyes on the salamander, focus on those few details that had enabled me to recognize it, believe that I am continuing the analysis that makes it more and more into *a* salamander, that is to say, an object of science, a reality that is structured by my reason and pervaded by language.]

Yet, in the intensity of its misplaced focus on the different parts of the salamander that allowed its identification, this second possibility leads to a frightening dislocation of the self; it leads to no longer seeing anything in the salamander but a terrifying series of meaningless, disconnected signs: 'dans ce contour d'une patte absolu, irréfutable, désert, qu'un faisceau effrayant d'énigmes' [in this shape, this shape of an absolute, indisputable, vacant leg, I no longer perceive anything but a terrifying knot of enigmas]. Bonnefoy links this crisis to the fact that the salamander has become 'pervaded by language', and writes that 'these things have a name, but suddenly, it is as though they have become strangers to that name' (*I*, 248). Tellingly, this horrifying sense of being cast entirely adrift in a meaningless universe is directly connected to Bonnefoy's contentious relationship with language and its theorization. He writes:

> Mais je viens en somme de découvrir l'angoissante tautologie des langues, dont les mots ne disent qu'eux-mêmes, sans prise vraie sur les choses — qui peuvent donc se détacher d'eux, s'absenter. J'appellerai *mauvaise présence* ce mutisme latent du monde. (*I*, 248)

> [In essence, I have just discovered the harrowing tautology of language; in it, words only say themselves and have no real hold on things, which can thus break away, absent themselves, from those words. *Evil presence* is how I will call this latent muteness of the world.]

Bonnefoy does not often speak or write about this *mauvaise présence*, but here, in a poetic materialization of the structuralist 'arbitrariness of language', he transforms what is a perfectly neutral linguistic analysis of the relationship between signifier and signified into a descent into hell. We have already seen Bonnefoy's ambivalence regarding structuralism, whose effect, he argues, had the impact of a 'bomb', making people believe that 'all communication was illusion or falsehood and that all that remained was to let language, seen now as its own self, manifest its autonomy' (*E*, 206). Yet, the hostility of his comment is mediated by his great familiarity with structuralist theories of language. From this perspective, it is fascinating to see him using theory itself to furnish the matter for poetic image. Clearly, *mauvaise présence* is the antithesis of *présence* and is linked through language to what might be considered as an emotional reception of conceptuality experienced at its utmost paroxysm. The fact that *mauvaise présence* should be so closely associated with language highlights once again the idea that the positive definition of *présence* would ideally be above or outside language and its 'latent muteness'. Indeed, after leading us through indifference and *mauvaise présence*, Bonnefoy finally presents a 'third path':

> Car voici la troisième voie: et que, par un acte toujours soudain, ce réel qui se dissociait, s'extériorisait, se *rassemble*, et cette fois dans une surabondance où je suis pris et sauvé. C'est comme si j'avais accepté, *vécu* cette salamandre, et désormais, loin d'avoir à être expliquée par d'autres aspects du réel, c'est elle, présente ici comme le cœur doucement battant de la terre, qui se fait l'origine de ce qui est. (*I*, 248)

> [Here is the third path through which by an always sudden act, that reality, which was breaking up, becoming alien, *binds itself together again*, but this time

in a plenitude where I am caught up and saved. It is as though I had accepted, *experienced* this salamander, and now rather than having to be explained by other aspects of reality, the salamander, here present as the softly beating heart of the world, becomes the origin of what is.]

Leaving aside for the moment the highly complex issue of the interaction between origin and *ce qui est*, Bonnefoy's 'sudden act', arguably figures a phenomenological approach to experience, a suggestion that is confirmed by the sentences that follow, where Bonnefoy writes:

> Disons — bien que cette expérience soit peu dicible — qu'elle s'est dévoilée, devenue ou redevenue *la* salamandre — ainsi dit-on *la* fée — dans un acte pur d'exister où son 'essence' est comprise. [...] tous les aspects, coagulations de visible, se sont dissous en tant que figures particulières, sont tombés comme les écailles d'une mue dans la connaissance, *ont découvert le corps de l'indissociable.* [...] J'appellerai cette unité rétablie [...] la *présence.* (*I*, 248)

> [Let's say — although this experience is barely say-able — that it has unveiled itself, becoming, or becoming again, *the* salamander — as one says *the* fairy — in a pure act of existing where its 'essence' is understood. [...] all appearances, which are coagulations of the visible have dissolved in their particularity, have, like scales sloughed-off into knowledge, *uncovered the body of the indissociable.* [...] I shall call this re-established unity [...] *presence.*]

Once again, Bonnefoy's italicization is purely essayistic, a hallmark of that community-building created by conscious but understated quoting that both reveals subjectivity and mutes it. The reference is perhaps to St John of the Cross, explicitly named later in the section, but the 'body' gives substance to the *présence* it describes. Without belabouring the point, I would suggest that it is almost impossible not to read in Bonnefoy's lexical choices and semantic trajectory (moving from unveiling and uncovering to knowledge and understanding) a subtext highly suggestive of Heideggerian disclosure and the philosophies of *présence* that subtend Bonnefoy's own. Just as clear, however, is his explicit equating of the notion of unity with that of *présence*. In some senses, there is nothing particularly surprising about that association; the references to Blanchot made in earlier chapters suggested that the correlation between *présence* and unity is by no means specific to Bonnefoy. Nonetheless, his notion of unity is particularized by his struggle to provide a theoretical and even rhetorical justification for the possibility of *présence* within language. Continuing his analysis of the salamander episode, he describes its effect upon him by saying that the essence of the salamander 's'est répandue dans l'essence des autres êtres, comme le flux d'une analogie par laquelle je perçois tout dans la continuité et la suffisance d'un *lieu* et dans la transparence de *l'unité*' [has propagated into the essence of other beings, like the flow of an analogy through which I perceive everything in the continuity and sufficiency of a *place* and in the transparency of *unity*] (*I*, 250). Once again, though the event of the salamander arguably took place, as I will show, in a real encounter, the place where this experience is described is an essay, which is also the final location of the salamander image, as it is indeed of the ivy leaf and the orangery. Thus the 1965 essay, 'La Poésie française et le principe d'identité', suggests that one can move beyond fragmentation, with Bonnefoy writing that language 'semble promettre au-delà de son moment conceptuel la même unité que celle que propose la vie au-delà des aspects qui ont fragmenté sa présence' [once past its conceptual moment, seems to promise the same unity as life offers when we move past those [partial] aspects that fragment its presence] (*I*, 251). Though it is certainly legitimate to recall Naughton's caveat concerning the evolution of Bonnefoy's positions over time, manifested by the poet's increasing confidence in the possibilities of image and language, it is equally legitimate to note that both *L'Improbable* and *Un rêve fait à Mantoue* were fused in the 1980 edition, with *Un rêve fait à Mantoue* even disappearing as a title, subsumed into *L'Improbable*.[34] That reprinting confirms what the 1975 poem, 'L'Epars, l'indivisible' [The Scattered, the Indivisable] also points to: that the dichotomy between fragmentation and unity has a permanent place in the Bonnefoyian imaginary, its Janus-like double image pointing to the paradox of a reality that can be neither wholly one nor the other.

This, of course, returns us to the double nature of *présence*, caught, in Bonnefoy's mental landscape, between fragmentation and unity. Both the leaf and the salamander passages point to experiences of *présence*; each seems to provide legitimate theoretical reasons for upholding fragmentation in the first case, or unity in the second. This paradoxical duality reiterates, of course, that double dimension of *présence* — both the underlying unity that gives meaning to everything and the fragment which leads us to that understanding. However, as the images provided in his essays show, the becoming of poetic *présence* is not a sinecure. In the leaf passage, allegory seems to be the precondition for our understanding of *présence*, and readers are told that they must read allegorically in order to connect the fragmentary leaf to an intuition of *présence*. But Bonnefoy's allegory is far more than that: it is the latent mechanism for his transfer of images from poetry to the essay, spurring my earlier suggestion that the essay is indeed a 'true place' where *présence* can become available and usable for readers.

★   ★   ★   ★   ★

Peter Berek cites Northrup Frye and Morton Bloomfield to point out that a number of critics have extended the concept of allegory to suggest that all forms of critical interpretation are allegorical, because all textual interpretation proposes to resolve the potential gap between the finished text and its intended meaning.[35] Berek is particularly interesting to the Bonnefoy reader because of the careful distinction he makes between author and reader, allegory and allegoresis. He writes that 'though its practitioners make interpretive statements which at first sound much like those made by interpreters of allegorical works', allegoresis 'ultimately makes claims to validity that have nothing to do with authorial intention, but rather with a truth the allegorizing reader knows which may well have been beyond the awareness, whether conscious or not, of the work's author'.[36] A rough distinction might then suggest that allegory is produced by the author as a means to read, while allegoresis is 'created' by the reader as an attempt to understand a structure; this, in turn, serves partly to explain why allegory is now so often defined as the post-modern 'trope of tropes'. Hence, to take an example from Bonnefoy's work we could, as critic

Matthieu Dubois has suggested, provide multiple interpretations of the 'character' of Douve, with some commentators interpreting it (her?) 'as an allegorical figure, others as a principle of knowledge, or even a poetic horizon determining its own aesthetic'.[37] The variability of these definitions, conjoined with Bonnefoy's own attempts to give an idea of the genesis of 'Douve', suggests that none of them is intrinsically false.

In contradistinction with *Douve*, Bonnefoy's 'Les Tombeaux de Ravenne' appears to be doing something quite different. Indeed, perhaps the most striking characteristic of the leaf passage is that it uses both allegory and allegoresis. This is clearly shown by its contrast with the primary question that the 'character' of Douve evokes in readers, with most of them wondering whether Douve is the allegorical representation of something else. For the leaf, by contrast, the allegorical dimension is patent. The question thus concerns allegoresis and the manner of reading and engenders a completely different question: why is this figure allegorical? And perhaps more cogently even: why does Bonnefoy so foreground the notion of allegory? Certainly the act of directly saying that one is speaking allegorically removes from it the idea of an oblique and hidden expression (*allos* and *agorein*) which the reader or hearer must decode by means of a given system of equivalences. It is, of course, Bonnefoy's chosen image, a leaf, that renders this necessary. Precisely because he is not engaging in some variant of personification allegory, which might be more easily visible through a 'character' such as Douve, there is no transparent allegorical gesture mapping one system of codes onto another set of referents. Thus, unlike the medieval and post-medieval allegorical texts that were so reviled by Romantic criticism, and in which the codes are patent and onomastically given by the names of the characters — Christian, Patience, The Giant Despair, and so on — the leaf has no immediately apparent codified meaning, forcing Bonnefoy to make the method of reading apparent. Indeed, a standard definition of allegory suggests that 'in allegory the objective referent evoked is without value until it is translated into the fixed meaning that it has in its own particular structure of ideas'.[38] This being the case, it is reasonable to assume that some indication must be given of the allegorical nature of the leaf; if no mention were made, the reader could not possibly grasp its allegorical import. But on the other hand — and this is really the central issue here — Bonnefoy, by inscribing the means of reading into his text, changes the emphasis of the reading, forcing the reader to look beyond the words on the page to an underlying meaning which is given as the *raison d'être* for the writing.

This question of guiding the manner in which the reader may read the text is vital to the allegorical gesture, and is particularly germane to my analysis because it replicates a number of the strategies connected to the generic functions of the essay, notably concerning subjectivity. However, in order to grasp this point more clearly, we need first to understand in what way Bonnefoy's text is allegorical. In other words, is it allegorical just because he tells us it is so, or are there some truly allegorical elements embedded in it? The short answer is the latter, for the allegorical dimension operates here both semantically, at the level of the word 'allegory' itself, and rhetorically, in the manner of structuring the syntax. In Bonnefoy's 'leaf' text, the physical position of the word 'allegory' itself embodies the allegorical process. Standing between the utterance 'I will say', and the real subject which follows the colon, it literalizes the notion of allegory, for it physically sets itself as an intermediary between the speaker and the subject. To see this more clearly, one has only to imagine the sentence without the transforming 'by allegory'. The result is a statement of future intent: 'I will say that it is the fragment of the dark tree', which has a much different tone and meaning than the 'allegorical' utterance.

Following the 'allegorical' introduction, the process reverses itself immediately thereafter through the repeated deixis, confronting the reader with a manner of contradiction. Indeed, if we return to Lewis's definition of allegory as concept dressed in *visibilia*, Bonnefoy's emphasis on 'this leaf' seems to fly in complete opposition to any conceptual perception of the leaf, pointing insistently instead at what is given as an identifiable element of concrete reality. It is difficult not to see the multiple reiterations of the deictic in such a short textual passage as having an effect similar to the use of any of the metalingual codes that might spontaneously be used to capture an interlocutor's attention: gesture, voice modulation, perhaps even physical contact. The net effect, of course, is to highlight the reality of the object being observed and anchor it in the text, rendering it, in Bonnefoy's own language, 'sense-able' that is, accessible to the senses ('the perceptible object [*object sensible*] is presence', *I*, 26). That this production of a textual 'here-ness' is rendered necessary by the image itself is shown by a comment in another essay, in which Bonnefoy contrasts 'leaf' and 'person', saying that the latter is always particularized by his or her individuality, while a leaf 'is closer to Idea' because it has a 'double image, simultaneously general and particular' (*I*, 84). The leaf passage works against this by overtly 'anthropomorphizing' the leaf, with Gasarian forcefully pointing out that it 'speaks', imputing to this the idea that it is an allegory of the poetic voice.[39] And indeed, though the leaf does speak, almost continuously ('I hear its unflagging voice'), it is further anthropomorphized because it 'constructs' ('using all its veins to construct its unchanging essence') and 'shows' ('shows in its wound'). Through these textual mechanisms, Bonnefoy creates a 'character', thereby undercutting the abstraction that is the 'true' meaning of the leaf. Nonetheless, its very 'leafness' stands in opposition to this anthropomorphization, begging the question whether the function it has is truly the allegorical one that Bonnefoy so adamantly imputes to it, or whether it might not be more aptly described by other rhetorical figures.

Paradoxically, useful understanding is gained by considering rhetorical elements with supposedly antinomic properties. Coleridge's oft-quoted distinction between allegory and symbol provides a plausible alternative for Bonnefoy's choice of the word 'allegory':

> Now an Allegory is but a translation of abstract notions into a picture-language, which is itself nothing but an abstraction from objects of the senses; the principal being more worthless even than its phantom proxy, both alike unsubstantial, and the former shapeless to boot. On the other hand a Symbol (ὁ ἐστιν ἀεί ταυτηγόρικου) is characterized [...] above all by a translucence of the Eternal through and in the Temporal. It always partakes of the reality which it

renders intelligible; and while it enunciates the whole, abides itself as a living part in that Unity of which it is the representative.[40]

This well-known passage describes not allegory, but symbol, using a series of terms that appear to be infinitely more suited to Bonnefoy's leaf. For instance, his insistent focus on rendering the leaf textually, almost materially present through deixis seems indeed to oppose Coleridge's idea of the insubstantiality of allegory. The leaf appears, like the Coleridgian symbol, expressly to 'partake of the reality which it renders intelligible', for it is the non-idealized reality of 'this blackening green leaf, broken and sullied' that provides 'intelligibility', precisely through the understanding of *présence* it furnishes. In addition, Coleridge's distinction between the whole and the part, with the symbol acting as 'living part', seems highly congruent with Bonnefoy's explicit description of the leaf as a fragment torn from the tree. Similarly, the Coleridgian 'it enunciates the whole' can fruitfully be conjoined with Bonnefoy's leaf that 'shows in its wound the *whole* depth of that which is' (my emphasis). Finally, Coleridge's 'translucence of the eternal through and in the temporal' is exactly the object of the leaf in the Bonnefoyian passage. It is because the leaf is damaged and dying that it can provide salvation, for its very destruction renders it inviolable: 'Qui pourrait m'arracher en effet que [cette feuille] a été mienne, et dans un contact au-delà des destins et des sites, dans l'absolu? Qui pourrait aussi bien détruite, la détruire? [Who could indeed wrench from me the fact that this leaf has been mine [...]. Who could destroy it, it having already been destroyed?] (*I*, 27). These parallels suggest that 'symbol' and not 'allegory' is the most appropriate term for Bonnefoy's description of the leaf. Which to choose? Our confusion is perhaps linked to the close proximity of the two figures, as indeed Paul Smith suggests when he notes that the commonly-held opposition between allegory and symbol is overstated since 'both eventually exhibit a similar nostalgia for a plenitude and security of reference, for "truth" as a stay against the individual's alienation from himself and from the world'.[41]

As the study of allegoresis in Chapter Four shows, this ambivalence between allegory and symbol certainly plays into Bonnefoy's overall project. Yet, his clear choice, reiterated and confirmed through the multiple editions of *L'Improbable*, is the word 'allegory'. His preference, moreover, cannot be imputed to lack of knowledge. Patrick Née has pointed out the poet's complete familiarity with theories of the symbol, evoking Bonnefoy's 'important article on the conception of the sign based in part on Coleridge and the Romantic theory of the symbol'.[42] Bonnefoy's choice must thus be assumed to be deliberate. Certainly, conscious decision plays into selecting allegory as a rhetorical strategy, as Coleridge himself points out:

> Of utmost importance to our present subject is this point, that the latter (the allegory) cannot be other than spoken consciously; whereas in the former (the symbol) it is very possible that the general truth represented may be working unconsciously in the writer's mind during the construction of the symbol.[43]

The fact that Bonnefoy's choice is a conscious one is confirmed by a comment made just a few pages before the leaf passage. Discussing his attraction for the tombs of Ravenna, he writes, 'qu'on ne s'étonne pas de la part que je fais aux monuments d'une ville. Ce n'est point par souci d'allégorie, ni simplement par le gout, d'ailleurs mystérieux, de la méditation des ruines' [let the reader not be surprised by the great interest I pay to the monuments of a town. It comes neither from a concern for allegory, nor yet simply by a liking — mysterious, withal — for meditating about ruins' (*I*, 21). Those tombs, he suggests, cannot be read as allegories of anything else, because their very ipseity renders them incompatible with conceptual thought (*I*, 20). Yet, in Bonnefoy's poetry, as Michèle Monte convincingly argues, it is often the bald ipseity of the thing described that impels an allegorical reading.[44] This renders Bonnefoy's explicit orienting of the manner in which the reader must read all the more pointed, and reinforces the idea that allegory is really the scrim through which he considers the leaf and its relation with *présence*. It is therefore all the more interesting that exploring more deeply the salamander image of *présence* hows that it too, like the leaf, is placed under the sign of allegory.

★ ★ ★ ★ ★

Perhaps more immediately (though not more completely, as we shall see) than the leaf image, the salamander episode shows an image from poetry actually finding its place in the essay, reinforcing thus my central idea that his essays are the 'true place' of writing, because there images acquire their dual dimension of experience and idea. As with the earlier 'orangery' image, the migration of the image takes place over a long period. Thus, although twelve years separate the 1953 *Douve* poetry cycle from the 1965 'La Poésie français et le principe d'identité', both texts contain what can only be read as identical images of a salamander. Patrick Née, who knew Bonnefoy personally, comments that all images in Bonnefoy's poetry correspond to real places and things in the world, indicating that the place Bonnefoy describes in 'Dévotion' as the 'city of kites and great glass houses that reflect the sky' is none other than New York.[45] When compared with the increasing metaphorization of the 'orangery' image examined earlier, the outlines of Bonnefoy's methodology become increasingly clear. They point to an originating salamander encounter that evolves and mutates in its displacement from one type of writing to another.

The importance of the image is patent. In a patient taxonomic study of the word patterns of Bonnefoy's early collections of poetry, Jérôme Thélot notes that the word *salamandre* appears no less than eight times in *Douve*, and then ceases to occur in subsequent collections of poetry.[46] It finally reappears in the essay, where, we saw, it is explicitly linked to *présence* and unity. In the poems, the strikingly high level of determination of the word *salamandre* (it is the title or a subject in no less than seven poems) parallels the fact that the image is directly associated with *présence* in the essay. As we saw in the Introduction, Bonnefoy himself is very clear about the fact that his poetry contains textual places that remain shadowy and obscure, even for him, thus requiring the 'clarification' of the essay (*E*, 63). Along the lines of his own argument, we could certainly read the relationship between the salamander occurrences in *Douve* and the later essay as the self-same process of addressing unresolved issues. And though the similitude between the texts lies essentially in lexical equivalences, it also exists in the semantic parallels between the poem and the essay and in the manner in which the image functions within the economy of each text. Indeed, from a lexical point of view, more conclusive, it would seem, than the actual occurrences of the word *salamandre* is the remarkable number of syntactic groups that appear in identical configurations in both texts.

The first cycle of poems, containing four Roman-numbered poems, is entitled 'La Salamandre', and occurs in 'L'Orangerie', the penultimate section of *Douve*. A title-less poem immediately follows the first four, and opens with the image of the salamander. After that, the salamander image disappears, only to appear again in 'Vrai lieu', the last section of *Douve*, in a poem called 'Le Vrai Lieu de la salamandre'. The first poem of the Salamander cycle is a prose poem that reads as follows:

> Une salamandre fuit sur le mur. Sa douce tête
> d'homme répand la mort de l'été. 'Je veux m'abîmer
> en toi, vie étroite, crie Douve. Eclair vide, cours sur mes lèvres, pénètre-moi!'
> (P, 96)

> [A salamander flees along the wall. Its gentle human head | diffuses the death of summer. 'I want to be engulfed | in you, narrow life' cries Douve 'Hollow lightening, run over my lips, pierce through me!'] (my translation)

The third poem of the cycle expands the description of that event into what might be read as its logical progression from flight into stillness:

> [...] Salamandre
> surprise, tu demeures immobile.
> Ayant vécu l'instant où la chair la plus proche se mue
> en connaissance. (P, 98)

> [Startled salamander, you freeze. | Having experienced that moment when the closest flesh sloughs | into knowledge.] (my translation)

And finally, 'Le Vrai Lieu de la salamandre' constitutes the crucial point of articulation between poem and essay. Condensing the themes broached in the previous poems, it projects them explicitly into an allegorical dimension linked to the mythological qualities associated with the figure of the salamander.

> La salamandre surprise s'immobilise
> Et feint la mort.
> Tel est le premier pas de la conscience dans les pierres,
> Le mythe le plus pur,
> Un grand feu traversé, qui est esprit.

> La salamandre était à mi-hauteur
> Du mur, dans la clarté de nos fenêtres.
> Son regard n'était que pierre,
> Mais je voyais son cœur battre éternel.

> O ma complice et ma pensée, allégorie
> De tout ce qui est pur,
> Que j'aime qui resserre ainsi dans son silence
> La seule force de joie.

[The startled salamander freezes
And feigns death.
This is the first step of consciousness among the stones.
The purest myth,
A great fire passed through, which is spirit

The salamander was halfway up
The wall, in the light from our windows.
Its gaze was merely a stone,
But I saw its heart beat eternal

O my accomplice and my thought, allegory
Of all that is pure,
How I love that which clasps to its silence thus
The single force of joy.] (P, 111; D, 151)

Naughton also cites that poem, reading it as 'stand[ing] for that which survives in the iconoclastic fury of Bonnefoy's early tendencies toward deconstruction and disillusionment'.[47] However, Naughton's depiction of the survival of images only takes on its full import if it is read in parallel with the later essay, where the identical images and syntactical expressions confirm the parallel between the *Douve* poems and the narrative it provides, as seen in the first line of the passage: 'j'entre un jour d'été dans une maison en ruine et vois soudain, sur le mur, une salamandre. Elle a été surprise, elle s'est effrayée et s'immobilise' [one summer's day I enter the ruins of a house and suddenly see a salamander on the wall. Taken by surprise, it is frightened, and freezes] (I, 248). The seven salamander poems of *Douve* demonstrate a clear trajectory going from what seems to be a 'real' encounter at the beginning of the cycle toward an increasing symbolization that reaches its apogee in the mythologizing and allegorizing dimension given to the image of the salamander ('mythe le plus pur' and 'allégorie de tout ce qui est pur'). As we saw earlier, the essay shows the salamander becoming indissociable from a unified whole that Bonnefoy describes as an epiphenomenological experience of *présence*. And though he insists on the fact that the encounter allows his consciousness to be 'saved', by becoming aware that it partakes in a larger whole, at the same time the salamander, qua salamander, having served as catalyst for conscious realization, is subsumed into the experience, much as the leaf was in the earlier text. This process of metamorphosis, of becoming an increasingly abstract figure is at work from the very beginning of the salamander poem cycle all the way through to the essay. More precisely, what we see over the course of the seven poems is a visible shift towards a mediated experience as the salamander image is increasingly absorbed into the more formal structures of language.

Two intricately enmeshed vectors allow the conversion of the hypothesized real encounter into the creation of a trope: first, its absorption into an increasingly structured linguistic paradigm, and second, its explicit integration into the structure of myth. From a purely formal perspective, the first four poems of the salamander cycle (P, 96–99) are prose poems, but the untitled salamander poem that follows them (P, 100) is in verse, as is the poem 'Le Vrai Lieu de la salamandre' quoted above. In the first four poems, Bonnefoy's use of more prose-like forms, his use of the indefinite article 'a salamander', of the present tense, as well as his repeated recourse to direct address all work to suggest that he is transcribing what seems to be a direct encounter. Over the course of the 'L'Orangerie' section, however, and culminating in 'Le Vrai Lieu de la salamandre', this unmediated encounter is increasingly integrated into a poetic paradigm: the last poem is visually structured so as to make it immediately identifiable as a poem; it begins with a five-line stanza regularized over the three subsequent stanzas into four lines. The increasingly formal structure of the poems into lines and stanzas, along with the recourse to alexandrines and other regular metres parallels the increasingly formal structuring of the narrative into coded linguistic structures whose apex, linguistically speaking, is the allegorizing and mythologizing of the salamander. From a semantic perspective, it is telling that the reference to the encounter with the salamander gives way to the imperfect tense only in the last poem, and then only after its association with myth. It is thus the recollection of the mythic resonance of the originating event that allows the salamander to become allegory, hence acquiring a meaning which, in turn, can become the transmissible idea that is reactivated in the essay.

Both the orangery and the salamander images demonstrate the struggle to give a written form to what appears in each case to be a single originating image. But if the orangery image was able to travel from narrative to poetry to essay in order to find its proper place, what is truly fascinating about the salamander image is that as it moves from poem to poem, and finally crosses the boundary between poetry and essay, it actually internalizes this quest for the true place. Indeed, the fact that the concluding section of *Douve* is explicitly titled 'Vrai Lieu', and that within it, the last use of the salamander image occurs in a poem entitled 'Le Vrai Lieu de la salamandre' suggests that closure can be attained when the object has 'found its place', and been integrated into it. In point of fact, it has been convincingly argued by a number of critics (Argyros, Née, Stamelman, and others) that the entire trajectory of the *Douve* cycle of poems indicates that the notion of place is the very objective towards which the whole collection tends. Yet, as the interaction between poetry and essay shows, the notion of place as the *telos* of poetry is itself highly problematic in Bonnefoy's work. In some highly significant way, the fact that the self-same salamander image recurs in the later essay indicates that the closure seemingly attained through poetic place cannot be maintained, and that the initial notion of 'true place' must not only be deferred, but also substantively rethought.

Where, then, is the true place? Generally speaking, one could define textual closure as the moment when the text can end because it is felt by the writer that the message it carries has been unambiguously transmitted. However, for a number of the poetic images, this clearly has not happened, and the message continues to seek its place. In a sense, we have come back full circle to the problem of the dual nature of *présence*, for if the salamander poems are structured to bring the reader to the implicit underlying idea that these images *are* the sign of *présence*, the crux of the problem lies in the fact that the same images have been transposed into the more conceptual prose of the essay, confirming once again that the images must contain both experience and idea. And the way in which that takes place is, as we have seen, the increasing absorption of the 'real' salamander of the first poems into the structured linguistic paradigm of the 'true place' poem, and finally into the idea-bearing image of the essay.

★   ★   ★   ★   ★

Unsurprisingly, as was shown through Bonnefoy's manner of introducing the example of the salamander, the problem is really one of communication, the fear of not having been clear enough. What he does not mention, but that we have seen through genre analyses of poetry and the essay, is that the problem of communicating through poetry collides with a number of factors that limit its range, notably the duality of *présence*, the intransivity of poetry, or the discrediting of the lyrical 'I'. Indeed, what seems to emerge inescapably from this very contemporary set of problems is the need for some form of writing that is more hospitable, perhaps even more efficient than poetry. That that form should be the essay seems confirmed by the intrinsic characteristics of the genre, its tentative nature, its permeability both to form and to idea, or, again, its creating of a common space where writer and reader come together to examine a topos. But — and this is an important 'but' — in Bonnefoy's case, it is also confirmed by the manner in which the essay genre enables the didactic impulse that subliminally structures his descriptions of *présence* and then carries over to his broader structuring of his essays.

Generally speaking, what have Bonnefoy's definitions of *présence* shown us? Primarily, of course, they have shown two life experiences that we believe to be his own. They invite the reader to relive the experiences of the authorial voice, and are narrated in that intensely personal manner that both poetry and the essay can muster in order to downplay their prescriptive dimension. Rather transparently also, especially in the case of the salamander, the two episodes assign a hierarchical value to the possible choices, with the goal of convincing the reader of the validity of that hierarchy. This is also the case in the leaf episode, where the repeated deixis makes *not* looking at the leaf a less desirable moral choice. In both instances, the underlying didacticism is patent, even though the subjectivity of the personal experience works to mask it partially. Secondly, Bonnefoy's descriptions (Chapter Four shows that this is equally true of the leaf image) have shown us the mobility of the images, and the fact that their displacement through genres is really only completely resolved when they reach the essay. But reading back through the transpositions of the salamander image from poem to essay has also shown that it connects to the leaf through two terms, 'salvation' and 'allegory', both of which, I argue, are connected to deeply-felt didactic ambitions that Bonnefoy can really only attain through the genre of the essay and its easy accommodation of the Austinian performative functions.

Both images are explicitly presented by Bonnefoy as means of salvation, a word which is of course derived from the theological roots of *présence*. In Bonnefoy's parlance, however, we know that it connotes not religious salvation, but something more diffuse, though no less serious: the possibility of escaping a grave, perhaps mortal danger. Indeed, from the 1980s to the end of his life, in many of his published texts Bonnefoy warned of the risk of the loss of poetry, equating it with a danger experienced not just by the individual, but by society as a whole. His choice of the word 'salvation' (as indeed of 'presence', or 'redeem', or any of his other uses of this lexical field) is thus calculated, and we have to look to Émile Benveniste to understand the illocutionary force of the term. In 'Nature du signe linguistique' [The Nature of the Sign], Benveniste challenges Saussure's 'arbitraire du signe', indicating that 'the action of a number of historical forces' transforms the relation between the sign and the object it represents.[48] Globally, he means that connotations inevitably accrue to words over time, justifying their preferential use in certain contexts. If we remember Bonnefoy's assertion about certain words such as 'bread' or 'wine', 'that mean *differently*' (E, 21), it is clear that in his *imaginaire* their passage through time has provided those signs with a motivation that Saussure denies.

As concerns the word 'salvation' itself, the significance of adopting a term so clearly derived from theological discourse lies in furnishing a moral imperative that undergirds Bonnefoy's work and provides, I believe, the grounds for the didactic cast of the two definitions of *présence*. More generally, however, the net effect on the reader of the use of such vocabulary is to consolidate Bonnefoy's position in a highly serious moral battleground where the stakes are those of thought and soul. A description of a textual 'act of presence' provides a good example of this moral dimension: although the question of what salvation might be remains unanswered, Bonnefoy says, 'nous avons reçu malgré tout le bien d'une certitude [...]. Désormais nous avons une raison d'être, qui est cet acte soudain. Et un devoir et une morale, au moins *par provision*, qui sera de le retrouver' [we have nonetheless received the boon of a certainty [...]. Henceforth, we have a reason for being, which is that sudden act. And a duty and a moral code — *provisionally*, at least — which will be to find it again] (I, 125). Here, beyond even the general gist of the passage and its evocation of salvation and moral duty, Bonnefoy's use of italics follows his standard method of using an approximate quotation. In this case, it echoes Descartes's proposal of a 'morale provisoire' by which to govern one's life during the intellectual process of determining the certitude grounded in the *cogito*.[49] Bonnefoy's recourse to the Cartesian phrase in the context of examining *présence* thus has a double thrust: on the one hand, it hints at a possible parallel between his own work and the didactic ambition so present in the *Discours de la méthode*, and on the other hand, it anchors Bonnefoy's own thinking within the Cartesian model of a philosophy informed by theological concerns, as indeed Steven Winspur argues, when he writes that 'a single matrix governs Bonnefoy's poetry of the *body* and Descartes's philosophy of the *soul*'.[50] Winspur's position can be further specified, for despite Bonnefoy's insistence on salvation as the *telos* principally of poetry, his view of writing as a guide for moral understanding factors far more substantively into his essays. It is therefore all the more interesting to see that Adorno also associates, albeit negatively, the essay with Descartes, defining it as a 'protest against the four rules that Descartes's *Discourse on Method* sets up'.[51]

The efficiency of that Cartesian-flavoured didacticism is really only made possible by the generic characteristics of the essay, in which didacticism, though perhaps not fostered, is undeniably allowed. The genre coalesces all the elements allowing the essayist to put forth what was qualified in Chapter One (with a nod to Adorno) as a 'methodless method'. That very 'unmethod' is Bonnefoy's response to the moral obligation he feels to transmit the notion of *présence*. The first, most obvious element is the essayist's subjectivity, which is transparently rendered by the way in which Bonnefoy makes the 'I' the central focus in both of his descriptions of *présence*. In both cases also, the authenticity of that 'I' is reinforced by the physicality of its actions, and by being enthymematically grounded in a physical place that the reader can recognize. 'Les Tombeaux de Ravenne' shows that physical 'placeness' of the 'I' walking through the streets of Ravenna, while in 'La Poésie française et le principe d'identité', we see the 'I' walking into the ruins of a house on a summer day. Similarly the careful reader would also note that when Descartes begins to outline his method in Part Two, he prefaces it with a description of his physical location, halted by winter in his travels through Germany, and then even more precisely 'enfermé seul dans un poêle' [holed up in a heated room]. Rhetorically then, these strategies capitalize on the generic characteristics of the essay to gain the reader's adhesion, for readers are meant to infer from the truly contingent, materially real experiences of a speaking 'I' the truth and authenticity of its physical experiences and these, in turn, should guarantee the truth and authenticity of the positions it conveys.

This brings us to the 'allegory' that also unites the two Bonnefoyian descriptions. As I suggested earlier, it functions at several levels in Bonnefoy's work inasmuch as it is both a straightforward figure that gives the manner of reading, and a tool inviting the reader to read through structure in order to see meaning. Once again, Austin provides the key to understanding what is happening at the level of word and intent. At the primary level, using his terminology of 'performative' speech shows Bonnefoy's 'I will say by allegory' to be a clear instance of an illocutionary act in the sense that it does not merely provide information, but tells us something about how the speaker is communicating. In his own work, Austin actually uses the term 'illocutionary force', but within the lexicon we have been building, 'intention' would speak more naturally to Bonnefoy's objectives and actions.[52] Indeed, the identical allegorical descriptor he uses for both leaf and salamander, combined with that Coleridgian dichotomy between allegory and symbol confirms the intentionality behind the term. For predicated on Coleridge's descriptions, it would certainly seem possible to describe the leaf as a symbol, with the whole notion immanent in its fragmentation. That, however, is a choice Bonnefoy eschews for philosophical reasons. A comment by Smith provides a means to understand Bonnefoy's position:

> It is the nature of allegory to stress discontinuity and to remark the irreparable distance between representation and ideas. Whereas the sense of the symbol is always given as wholesome and natural, the sense of allegory is arbitrary and conventional since allegory specifically marks its distance from an original truth.[53]

The net effect of Bonnefoy's choosing (and reiterating) allegory as the figure that defines his images is to reinforce the basic tenets of his own position regarding the unreliability of images, their inability to give us an authentic experience of *présence*. My hypothesis that the salamander and leaf images found in the essays are grounded in events that really happened in Bonnefoy's personal history corroborates the intellectual honesty of his 'allegorical' choice, for by materializing that distance between the text and the original event, he emphasizes the essay's 'truth potential'.

He also does more than that. If we look even more closely at the statement, we see that it goes beyond the illocutionary to encapsulate a perlocutionary dimension. In Austin's typology of speech acts, the last category, the perlocutionary, addresses statements that effect a change in the behaviour of the message's recipient. For readers of the leaf passage, Bonnefoy's 'I will say allegorically' literally works as an act, changing the way we read the text, for by introducing the statement as he does, he disallows the possibility of reading the leaf simply as leaf, even had we so wanted. In a sense, his words have become an act, and perhaps even more a prescriptive act that reinforces the didactic dimension seen in both the texts. Like all didacticism, Bonnefoy's didacticism is purposeful, linked in part to that moral obligation to convey *présence*, and in part to the essay's greater capacity to effect the transformation of the reader into that good reader so necessary for the survival of an increasingly embattled poetry. In *Entretiens sur la poésie* he writes, 'de mon côté du poème, j'ai surtout l'expérience d'images qui me viennent obscures et qui le restent, et de contradictions que je n'arrive pas à lever' [from my side of the poem, my experience is one of images that are obscure when they come to me and remain so afterwards, of contradictions I cannot resolve] (*E*, 63). This could almost be a description of the experience of the reader confronting Bonnefoy's essays. Once again, it is the generic characteristics of the essay that enable this, for the paradox and syntax that are his tools of predilection represent perhaps to the highest degree the poetic language that can inhabit the essay, thereby consolidating and affirming its didactic potential. In many ways, Pearre's idea of the proximity of Bonnefoy's poetry to the Buddhist *koan* provides a useful image of what is happening in his essays as well. The reader will remember that the specificity of the *koan* is to provide the basis for meditation through the contradiction or paradox it presents. That meditation, however, is active; it aims to teach through the act of resolving the paradox. The salamander text provides a good example of this very Bonnefoyian strategy.

In the *mauvaise présence* section of the text, we saw Bonnefoy annexing the theoretical expression *l'arbitraire du signe*, and transforming it into a poetic image. A paragraph later in, when describing the apotheosis of unity, he puts the salamander image in parallel with another image, 'the fairy', written '*the* fairy', just as the salamander is written '*the* salamander' ('qu'elle s'est dévoilée, devenue ou redevenue *la* salamander — ainsi dit-on *la* fée — dans un acte pur d'exister où son "essence" est comprise' [it has unveiled itself, becoming, or becoming again, *the* salamander — as one says *the* fairy — in a pure act of existing], *I*, 248). This usage cannot but startle. There is no doubt that Bonnefoy intends the definite article to carry a semantic weight far beyond its ordinary grammatical purpose: its italicization and repetition force us to focus on it. Immediately, however, Bonnefoy associates it with '*the* fairy', enclosing the term in dashes which rhetorically indicate that he is providing a further illustration of his point. His choice is puzzling, for though the shift from 'a salamander' to '*the* salamander' appears as a transparent evocation of the increasingly specific relation that is the point of the whole text, the same cannot be said for '*la fée*', which does not, in fact, clarify the definite article of the salamander. Indeed, it requires some effort — that meditative focus of the *koan* — to work through Bonnefoy's reasoning.

Née points to the importance of proper names in Bonnefoy's goal of transmitting *présence*, writing, 'if there is a chance that 'presence' might appear within the words of language [...] it is on the condition that these poetic words be like proper names'.[54] His point is corroborated by the fact that the proper name becomes the theme of a *récit*, 'Le Prénom', found in the much later collection of poetic texts.[55] Née links proper names with Bonnefoy's predilection for using metonymy rather than metaphor as a means to integrate *présence* into poetic texts. He consolidates the idea by pointing out that this is supported by linguistics because proper names coalesce the signifier, the signified, and the extra-linguistic referent into one word.[56] Winspur also addresses the capacity of proper names to act as linguistic artefacts able to point directly to the 'thing-in-itself'. He concludes however that proper names are not special elements of language because 'even the so-called proper names are signs', our perception of the higher poetic value of proper names is a myth that we tell ourselves about how language works.[57] His evocation of myth with respect to proper names is fascinating because in Bonnefoy's text, what we see is the exact opposite of proper names becoming signs, and the way it works is precisely by going through myth and reactivating the metonymic relationship between language and reality pointed out by Née.[58]

What does the text give us? A common noun, *fée*, associated with a definite article for which we have no textual referent. In other words, in the immediate vicinity of the passage, there is no other place where Bonnefoy has previously referred to the word *fée*, thus allowing us to understand his use of the definite article. Moreover, his italicizing of the article clearly indicates that the word cannot, in the French context, be taken in its generic sense of 'fairies'. From a purely grammatical perspective, the use of a referenceless definite article is possible only in the context of a shared culture allowing writer and reader to refer to the same reality. Thus if one can easily speak of 'the' moon or 'the' sun to any person on earth, the words 'the' nation or even 'the' river require a closer cultural connection, each socio-cultural sphere delimiting the grammatical possibility of the definite article. Bonnefoy's use of '*the* fairy' thus compels the reader to search within his or her cultural construct to find the missing referent, which, it will occur to most French readers, must be a proper name because *fée* can only point in that direction. Given the image of the salamander, the serpent/ lizard-tailed Mélusine fits rather better in the context than Morgane, but this hardly matters, because what is important is how Bonnefoy has made his text point to a proper name without himself furnishing it.

It would, of course, have been easy to provide the name. The question is: why did he refrain from doing so? The answer, I believe, is that Bonnefoy is trying to open a breach in language. He has structured his text to elicit a specific response from the reader, namely searching through myth and tales for the missing referent. This, in turn, allows the text to involve the reader because by supplying the name, he or she participates in the construction of the meaning that is given. Moreover, Bonnefoy's seemingly casual use of the construction 'as one says', reinforces this sense of participation by providing a clear sense of inclusiveness — the 'we-ness' we saw earlier. The whole structure works in the following manner: by activating the larger cultural context of tale/myth while simultaneously suppressing it, Bonnefoy uses the absent proper name to create a direct connection between his own use of language and the exterior reality shared by both writer and reader. The specificity of proper names is that they are not the metaphorical equating of two different elements of reality, but that they the *exact* equivalent of the reality they point to. Metonymically, thus, the proper name the reader must provide becomes identical to the textual fairy. It *is* 'the fairy'. And so, remarkably, Bonnefoy has textually created a space with a greater potential to include *présence*, inasmuch as the referent has literally managed to escape language.

Tellingly, this use of an absent proper name and its metonymic connections has happened in an essay; and it is not an isolated instance, for something of the same nature takes place with the leaf, as we will see in Chapter Four. One might therefore go further and suggest that looking for the missing referent is only feasible in an essay insofar as the hermetic nature of poetry precludes as active a search for the missing referent. Would readers of poetry not simply accept the opacity of the word, as, for instance, they do for 'Douve'? As a corollary to that question, can it be that it is the nature of the essay, its supposed transparency, that makes the reader resist a perceived lack of information and thus seek to fill it? Thus, the concept, after having undergone a poetic metamorphosis, which the essay is eminently able to integrate, can actually become form in Bonnefoy's essays.

The function of this hard-won form lies in challenging the reader. In those frequent moments of incomprehension where the text presents a paradox, the reader must really look at what language is doing, and reflect on what that means in terms of understanding *présence*. That we should gain this understanding is Bonnefoy's fundamental goal. The examples given throughout this chapter encompass the spectrum of Bonnefoy's didactic strategies: they both describe cognitively the path to *présence*, and they show literally how the deep rhetorical structures of language can be shaped to materialize something resembling textual *présence*. Could he have achieved this through poetry? Perhaps not, and that for many reasons, including contemporary poetry's dissociation from idea, and the change in our socio-cultural relation to poetry. But the essay, because it invites a different relationship to the text and its author, allows that latent, though powerful form of teaching. Its strength lies in the fact that it can accommodate these two perspectives. It is even the faithful replica of the multiple ways to teach: by telling, by showing, and by eliciting the thinking process that will allow the reader to absorb, really make his or her own the material learnt and thus be able to transpose this acquired competency into other circumstances. Bonnefoy's subliminal goal is the rehabilitation of poetry through the reactivation of the desire *and* the capacity to read poetry, and this can only work through that '*koan*-like' grappling with the complexities of the text. All these textual images and the language of their description are complex because of the extremely constructed nature of Bonnefoy's writing, which nests each image, reference, or phrase within numerous other references, in what seems like a complex textual kaleidoscope that can leave the reader with a dizzying impression of disorientation. There are so many instances requiring either that circular reading we saw earlier, or a determined search for the linguistic and cultural ramifications that confirm the purpose of a word. My point is that Bonnefoy's lexical, syntactical, and imagistic choices are never random; they are always motivated by that greater goal of bringing readers to *présence*. Far from being a kaleidoscope of disparate luminous pieces, his work resembles more a densely woven fractal tapestry whose intense colours and patterns repeat at all levels, but that can only be seen properly from a distance. After this chapter's microanalyses of specific images and words, Chapter Four shows that the teaching of *présence* also conditions the structuring of Bonnefoy's essay collections, with each essay providing an additional stone to build the reader's understanding of the notion.

Notes to Chapter 3

1. Yves Bonnefoy, 'Entretien avec Fabien Scotto', *Europe*, 890–91 (June-July 2003), 49–63 (p. 52).
2. Adorno, 'The Essay as Form', p. 12.
3. Alex L. Gordon, 'From *Anti-Platon* to *Pierre Ecrite*: Bonnefoy's "Indispensable" Death', *World Literature Today*, 53.3 (Summer 1979), 430–40 (p. 433).
4. Cavallini, *Langage et poésie*, p. 140.
5. Korhonen, *Essaying Friendship*, p. 245.
6. See, among others, Richard Stamelman's work *Lost Beyond Telling* (Ithaca, NY: Cornell University Press, 1990); Yves Bonnefoy, *The Lure and the Truth of Painting*, trans. by Richard Stamelman (Chicago: University of Chicago, 1995); Patrick Née, *Yves Bonnefoy, penseur de l'image* (Paris: Gallimard, 2006); Murielle Gagnebin, *Yves Bonnefoy: lumière et nuit des images* (Seyssel: Champ Vallon, 2005); Pierre Dubrunquez, 'La Fonction ontologique de l'image chez Yves Bonnefoy', *Revue d'esthétique*, 7 (1984), 85–90.
7. Bonnefoy, 'Le Carrefour dans l'image', p. 12.
8. Adorno, 'The Essay as Form', p. 11.
9. Jean-Michel Gouvard, 'Éléments pour une grammaire de la poésie moderne', *Poétique*, 129 (2002), 3–31 (p. 3).
10. Vernier, 'Un récit d'Yves Bonnefoy', p. 37.
11. Gasarian, *Yves Bonnefoy*, p. 32.
12. Lukács, *Soul and Form*, p. 7.
13. Yves Bonnefoy, *Récits en rêve* (Paris: Gallimard, 1987), pp. 191–92.
14. Franck Merger, *Les Planches courbes* (Paris: Bréal, 2005), p. 27.
15. Bonnefoy, *Récits en rêve*, p. 251.
16. Steven Winspur, 'The Poetic Significance of the Thing-in-itself', *SubStance*, 41 (1983), 41–49 (pp. 41, 42, 44).
17. This image, too, connects back to *L'Ordalie*, where it is not lightning, but the first ray of sunlight that suddenly 'tears the site', revealing the previously hidden landscape (Bonnefoy, *Récits en rêve*, p. 190).
18. Lukács, *Soul and Form*, p. 9.
19. Obaldia, *The Essayistic Spirit*, p. 18.
20. Blanchot, *L'Entretien infini*, p. 525.

21. Richard Stamelman, 'The Syntax of the Ephemeral', *Dalhousie French Studies*, 2 (1980), 101–17 (p. 103).
22. Adorno, 'The Essay as Form', p. 19.
23. Paquette, 'De l'essai dans le récit au récit dans l'essai chez Jacques Ferron', p. 623.
24. Bonnefoy, *Récits en rêve*, p. 131. Jean Racine, *Phaedra*, trans. by Bruce Boswell <https://www.gutenberg.org/files/1977/1977-h/1977-h.htm> [accessed 24 October 2021].
25. Gasarian, *Yves Bonnefoy*, p. 20.
26. C. S. Lewis, *The Allegory of Love: A Study in Medieval Tradition* (New York: Galaxy, 1966), pp. 44, 45.
27. Naughton's translation uses 'shall', which is certainly the correct modal, perhaps even more so than 'will'. I have preferred 'will' because of a possible prescriptive ambiguity created by 'shall' that is not present in the French *dirai*.
28. Indeed, this use is so surprising that I checked all three editions of *L'Improbable* to confirm the spelling (and thus the verb tense).
29. Larroux, 'L'Essai aujourd'hui', p. 468.
30. Ibid., p. 36.
31. Gérard Genette, *Thresholds of Interpretation*, trans. by Jane E. Lewin (Cambridge: Cambridge University Press, 1997), p. 315.
32. Gouvard, 'Éléments pour une grammaire de la poésie moderne', p. 3.
33. See, on this point, Dominique Combe, *Poésie et récit: une rhétorique des genres* (Paris: José Corti, 1989), p. 26.
34. Naughton, 'The Notion of Presence in the Poetics of Yves Bonnefoy', pp. 43–44, 54.
35. Peter Berek, 'Interpretation, Allegory, and Allegoresis', *College English*, 40.2 (1978), 117–32 (p. 117).
36. Ibid., p. 118.
37. Matthieu Dubois, *Figuration contemporaine de la poésie amoureuse: du mouvement et de l'immobilité de Douve d'Yves Bonnefoy* (Paris: L'Harmattan, 2011), p. 11.
38. William Harmon and C. Hugh Holman, *A Handbook to Literature*, 8th edn (Upper Saddle, NJ, & London: Prentice Hall, 1999), p. 498.
39. Gasarian, *Yves Bonnefoy*, p. xxx.
40. Samuel Taylor Coleridge, *The Statesman's Manual* (Burlington, VT: Chauncey Goodrich, 1832), p. 40.
41. Paul Smith, 'The Will to Allegory in Postmodernism', *Dalhousie Review*, 62.1 (1982), 105–21 (p. 108).
42. Patrick Née, *Yves Bonnefoy* (Paris: Association pour la Diffusion de la Pensée Française, 2005), p. 13.
43. Coleridge, *The Statesman's Manual*, p. 107.
44. Michèle Monte, '*Runes* de Jean Grosjean et *La Grande neige* d'Yves Bonnefoy: de l'étrangeté pragmatique à la lecture allégorique', in *Sens et présence du sujet poétique*, ed. by Michael Brophy and Mary Gallagher (Amsterdam: Rodopi, 2006), pp. 227–41 (p. 238)
45. Patrick Née, *Rhétorique profonde d'Yves Bonnefoy* (Paris: Hermann, 2004), p. 7.
46. Jérôme Thélot, *Poétique d'Yves Bonnefoy* (Geneva: Droz, 1983), p. 141.
47. Naughton, 'The Notion of Presence in the Poetics of Yves Bonnefoy', p. 54.
48. Émile Benveniste, *Problèmes de linguistique générale*, 2 vols (Paris: Gallimard, 1966–74), I, 49–55. It must be noted that challenges to Benveniste's reading of Saussure have been presented, notably by Simon Bouquet, 'Benveniste et la représentation du sens: de l'arbitraire du signe à l'objet extra-linguistique', *Linx*, 9 (1997), 107–23 <https://doi.org/10.4000/linx.1008> [accessed 28 May 2022].
49. Adorno also refers to Descartes with respect to the essay, holding the method of the *Discourse* as a negative mirror for goals of the essay ('The Essay as Form', p. 161).
50. Steven Winspur, 'Bonnefoy cartésien?', *French Forum*, 9.2 (1984), 236–50 (p. 244).
51. Adorno, 'The Essay as Form', p. 161.
52. Austin, *How to Do Things with Words*, p. 98.
53. Smith, 'The Will to Allegory in Postmodernism', p. 106.

54. Née, *Yves Bonnefoy*, p. 49.

55. Yves Bonnefoy, *La Longue Chaîne de l'ancre*, in *L'Heure présente, précédé de La Longue Chaîne de l'ancre et suivi de Le Digamma* (Paris: Gallimard, 2014), pp. 53–61.

56. Née, *Yves Bonnefoy*, p. 49.

57. Winspur, 'The Poetic Significance of the Thing-in-itself', pp. 44–45.

58. Née, *Yves Bonnefoy*, p. 50.

CHAPTER 4

❖

Being the Bad Reader

The Act and the Place of Poetry, John Naughton's carefully curated translations of Yves Bonnefoy's essays, appeared in 1989, bringing together a number of essays that finally allowed English-language readers a structured contact with this most important aspect of Bonnefoy's poetics. Naughton's selection includes a number of essays that had previously been translated for various academic reviews; some, however, were translated specifically for this collection. He amply defends his selection in the introduction, explaining that it was guided by the desire to offer 'a coherent statement of poetic philosophy and intent' that reflected the 'continuity and coherence' in Bonnefoy's essayistic practice (*APP*, xvi). This position motivates the decision to include essays written over a thirty-year period. His choices, moreover, are very well adapted to his rhetorical purpose, which is to bring Bonnefoy into the purview of English-language readers. Thus three essays on Shakespeare are included, as are several on well-known French literary icons such as Baudelaire, Valéry, and Mallarmé. Similarly, in order to establish a discussion on 'what amounts to almost the whole sweep of French poetic tradition' (*APP*, xvi), Naughton organizes the essays chronologically by their subject matter: the 1965 essay on the medieval *Chanson de Roland* precedes, for example, the 1955 essay on Baudelaire, which itself precedes the 1963 'Paul Valéry', and so on. Richard Stamelman, in his roughly contemporaneous volume of translations of Bonnefoy's essays on the plastic arts makes a very similar chronological choice, dividing his book into three sections that trace art through its 'classical', 'modern', and 'contemporary' periods. The choices made by Naughton and Stamelman are certainly legitimated by their rhetorical objectives, but I would suggest, as Bonnefoy himself does in his preface to Stamelman's book, that reading these essays in isolation from their original structure might compromise the reader's understanding of the meaning he originally intended through his own organization.[1] Moreover, in a comment that reinforces my hypothesis that his use of the form of the essay is a conscious strategy furthering his moral obligation to bring readers to a complete understanding of *présence*, he also suggests there that readers who have not been steeped in the idioms and thought patterns of French might not understand his work. He writes: 'despite the quality of the translations, the essays in the present volume are deprived of the kind of help that a reader's familiarity with the language in which they were written might bring to his or her reading, let alone acceptance of them'.[2] Bonnefoy's comment reveals his absorption of a number of the defining elements of the essay as form. Indeed, while the notion of 'reader acceptance' evokes that low-key persuasive dimension almost automatically carried by the essay, the question of the 'idioms and thought patterns of French' is even more striking, ineluctably recalling the enthymematic construction Bonnefoy uses to elicit the proper name in the fairy example given in the previous chapter. Less explicitly in Bonnefoy's comment, but no less important generally, the thematic reorganization of his essays in their English translations deprives them of a structuring mechanism that is the hallmark of the essays of *L'Improbable*.

This chapter focuses specifically on that mechanism, showing that his purposeful organization of a number of his essays into a much larger set of structures, his collected essays, relies heavily on the images and characteristics that describe the genre, notably the notions of wandering and fragmentation whose tentative underpinnings seek to minimize any authoritative stance. Overall, Bonnefoy's deliberate organization contributes, of course, to his primary goal of conveying *présence*. In conjunction with that goal, however, this chapter shows that reading his collected essays through that trope of allegory so explicitly foregrounded in his descriptions of *présence* provides here also something resembling an act of *présence*. Indeed, like the fairy example, which made the reader provide the name allowing the character to become textually present, the reader's action of reading the collected essays through allegoresis reveals the centrality of the authorial presence and voice, thus countering, sotto voce as it were, deconstructionist claims concerning the putative 'death of the author'.

★   ★   ★   ★   ★

In his 'Leçon inaugurale au Collège de France', Bonnefoy remarks that 'il n'y a pas que des livres, il y a des destinées littéraires, où chaque ouvrage marque une étape' [there are not only books; there are literary destinies, where each work marks a way-station] (*E*, 193). His comment compels interest, for the notion of way-stations on a path is an image that is particularly germane to the essay and its capacity to engage the reader through what appears as random meandering. As Riendeau writes, 'essay-writing can be apprehended through the metaphorical concept of *drifting*'.[3] We remember that Bonnefoy also explicitly formulates the ontological value of wandering when he gives it as the only way to return to the 'true place' (*I*, 130). And indeed, the collecting of the essays appears on the surface to replicate the notion of wandering, for though each volume of the ur-structure of *L'Improbable* corresponds roughly to a ten-year time span (*L'Improbable* contains essays from the 1950s, *Un rêve fait à Mantoue*, those dating from the 1960s, while *Le Nuage rouge* and *Vérité de parole* respectively collect essays from the 1970s and the 1980s), the organization of each does not give the impression of adhering to a rigid structure, instead shifting apparently randomly between essays describing voyages, places, or the works of specific artists or writers, to essays dealing with abstract notions such as perspective in painting.

However, although Bonnefoy materializes the value of wandering through the structure of the collected essays, the most noteworthy dimension of his choice is that 'wandering' is itself no more than a trope. In rhetorical terms, it is an image that has a functional potential: that of subtly obtaining reader collusion through the innocuousness of its positions. For the real function of his collected essays is by no means arbitrary; it is a conscious framework constructed for a purpose. The organizing principle of *L'Improbable* lies in that double faculty I evoked in the Introduction, that capacity of the essay to employ *présence* as a *telos* and as a tool: *présence* is both a means to evaluate the work of other artists ('Valéry a méconnu le mystère de la présence'), but at the same time, as we saw in the leaf, salamander, and fairy examples, showing it becomes the *telos* of those passages. And in terms of this tool-*telos* duality, the notion of wandering is another tool masking the purposefulness that is so important to Bonnefoy. Like Descartes, who tells us that his objective 'is not to teach the method which each ought to follow [...] but solely to describe the way in which I have endeavoured to conduct my own', Bonnefoy repudiates the idea of a didactic purpose.[4] For both writers, the way to circumvent a patently didactic position that might be rejected by the reader is to present their own experience as no more than a possible model. Hence the seemingly random organization of the essays ostensibly points to the path that Bonnefoy himself took: the fact that they speak about very different subjects and seem to be arbitrarily juxtaposed suggests that their ordering replicates their occurrence as chance 'encounters' in his life, a structure that is philosophically undergirded by Bonnefoy's comment in *La Vérité de parole* that 'le hasard est consubstantiel à l'immédiat, ne l'oublions pas' [happenstance, let us not forget, is consubstantial with immediacy] (*VP*, 49). All of this is profoundly anchored in the essay's ostensibly anti-didactic function, and returns us to the question of the personal subjectivity that is so germane to it.

Bearing in mind Obaldia's caveat about the difference between the flesh-and-blood essayist and the essayist made of words, we could say that the essay, much more than poetry, gives the impression of allowing the author to be him or herself completely.[5] Indeed, inasmuch as the essay can integrate the sensed as well as the intellectual forms of personal experience, the 'total approach' that it provides works to guarantee the truth of the experience, thus allowing for its greater acceptance and a heightened didactic potential that would appear paradoxical had we not seen this as one of the underlying possibilities offered by the tentative qualities of the genre itself. As Bonnefoy frequently reminds us, one of the signal characteristics of 'flesh-and-blood' individuals is that they are subject to time, to the *hic et nunc* of embodied existence. His comments regarding his different volumes of poetry are particularly apposite for the essay collections as well:

> Quand j'ai commencé à écrire, j'ai perçu que j'avais plusieurs ouvrages à produire, à produire, disons, *d'un même souffle*, la fragmentation en plusieurs volumes venant du fait que c'est la vie même qui doit y jouer son rôle, de par ses différents âges. (*YB*, 330)

> [When I began to write, I realized that I needed to produce several works, *all in the same breath*, let's say. The fragmentation of the work into several volumes comes from the fact that life itself has a role to play through the different periods we experience.]

The semi-autobiographical quality of the collected essays incorporates this notion, as the progression through the different collections reinforces the notion of the integrity of the writing subject via the essays' movement through time. Nowhere is this more apparent than in Bonnefoy's 1980 conjoining of *L'Improbable* and *Un rêve fait à Mantoue*, which shows more clearly than the later collections a shift in Bonnefoy's position concerning language.[6] It is in this volume that the essay carves out its difference from poetry and, by refraction, reveals its value as genre. We saw earlier that Derrida's notion of the 'supplement' produced by the parergon responds to a perceived lack, to something missing in the grounding work. Given Bonnefoy's discourse on the primacy of poetry in providing access to *présence*, the essay fulfils the role of parergon in his work, for by contrast with the atemporal, universal qualities of poetry, one of the strengths of the essay lies precisely in its ability to inscribe the essayist and his experiences into the flow of time. This closer attachment to historicity is, in turn, precisely what is highlighted and reinforced through Bonnefoy's act of collecting his essays. It follows from this that the topics we see in Bonnefoy's essays are presented as authentic time-bound encounters with various cultural constructions. This, indeed, is exactly how they are received by the reader, who is rhetorically guided not only to believe in the veracity of the information furnished, but also to perceive the essay as a sort of work in progress being directly observed. Statements conjuring a rhetorical wandering ('je me suis égaré, si tant est que la vérité que j'appelle contredise de tels égarements' [I have lost my way; but the truth that I'm invoking is at variance with [the possibility of] such straying], *I*, 22) use the generic possibilities of the essay — wandering, losing one's way, finding it again — to reinforce this impression of a mind in the process of constructing its ideas and thereby subtly authenticate the truth of the *présence* that is the object of the textual quest.

These rhetorical tactics notwithstanding, several concrete factors confirm the intuition that the collections are deliberately constructed. Née points out that Bonnefoy's literary corpus contained a great number of essays that were never collected nor even, for some of them, published.[7] Consequently, the fact that the essays included in the various collections were selected from a much larger body of possible alternatives underlines the idea that their choice and position was the object of a conscious consideration. This deliberation is further focused by Bonnefoy's calculated use of paratexts: at the end of each collection (with the exception of the 1959 *L'Improbable*), he faithfully gives bibliographical information about the provenance of each essay, recording whether it was initially a talk or an article, and providing precise references for each. Here again, Genette's discussion of paratexts proves particularly illuminating, for he considers the paratextual apparatus of a text as a zone of:

> *Transaction*: a privileged place of a pragmatics and a strategy, of an influence on the readership, an influence that — whether well or poorly understood and achieved — is at the service of a better reception for the text and a more pertinent reading.[8]

Bonnefoy's numerous paratextual strategies certainly seem to confirm Genette's point.

My focus here turns more specifically to the 1983 Gallimard 'livre de poche' edition of *L'Improbable* because it takes to their logical endpoint the functions of the paratextual elements initiated in the 1980 Mercure de France edition. Indeed, the 'poche' [pocket] format itself has paratextual meaning, as Genette points out, when he equates the format with the canonization of the work, and writes that in and of itself, the 'pocket format is [...] a formidable paratextual message'.[9] Considering the vituperative French debate that took place in the fifties about whether the pocket format represented the 'debasement' or the 'democratization' of culture, Bonnefoy's choice to make his work accessible in this way has significance. Concerning the text itself, two phenomena characterize the 'definitive', 1980 *L'Improbable* and reveal its careful composition. At the micro-level, first, comparing the 1980 edition with the original 1959 and 1967 editions shows the great number of changes made to the text. There are literally changes — sometimes a dozen or more — to the wording on every page. Space precludes analysing all of them, but I mentioned earlier one of the most significant: the change from *sensible* to *présence*. The quantity of the changes suggest that Bonnefoy's essayistic project was substantially rethought in the light of his evolving philosophical position. Second, as I have indicated, the original *Improbable* and *Mantoue* collections were fused into a single volume for the 1980 edition, the two bridged by four additional essays, which are critiques of art history books on Fra Angelico, Michelangelo, Caravaggio, and Degas. Among the parallels that can be drawn between these last four essays, not least is that in each of them Bonnefoy positions himself as the reader of another text. This stance recalls his comment to Jackson about the quest for *présence* being a collaborative effort shared by all (*E*, 58), and places him in a position identical to that of the 'ordinary' reader of his essays, bolstering thus the enthymematic, shared quality of the essay. Finally, more structural changes concern the essays themselves. Indeed, though the essays from the original *Improbable* remain identical, the 1980 edition adds two essays to the *Un rêve fait à Mantoue* section, 'Note sur Hercule Seghers' and 'Des fruits montant de l'abîme' ['Fruits emerging from the abyss', an essay on the artist Raoul Ubac]. These essays are similar in their positive view of the possibility of *présence* in the visual arts, a possibility Bonnefoy equates with language, giving, for example, the materiality of the slate Ubac sculpts as a metaphor of the difficulty of *la parole* (*I*, 305). All these changes reinforce my argument that Bonnefoy's collected essays are the outward manifestation of a structure that is itself semantic, obeying a didactic impulse to show, almost materially, the path he himself took to reach his understanding of the dialectic opposing *présence* and its representation in language.

This path is substantively consolidated by the paratextual elements Bonnefoy brings into play, of which two stand out particularly starkly (albeit from different perspectives): the dedication of *L'Improbable*, and the bibliographical material mentioned above. While the latter is unobtrusive, requiring a certain amount of reader commitment to acquire it, the dedication, thanks to what Genette calls 'the publisher's peritext' (its printing, discussed below, on the back cover of this 'pocket' edition) can hardly fail to escape the reader's attention. Once again, Genette's observations allow us to perceive how the peritextual elements of the essays allow Bonnefoy to shape the reader's reception. Genette makes a point of mentioning that one of the functions of a table of contents is to highlight 'the fact of the *book* as such'. As his translator reminds us in a note, contemporary French practice, unlike German or English custom, puts the table at the end of the book. To this Genette adds that whether a table is a reminder of the contents or their announcement is not the same thing.[10] This is why it is so interesting to see the shift from the 1959 *Improbable* to the later 'pocket' versions, which add a table of contents to the front matter. Additionally, the 1967 *Un rêve fait à Mantoue* had already broken new ground by adding bibliographical notes at the end of the book, along with the table of contents. For the 1980 *Improbable,* Bonnefoy 'mends' the 'deficiency' in the original 1959 volume by furnishing readers with bibliographic notes for each text. Careful perusal of these notes over all the volumes shows that only two texts were specifically written for the *Improbable* collections: 'Dévotion', the poem from the first volume, and 'Quelques notes sur Mondrian', the essay whose object furnishes the title of *Le Nuage rouge.* This choice reinforces the collective community-building and anti-solipsistic quality of his essayistic project in the sense that the essays Bonnefoy chose to collect had already received the imprimatur, as it were, of the community. Moreover, it is noteworthy that Bonnefoy's careful bibliographical record exemplifies the conventions of academic discourse, subtly reinforcing the legitimacy and 'truth-value', not only of the content, but also of its arranging. Finally, and most significantly, Bonnefoy uses the bibliographic notes to furnish capital information regarding the constructed nature of the project. The notes to *La Vérité de parole,* the last volume of *L'Improbable,* provides a truly fascinating instance of what appears to be an *ex post facto* creation of structure. As I suggested earlier, it is in this volume that the reader is finally informed of the overarching construction of the essay collections through Bonnefoy's statement that '*La Vérité de parole* is the third volume of *L'Improbable,* a collection of essays on poetics whose two first parts are *L'Improbable* (followed by *Un rêve fait à Mantoue*) and *Le Nuage rouge* (*VP,* 331). It is possible, of course, that Bonnefoy always saw the essays on poetics as a single unit. For readers, however, this late information, received literally in the closing moments of the reading, completely reorients their reading, almost *requiring* a re-evaluation of the whole, as indeed Genette suggests when he gives the example of Zola's *L'Assommoir* to show that reading it 'as a self-contained work is very different from reading it as an episode of *Les Rougon-Macquart.*[11] This rereading constructs the essays as a much larger project encompassing, perforce, decades of work. There is, nonetheless, a deep paradox in the way in which the information is delivered, the impulse to provide it contrasting with the obscuring nature of its placement. This very contrast, its 'there/not-there' quality replicates the overall function of the collected essays, hinting already at the dimly seen, yet discernible autobiographical dimension that hovers beneath their surface.

⋆   ⋆   ⋆   ⋆   ⋆

What, in the end, do Bonnefoy's collected essays do for us? The simple answer is that they show us a series of personal experiences, which, at a first level, might appear as a self-absorbed attempt by Bonnefoy himself to understand these encounters. But all that has been said on the urgency of transmitting the notion of *présence* indicates that Bonnefoy capitalizes on the possibilities of the essay — the way it works to create a common ground, its openness to relation with the other — by constructing a demonstration of how he himself arrived at his reflection on *présence*. Each essay marks a milestone on the path of his thought process. The essay genre provides precisely that capacity to extract himself from the potential solipsism of poetry and engage with the world. With respect to poetry, he says that:

> Au cœur du poème est cette relation même du JE au TU en tant que rapport difficile, parce que ce qui se cherche dans le poème, ce qui en constitue le drame, c'est la façon dont le JE va briser sa clôture, va s'arracher aux mythes du moi.

> [At the heart of poem lies the difficulty of that relation between the 'I' and the 'you' because the quest of the poem — which is also its tragedy — is how to make the 'I' break out of its closure, wrench itself from the myths of the self.] (*YB*, 331)

The images Bonnefoy uses to describe the 'I' freed from its narcissistic self-absorption coincide precisely with the attention to exterior objects, to that 'corpus culturel', from which the essay springs. It is that corpus that provides the markers of his path.

If the notion of 'itinerary' shows the directions he has taken, Bonnefoy himself is pertinently aware of the symbolical path that his own experiences must chart in order to become useful for others; without this step, his encounters remain ineluctably linked to personal existence and cannot but have limited value. As he says, 'Pour que se reforment les symbols, j'ai à méditer les événements de mon existence où ce qu'ils enseignent s'est révélé de soi-même, à mi-chemin entre ma particularité et les constantes de toute vie' [for symbols to create themselves anew, I must meditate on the events of my existence whose teaching spontaneously revealed itself, halfway between my own particularity and the constants of any life] (*E*, 22). These elements that he himself learnt must, through the diverse rhetorical techniques that he musters, including allegory, the fragment, and the essay, find their place in language so that they can serve as tools for others, transforming the itinerary of his own intellectual progression into something resembling a usable map to guide readers in their own encounters with *présence*. The fragmentary identity of the essay, its 'inner fragmentariness and its quality as a fragment' allows him to foreground the ontologically and even morally significant notion of fragmentation to reach the more meaningful issue of the underlying unity of *présence*.[12] He repeatedly stresses the importance of the unity that can be glimpsed through fragmentation, writing, for instance, in a passage where he evokes the kinship between prose and poetry, 'ce que j'écris ce sont les ensembles dont chacun de ces textes n'est qu'un fragment: car ces derniers n'existent pour moi, dès leur début, que dans leur relation avec les autres' [what I write are structures where each of the texts is just a fragment; from their inception, these fragments only exist for me in their relation with the others] (*E*, 19). Thus each collection of essays is part of a progression that represents an intellectual trajectory. This point is capital, for it contributes to the underlying didactic purpose that not only characterizes the tone of Bonnefoy's individual essays, but also configures the structure of the collections. Indeed, Georgia Johnston confirms this intuition, suggesting that 'the writing of essays as a group expands an author's ability to highlight subtleties of theme and style, allowing the author to guide a reader, whether didactically or unobtrusively, more easily toward that author's philosophy or theory'.[13] This guiding toward a larger idea is precisely the effect of Bonnefoy's collected essays.

Primed by the recursive reading needed for the individual essays or for the poetry, we can see that certain elements of the collected essays do indeed demonstrate patterns of this nature, reproducing at times Gouvard's 'principle of repetition', or echo, that we saw functioning within individual essays.[14] Thus, as I suggested, a stronger parallel exists between the 1959 *L'Improbable* and *Un rêve fait à Mantoue* collections because both end with an imaginative text, more obviously then legitimating their fusion into the single volume of the 1980 *L'Improbable*. Those earlier collections thereby provide a clearer intimation that the essay is intended to bring the reader back to poetry or poetic forms. When we remember, however, Bonnefoy's comments regarding the broad, almost ineffable nature of *poésie*, which he describes not as text, but as the relation between the 'I' of the author and the 'you' of the reader, we see that even the return to poetry is not the final objective of his writing. On the contrary, as his later writing shows, poetry is an important part of the process that provides the means for an authentic being-in-the-world. Engaging with that process through language requires the guidance provided by the collected essays that replicate at the level of volumes a fragmentation that is countered and unified through intellectual effort.

At the level of single volumes, the 1959 edition of *L'Improbable*, as I indicated earlier, puts into direct relation the dedication that opens the volume and 'Dévotion', the poem that closes it, through the structures common to both of them. Before addressing these parallels, however, it behoves us to examine what the dedication is doing in itself. Many elements of the 'Dédicace' have been mentioned in previous chapters because it provides such a strong framing device for understanding the interaction between Bonnefoy's philosophical positions and their transposition into language. In many ways, Lukács's discussion on parerga reflects rather precisely what Bonnefoy is doing with the 'Dédicace'. Lukács writes

> The Parerga written before the system create their preconditions from within themselves, create the whole world out of the longing for the system so that, it seems, they can give an example, a hint; immanently and inexpressibly, they contain the system.[15]

In the case of Bonnefoy's essays, Lukács's 'system' transposes, of course, to the very collection of these essays. Within that framework, the 'Dédicace' is particularly interesting because it projects a type of purpose that Genette pinpoints when he writes of paratexts, quoting Philippe Lejeune, that they are 'a fringe of the printed text which, in reality wholly determines the reading.[16] Reading Lukács and Genette together shows that the 'Dédicace' does more than that. The fact that that single dedication extends to the four-volume ensemble (none of the other works contain a dedication) shows its double function, both on reader and author, for while it determines the reading, it also confirms Lukács's idea that a perergon written before constituting the system conditions the choices made in creating the system.

★   ★   ★   ★   ★

Both in form and content, the dedication to *L'Improbable* presents a distillation of the major concerns that determine Bonnefoy's writing, making it difficult not to see this quintessentially paratextual piece of writing as a metatextual outline of his project. Its sheer lyricism is so immediately striking, its intellectual structures so disorienting, that it unmistakably signals its own significance — something that has not escaped the attention of readers and editors alike — and helps to explain the curious, doubly paratextual position it acquired in that 1983 'pocket' edition of *L'Improbable* mentioned above. There, it literally appears twice: conventionally, in the front matter, and repeated on the back cover, thus consolidating its inherently independent and extra-textual potential. Doubtless, the need to market the book impelled the decision. That choice nonetheless, confirms the overarching significance of the 'Dédicace'. Far more than just a minor adjunct, it can stand alone and provide a path of access to guide the reading of Bonnefoy's essays. Naturally, its importance is further emphasized by the fact that the 'improbable' to which it is addressed generates the title of the entire four-volume collection of essays: as Jean Starobinski indicates, in his preface to the *Poèmes*, the *hors-texte* is never insignificant in Bonnefoy's work (*P*, 8). Reading the dedication, however, it becomes rapidly clear that its form also conveys intent, both its form *qua* dedication and the explicitly poetic rhythms and structures of its syntax.

The 'Dédicace' reads as follows:

> Je dédie ce livre à l'improbable, c'est-à-dire à ce qui est.
> A un esprit de veille. Aux théologies négatives. A une poésie désirée, de pluies, d'attente et de vent.
> A un grand réalisme, qui aggrave au lieu de résoudre, qui désigne l'obscur, qui tienne les clartés pour nuées toujours déchirables. Qui ait souci d'une haute et impraticable clarté.

> [I dedicate this book to the improbable, in other words, to that which is.
> To a spirit of wakefulness. To the negative theologies. To a poetry desired, of rain, of waiting, and of wind.
> To a great realism that exacerbates rather than resolves, that designates the obscure, that sees all transparencies as nebulae to be torn. That is concerned with a high and impracticable transparence.]

The text startles because it clearly eschews the convention of dedicating the work to persons whose support allowed the authorial objectives to be attained. By directly addressing instead an abstract substantive, 'l'improbable', the text undercuts the 'normal' dedication's connection with an extra-diegetic reality. Addressing a dedication to the work itself via its title is thus a form of closure that sets itself off from standard practice. What sets Bonnefoy's work apart, however, is that this closure, the reader will realize much later, is incomplete. More immediately striking in the text is the equating of *ce qui est* with the notion of improbability, a parallel which caused Gasarian to characterize the dedication as 'bewildering' or even *'astounding'*.[17] What also immediately attracts attention is the poetic style of the text, and, as I indicated in Chapter Three, the reciprocal echoes it creates with the poem 'Dévotion'. Both use the insistent reiteration of an anaphoric invocation as a technique that not only invites the reader to enter the text, but also hearkens back to the structure of many prayers addressed to divine figures. In Chapter Two, I gave the opening statement of the 'Dédicace' as an example of Bonnefoyian paradox, suggesting that the apparent aporia is resolved by comparing the etymology of its antonym *le probable*, whose Latin root, *probare*, evokes that which can be proved, or, more accurately perhaps, that whose existence might be affirmed more easily than the existence of other things. Although the etymological dependency on the action of proving seems ineluctably to orient our interpretation, in reality, *le probable* is precisely that which persistently slips out of the definition: it is that which is likely rather than that which is a fact. This constellation of problems, both of theoretical definition and of practical use, applies equally to *l'improbable*, equating it with that which cannot be disproved, or that which persists and cannot be easily dismissed, even in the absence of proof. Within this structure, *le probable* thus logically becomes that which though likely, does not, in fact, exist, while *l'improbable*, on the contrary, is linked with that which, however precariously and against all odds, continues to exist. And this is exactly the category of reality that Bonnefoy equates with *ce qui est*. It is significant, however, that the ontological quality of this *ce qui est* is tempered by the rhetorical nature of the opening. For although it cannot be denied that uniting the notion of *l'improbable* with that of *ce qui est* has a disruptive, even startling function, Bonnefoy's decision to link the two seemingly discordant terms is a rhetorical strategy that is essentially poetic, much as Eluard's paradoxical uniting of orange and blue ('La terre est bleue comme une orange' [The earth is blue like an orange]) produces a poetic explosion suggestive of a truth that lies beyond appearances ('Jamais une erreur les mots ne mentent pas' [No error there ever words do not lie]).[18] Similarly, uniting improbability and existence suggests that they are symbiotically linked in Bonnefoy's mind as the very shape of reality.

The beginning of the dedication is thus already a first step in the 'training' of the good reader, for it shows that the *koan*-like meditation required to resolve the paradox is analogous to the receptivity and intellectual effort required not only to read poetry, but to produce it as well. Indeed, the specificity of the 'Dédicace' lies in the fact that it deliberately interweaves a distinctly poetic message with explicitly philosophical and theological concerns, thereby producing a microcosm of the essayistic work to come. Reading it, one becomes aware that Bonnefoy uses the thrust of poetic language to forge the outlines of an intellectual and moral *prise de position* characterized here by the uniting of such seemingly disparate ideas as 'théologies négatives', 'une poésie désirée', and 'réalisme' in a sequence that reproduces the sequence of the intellectual process. Unsurprisingly, then, resolving the initial paradox paves the way for the second section of the dedication whose 'poeticity' is made manifest both in the vocabulary and the assonances I described in Chapter One. Taken for itself, the segment produces something resembling a '*mise en abyme*' in the sense that its intensely poetic forms ('de pluies, d'attente et de vent') echo and reinforce its message, that is, Bonnefoy's call to poetry. The 'poetic turn' of language demonstrates the function of the essay as messenger for poetry. It is thus completely congruent that the dedication does not end simply by generating the poetic section. On the contrary, it continues, segueing into the last section, which clearly flags a philosophical intent invoked through its addressee, the 'grand réalisme'. The tenor of the third section returns to a form of paradox located in a poetic description of the dichotomy between 'clartés' which, when torn, reveal a final transparency. The image is identical to that image of rending seen in other Bonnefoyian contexts, and invokes a true realism whose resolution echoes the circular instability the reader will encounter in *L'Improbable*: the poetry that leads to essay, that in turn leads back to poetry, in an endless quest for the 'true place'.

The importance of this 'placeness' is confirmed by the etymology of the word 'dedication' itself, whose original meaning, now mostly lost, concerned not text, but place, and referred to the consecration of a sacred area. Seen through the prism of Bonnefoy's writing, both the notion of consecration and that of place are of importance, for they involve the transforming of something ordinary into something sacred through the incantatory power of language. For although traditional religious practices typically involve an agent (holy water, chrism, burnt offerings, etc.), these actions culminate in the voicing of special dedicatory prayers, which, in a clear example of those Austinian illocutionary performative acts, explicitly accomplish the dedication of the physical space. Similarly, any book dedication is an illocutionary act, for it does what it says it is doing: it dedicates by saying it dedicates. But, as Austin reminds us, certain preconditions are necessary:

> It is always necessary that the *circumstances* in which the words are uttered should be in some way, or ways, *appropriate*, and it is very commonly necessary that either the speaker himself or other persons should *also* perform certain *other* actions, whether 'physical' or 'mental'.[19]

In the case of dedications, their physical disposition at the beginning of a work creates the framework of the 'appropriate circumstances' to identify the act being performed. The robustness of this mental framework is confirmed by the fact that many dedications begin not with an explicit statement of dedication, but simply with a preposition (e.g. '*To* my parents', '*For* Professor X'). As with the 'allegorical' leaf, Bonnefoy's choice to explicitly foreground the illocutionary act is doubtless linked both to the immaterial nature of the object of the dedication and the ambiguity of its status as either notion or text. However, it can also be seen as an act consecrating the space to come, the 'place' of the text, and thereby inviting the reader to enter it almost as though entering a sacred space where author and reader have come together to provide acts: the author by the act of dedicating, and the reader through the act of resolving the paradox of the opening line.

More broadly, the close rhetorical parallels between the dedication and 'Dévotion' put the two texts on the same plane, proposing the essays that they frame as the path toward the apotheosis of poetry. The characterization of 'Dévotion' as a poem is confirmed by the fact that it figures in the 1978 collection *Poèmes*, which consolidated all of Bonnefoy's then-extant poetry collections in a single volume. The poem's homage to Rimbaud's 1873 poem of the same title is palpable. Considering Bonnefoy's real engagement with Rimbaud, borne out by the number of studies in which he reflected on that 'poète maudit' (full-length works such as *Rimbaud par lui-même* (1961) or *Notre besoin de Rimbaud* (2009), or single essays such as 'Madame Rimbaud' from *La Vérité de parole*), it is impossible not to see echoes of Rimbaud's 'Dévotion' in Bonnefoy's poem. Both, indeed, engage in a 'secular litany' organized around the direct address *à* and a constellation of seemingly disconnected events that lead, at the end of Rimbaud's poem, to 'metaphysical voyages', a notion that we know to be impossible in Bonnefoy's own philosophy. Indeed, the end of Bonnefoy's 'Dévotion' reverses the anti-theological tenor of the Rimbaud poem to make a place, both humble and mundane, for the *présence* of the divine: 'à ces deux salles quelconques, pour le maintien des dieux parmi nous' [to those two ordinary rooms, so to preserve the gods among us]. This specifically theological anchoring echoes, of course, the 'negative theologies' seen in the dedication, but also provides a link to the dreamlike narrative of 'Sept feux' [Seven Flames] that closes *Un rêve fait à Mantoue*.

Partway between prose poem, reminiscence and dream, 'Sept feux' foregrounds explicitly its oneiric dimension: each segment of the seven it contains (like the flames of the title) juxtaposes spatial displacements in that strange irrational shifting we experience in dreams. As Bonnefoy informs us, a first version appeared in *L'Ephémère* in 1967; its incorporation into *Un rêve fait à Mantoue* was thus almost immediate. Regrettably, space precludes undertaking a full analysis of the text here; in any case, my focus is on its interactions with the other texts of the volume. At a purely thematic level, 'Sept feux' connects to the dedication and 'Dévotion' through its explicit evocation of the divine: in section II of the text, the narrator is in what is 'doubtless a disaffected church', listening to music coming from the sacristy. Indistinct people around him express great excitement, whispering '"Écoutez, me dit-on à voix chuchotante, écoutez! Voici enfin la prevue de l'existence de Dieu"' ['Listen! Listen!', someone whispers to me, here at last is the proof of the existence of God!] (*I*, 333). After describing the form of synesthesia created by the singing voices and colour as 'the voice of God' (in inverted commas in the text), Bonnefoy subverts the theological dimension, writing: 'Je revois l'électrophone, sur cette table, et le disque enfin arrêté, que quelqu'un a pris en main, examine. Mais le rêve change et soudain c'est ma sombre ville natale' [I see again the gramophone on the table, the disk that has stopped playing, that someone has taken in hand to examine. But the dream changes, and suddenly it is my dark native town] (*I*, 334). As in 'Dévotion' (and as, more generally, throughout his work), this sentence suggests that undercutting the divine, paradoxically does not erase it, but makes it more accessible, demonstrating that it can be sought and found in the ordinary elements of daily life.

From a structural perspective then, these three texts, precisely because of their radical difference from the essays they textually enclose, reinforce the latent theo-philosophical dimension also so present in the essays. In an essay discussing Bonnefoy's essays on art, Patrick Née indicates that 'on the path that he believes leads to the mythical "arrière-pays", Bonnefoy continuously strews those little white stones that will help him get back to his own existence'.[20] These white stones are there for the reader also, but the path they make join the different pieces of Bonnefoy's work. Hence, a number of tendrils connect 'Sept feux' back to the first volume of *L'Improbable*, legitimating the closure it provides to the combined 1980 edition. A case in point is the narrator's description, in section III, of his voyage between Rimini and Ravenna. The latter place, of course, echoes 'Les Tombeaux de Ravenne', while Rimini is evoked in section III of 'Dévotion' where Bonnefoy writes, 'Aux peintres de l'école de Rimini. J'ai voulu être historien par angoisse de votre gloire. Je voudrais effacer l'histoire par souci de votre absolu' [To the painters of the School of Rimini. I wanted to be a historian by anguish of your glory. I would like to erase history by concern for your perfection] (I, 136). Finally, the very last line of 'Sept feux' is striking: 'Au souvenir du Bernin, sculpteur de la *Vérité* du tombeau d'Alexandre VII — celle qui se redresse comme une flamme soufflée — , que soient dédiés ces pas au-dehors, dans la fumée des sept feux' [To the memory of Bernini, the sculptor of *Truth* on the tomb of Alexander VII — she who rears up like the flame blown out — , dedicated be these footfalls outside, in the smoke of the seven flames] (I, 343). The text forms a perfect structural echo, both to the 'Dédicace', through the repetition of the identical performative act of dedication, and to 'Dévotion', through the reiteration of the direct address.

Taken together then, these three short 'peripheral' texts powerfully consolidate the unity of *L'Improbable*, inscribing in it that circular reading Bonnefoy's poetry requires of the reader: the *vrai lieu* that closes *Douve* does not provide true closure, devolving instead into the essay's depiction of the event, and bringing us to understand that poetry leads to essay. *L'Improbable* and *Un rêve fait à Mantoue* show that the reverse is also true, for each culminates in a poetic text meant to send us back to the place of poetry. The trope of this 'text-faring' takes on further resonance, for it shows up in the metaphorical starting point of each of the volumes of *L'Improbable*. This is more clearly apparent in *L'Improbable* and *Un rêve fait à Mantoue*, for the essays beginning each volume depict an 'elsewhere', Ravenna for *L'Improbable*, and Byzantium for *Un rêve fait à Mantoue*, that instigates the intellectual and spiritual peregrination. The importance of displacement is also present in the first essays of *Le Nuage rouge* ('Baudelaire contre Rubens') and *La Vérité de parole* ('Marceline Desbordes-Valmore'), though this displacement is more latent, filtered through the scrim of other travellers. In *Le Nuage rouge*, it is Baudelaire's trip to Belgium which prompts his criticism of Rubens, while Marceline Desbodes-Valmore's ill-fated voyage to the Antilles sets the scene for the tonalities of her poetic voice.

Finally, the very brief closing essay of *La Vérité de parole* (the last volume of *L'Improbable*), proves particularly interesting in that its terminal position provides a form of closure that is riddled with covert connections to the very notion of 'essay'. On the surface, that essay reads much like a postliminary *captatio benevolentiae* seeking retroactively to inflect readers' perceptions of the critical essays comprising the four volumes of *L'Improbable* and defending the value of a 'properly constructed' critical essay. In it, Bonnefoy reiterates many of his central positions, notably regarding the priority of reality and lived experience over text, and the possibility for language to account for the duality of *présence* through the capacity that some 'greater' words have to coincide 'à nouveau avec les choses qu'ils nomment' [again with the things they name], thus allowing the sign to be 'd'un même soufflé le singulier et l'universel' [in the same breath, the singular and the universal] (*VP*, 322–23). Once again, he evokes here the potential deficiencies of a poetry given as ambivalent, its 'desire to address others' warring with 'its apathy in doing so', 'its concern for the presence of the world' at odds with 'its love of language' (*VP*, 324). It is not insignificant that these deficiencies are embedded in a discussion about the value of the critical essay, and its insistence on communication. Moreover, it is also noteworthy that this final discussion re-evaluates the primacy given to allegory in the descriptions of *présence* we saw earlier.

This begs the question: is this last essay of *L'Improbable* Bonnefoy's own 'essay on the essay'? For readers attuned to the parallel, Bonnefoy's title, 'Quelque chose comme une lettre', reads very much like a nod to Lukács, whose 'On the Nature and Form of the Essay' is in fact a letter to Leo Popper. In both cases, the choice clearly conforms to a rhetorical strategy, one that de Obaldia qualifies as 'dialogic', insofar as the letter-essay involves both an obvious interlocutor and, she says, 'a "trying out" of ideas revealing a "thought in progress"'.[21] Certainly, the 'essay-letter' contains a dialogic element; I would suggest however that the drama term 'double enunciation' might provide a more appropriate qualification. Indeed, here, as in theatre, where the actors seem to speak exclusively to each other but are actually speaking to the audience, readers partake in a one-sided exchange addressed ostensibly to the nominal addressee, but 'really' to them. This strategy is profoundly essayistic in that it reinforces the authenticity of the ideas involved while stressing the presence of both interlocutors, given as real persons. But while Bonnefoy's echoing seems to validate Lukács's rhetoric, he also seems to deny Lukács's conclusion that 'the essay is an art form, an autonomous and integral giving-of-form to an autonomous and complete life'.[22] For Bonnefoy, the essay is inherently auxiliary. But this is not to say that it has no value. On the contrary, poetry needs the essay's critical gaze which, because it remains 'outside of the economy of [poetry's] dream', can undo 'the immuring of poetry' (*VP*, 325). This, however, is only possible through a specific type of gaze, which Bonnefoy associates with the subject of his essay, his friend and fellow-essayist Jean Starobinski.

The choice to publish in essay form a letter to Starobinski factors also into the *mise en abyme* of the genre of essay being accomplished here, for Starobinski, a renowned specialist of the father of all essayists, Montaigne, is also distinguished by his own essayistic production: not only was he the 1982 recipient of the Grand Prix européen de l'essai, but he is also the author of theoretical work seeking to define the essay. In Bonnefoy's essay, Starobinski is presented as a good reader by refraction with (very likely) Paul de Man, who appears in an oblique reference to 'one of [our] closest friends' (Bonnefoy was among those who contributed to the *in memoriam* essays written upon de Man's death in 1983). Like de Man, the anonymous friend in Bonnefoy's essay denigrates the symbol, defining it as illusion, as 'the Romantic dream of an absolute', and defending instead the greater courage and truth of allegory, whose lucidity reveals the desert separating the being of the world and the sign (*VP*, 322). In 'Quelque chose comme une lettre', which appeared, of course, several decades after the 'allegorical' definitions of *présence* found in the first volumes of *L'Improbable*, Bonnefoy directly rejects allegory in favour of symbol, and argues that allegory is the mark of a critical gaze which:

> [ne rendra compte d'un fait qu'à l'aide d'un instrument de signification emprunté à un système de representations, de valeurs, [la critique-allégorique] est et reste celui d'une personne bien installée dans ses choix méthodologiques, bien décidée à en faire le vrai objet de sa réflexion. (*VP*, 323)

> [Only assesses a circumstance through an instrument of signification borrowed from a system of representations and values; [la critique-allégorique] is that of a person thoroughly set in his methodological choices and bent on making these the true object of his reflection.]

By contrast, 'la critique-symbole' said to be characteristic of Starobinski is one which would approach a work with 'le désir de subordonner ses points de vue propres à cette parole qui a son unité tout de même, son ardeur, son besoin de vérité' [the desire to subordinate its own points of view to this *parole* that indeed has its own unity, its own ardour and need for truth] (*VP*, 324). In short, through the filter of Starobinski, Bonnefoy seems to reclaim the theoretical definition of allegory as 'supplement', that is, as meaning not necessary to the narrative drive, to give here a fairly impassioned defence of a 'proper' criticism that respects and amplifies the elements that an author has consciously placed in a work, and contrasting it with a bad, 'aggressive' criticism that reads through the work and sees in it a design the author never intended.

Though one can certainly understand Bonnefoy's disinclination to be misinterpreted, his position is problematic from a critical standpoint, for it seems to disallow substantive divergence from a prescribed path. What to do, for instance, with the allegorical reading that so obviously orients the earlier texts if it later becomes analytically *non grata*? I propose at this juncture to become the bad reader Bonnefoy warns against and embrace the discordance between that explicitly foregrounded allegory of the earlier texts and its rejection here. My suggestion is that rather than a fortuitous oddity, that foreclosed allegory reverberates at numerous psychological and aesthetic levels of Bonnefoy's work, truly permitting an understanding of its multiple facets. Craig Owens, using vocabulary that has immediate resonance for readers who remember Bonnefoy's strongly reiterated 'imperfection is the summit' (*P*, 139), tells us that 'allegory is constantly attracted to the fragmentary, the imperfect, the incomplete'.[23] This thematic parallelism is consolidated by Serge Canadas's definition of Bonnefoy as 'an allegorician'.[24] More technically, my interest in the discarded though potent figure of allegory lies in its close parallels with two of Bonnefoy's recurring choices, namely, his predilection for the essay and his preference for metonymy over metaphor. Also at play is allegory's desire to redeem and revitalize textual pasts while imposing reading constraints and a certain didacticism on readers. Finally, also of capital importance is the way in which Bonnefoy's collected essays can be read allegorically as a veiled form of autobiography. Indeed, the double description of allegory as 'a means of constructing the world, and as a means to decipher it' evokes precisely the distinction between allegory and allegoresis that provides the interpretative structure for the subsequent sections of this chapter.[25]

★   ★   ★   ★   ★

The past decades have seen a strong revival of interest in allegory, driven in part by its contemporary identification as the post-modern or structural figure of speech, par excellence.[26] With respect to my own analysis of Bonnefoy's work, what is striking is the manner in which many of the theoretical discussions on allegory use terminology and assign motivations that are, in many cases, highly congruent with those associated with the essay. This is seen particularly clearly in the idea that 'the allegorical work is synthetic; it crosses aesthetic boundaries'.[27] The essay, as we saw, is also frequently praised or taxed for these very qualities. And along similar lines, but in what is perhaps an even more prominent coincidence of descriptive adjectives, Angus Fletcher's opening words to his *Allegory: The Theory of a Symbolic Mode*, are: 'Allegory is a *protean* device, omnipresent in Western literature from the earliest times to the modern era'.[28] The essay, it will be remembered, is also identified with that rather unusual term 'protean', thus suggesting the variability associated with both genres and consequently their parallelism.

The traditional definition of allegory describes it as an extended metaphor developed over an entire narrative structure. Joel Fineman, countering Roman Jakobson's *Fundamentals of Language*, suggests however that this association is too simplistic, and that allegory must be treated as a particular case. Jakobson, it will be remembered, associates metaphor with the paradigmatic y-axis on which words substitute for each other based on a perceived similarity, while he puts prose into parallel with metonymy along a syntagmatic x-axis driven by structure. These distinctions bear upon and define different literary forms: 'The principle of symmetry underlies poetry [...] Prose, on the contrary, is forwarded essentially by contiguity. Thus for poetry metaphor, and for prose metonymy is the line of least resistance'.[29] These aspects of structural linguistics are vital elements of Bonnefoy's own theorization of language and poetry, consequently impinging both upon their relationship to allegory, and, by transfer, to the essay. Perhaps the most important aspect of metaphor is the apparent un-relatedness that habitually characterizes its two parts: 'the linking of a particular tenor and vehicle is normally unfamiliar: we must make an imaginative leap to recognize the resemblance to which a fresh metaphor alludes'.[30] In order for metaphor to 'work' properly, thus, the necessary distance between the two terms must be decoded by the observer, and this deciphering relies on the suppressed image connecting them. For instance, Apollinaire's 'Bergère ô tour Eiffel le troupeau des ponts bêle ce matin' ['Shepherdess, o Eiffel Tower, the flock of bridges is bleating this morning'] requires the latent image of Paris.[31] As a result, through an initiating creative impulse, the content of the metaphor is subordinated to an image that creates a connection by analogy: A *seems* like B through image C.

When one considers the theoretical primacy Bonnefoy gives to *parole*, seen as the authentic, individuated expression of each speaker, the negative value he assigns to metaphor, which he associates with closure and stasis, seems paradoxical. In this also, the essay and its values provide a helpful benchmark for his positions. Indeed, his opposition to metaphor is structured around notions of communion and community that are intrinsic to the essay. In his very adverse reaction to Nietzsche's reification of metaphor-creation, Bonnefoy, as we saw, constructs his repudiation along lines highly germane to the essay, namely its rejection of the individualism and solipsism that deny shared access to some form of communion. Generally speaking, it is on this point that he is most critical of Nietzsche, for, as he argues, an attachment to metaphor, that is, to the signifier alone, engenders the isolation of the individual, and through it, the negation of community. He writes: 'la danse de qui, à la suite de Nietzsche, se donne au signifiant dans sa virtualité, est un acte de solitude, dans lequel le rapport à autrui ne peut plus s'établir' [the dance of those who, in the tracks of Nietzsche, give themselves over to the signifier in its virtuality, is an act of solitude within which the relation to the other can no longer be established] (*YB*, 25). Metonymy, by contrast, relies on shared knowledge, as Hugh Bredin stresses when he writes: 'metaphor *creates* a knowledge of the relation between its objects; metonymy *presupposes* that knowledge.[32]

Metaphor appears thus as reductionist, and Bonnefoy uses the linguistics codes co-opted from Saussure to suggest that it discounts the 'signified' to focus on the 'signifier' alone, making it inadequate to transmit *présence*, which is carried in both the signifier and signified. Closer analysis of his position shows, however, that his position is also fundamentally dependent on Jakobson's metaphor-metonymy distinction. In a lengthy response to a question on the function of prose, Bonnefoy analyses in *Entretiens sur la poésie* why metonymy takes philosophical precedence over metaphor in his work. His answer involves a re-categorization of Jakobson's work that is very similar to his re-evaluation of Saussurian linguistics, for he assigns positive and negative values to eminently neutral linguistic analyses, based on their capacity to engage with *présence*. In the Jakobsonian paradigm, metonymy is indeed substantively different from metaphor in that it operates by contiguity, and thus presupposes a perceptible connection between the elements put into relation. Depending on the literary theory being invoked, classic examples (among many) include synecdoches, such as 'boot' for 'soldier', that take the part for the whole, or metalepses such as 'lead foot' that combine metonymies to mean 'fast driver'. Taking this a bit further, Tristan Todorov indicates that metonymy uses 'a word to designate an object or a property which occurs in an existential relationship with the habitual reference of this same word'.[33] This 'existential relationship' strikes at the heart of Bonnefoy's preoccupations; its relation to *présence* is suggested even more explicitly in Jakobson's reading of Saussure, where metonymy is described as being '*in presentia*: it is based on two or several terms jointly present in an actual series', whereas metaphor 'connects terms *in absentia* as members of a virtual mnemonic series'.[34]

This crucial point, linking metonymy to *présence* through its more immediate connection between language and object, is substantiated by Née's suggestion that

Bonnefoy's predilection for metonymy stems from the fact that it is perhaps the only rhetorical figure allowing him effectively to integrate *présence* into language.[35] Née writes that in Bonnefoy's work, metonymy 'has an extension that is truly revolutionary', for rather than being 'a [rhetorical] figure like all the others, it *embodies* "presence", primarily by the contiguity it establishes (at the level of an ontology of utterance [*la parole*]) with that which, because it is both underneath and beyond language, escapes language itself'. In a complementary point regarding a Bonnefoyian connection between metonymy and *présence*, Née refers to poetic words that would be 'like proper names, or even given names, within which 'coincide the three poles of the sign (signifier/signified *and* extra-linguistic referent)'.[36] In essence, this is precisely what we saw happening with the absent proper name of Mélusine, which allowed Bonnefoy to take to a higher level the 'ordinary' relation of contiguity that names create by connecting a word directly to an 'extra-linguistic referent' that has a real, physical existence outside of language. The 'truly revolutionary' element evoked by Née refers to Bonnefoy's extension of linguistic analysis into the realm of ontology, reading Jakobson's metaphoric/paradigmatic y-axis and his metonymic/syntagmatic x-axis through their capacity to harbour *présence*. What does the 'poetic' y-axis give us? A vertical set of substitutable terms that exist *in absentia*, that is, only in the mind of the metaphor creator. Bonnefoy associates this verticality with stasis, with a 'decision of the past' (*E*, 51). By contrast, the 'prosaic' x-axis is driven by contiguity, meaning that it creates syntagms by conjoining dissimilar elements structured *in presentia* within a schema that James McAllister, using the rhetorical analyses of the Groupe μ, describes 'as construed spatially or, by extension, temporally'.[37] Indeed, along the syntagmatic axis, meaning is constructed by the place each word occupies ('the cat ate the fish' is not the same as 'the fish ate the cat'), but also by its development in the time needed to follow the syntagmatic path, which unfolds sequentially. The syntagmatic axis thus spontaneously integrates precisely those deictic *hic et nunc* dimensions that are key to Bonnefoy's philosophical positions, and play so strikingly into characterizations of the essay. This theoretical grounding plays out at all levels of Bonnefoy's work, with the apotheosis of the metonymic gesture reached through his structuring of his essays into collections. Indeed, by placing what were initially single texts into unified collections, he positions each original 'fragment' in a syntagmatic structure that has both temporal and spatial extensions. The temporality of the collections, as we saw, is clearly present in the rough categorization of each with respect to the decade of its publication. Again, it bears mentioning that without the note at the end of *La Vérité de parole*, the full arc of the temporal structuring would not be visible to readers. The spatial structuring is also made evident through the different points evoked earlier: the purposeful mix of prose and poetry; the thematic structuring, seen, for example, in the notion of travel, or displacement, that begins each collection; and the logical connections made through the sequence of essays that take readers on a journey toward *présence*, where the different way-stations are the patient essayistic construction of the 'places' where Bonnefoy has encountered or failed to encounter (see 'Paul Valéry') *présence*.

This metonymic structuring notwithstanding, Bonnefoy still cannot completely eschew metaphor, as we saw for instance in his use of the figure of Phaedra, or even the 'allegorical' leaf, which also requires both symbolic and metaphorical readings. The ambivalence he demonstrates is native to the theoretical distinctions drawn between metaphor and metonymy, which is indeed Bredin's central point when he reads through the elegance of Jakobson's metaphor-metonymy dichotomy and affirms that it is inadequate because all language requires the 'equal cooperation' between the two figures.[38] This, in fact, brings us back to allegory and its theoretical significance to Bonnefoy's work because, as Fineman suggests, allegory differs from the trenchant distinction between metaphor and metonymy, for it can:

> Cut across and subtend all such stylistic categorizations, being equally possible in either verse or prose, and quite capable of transforming the most objective naturalism into the most subjective expressionism, or the most determined realism into the most surrealistically ornamental baroque.[39]

Owens is even more direct, saying that allegory, 'with blatant disregard for aesthetic categories', 'implicates *both* metaphor and metonymy'.[40] These critics thus imply that something specific about allegory allows it a span of freedom that other rhetorical figures can acquire only with great difficulty. Their claim puts allegory once again into close relation with the essay, whose sense of freedom is also widely asserted. More importantly perhaps, the fusion of metaphor and metonymy in the figure of allegory provides a robust theoretical grounding for Bonnefoy's own perspectives on language and its capacities. As the preceding chapter showed, Bonnefoy makes a clear distinction between words that are 'naturally poetic', and others that are less so: '*brique*,' he writes, 'déjà, parle à l'esprit de poésie de façon moins évidente que *pierre*, parce que le rappel du procédé de fabrication l'emporte, dans la donnée de ce mot' [already speaks less clearly to poetic spirit than *stone*, because the reminder of the manufacturing process takes over in the basic idea of the word] (I, 255). But this difference is not immutable, and he gives the example of words that can be 'redeemed' by the poetic gesture, allowing them to express a *présence* that had been previously foreclosed to them (I, 256). Once again, this redemption of the words is made possible by Bonnefoy's re-evaluation of the Saussurian arbitrariness of language, redefining it to include a positive form of differentiation between certain words based on their relationship to *présence*. Allegory can be seen similarly to transform the arbitrary quality of language.

Indeed, Fineman, following Benveniste, argues that contrary to the completely arbitrary coupling of 'signifier' and 'signified' postulated by Saussure, the very passage of language through history transforms the relations between these two parts of the sign.[41] Fineman writes: 'Once the signifier's relation to the signified, i.e. the sign as a whole, is understood [...] to be relatively motivated, rather than utterly arbitrary as in Saussure, it is possible to make the sign itself into an index pointing to the structure it embodies and supports'.[42] In substance, he argues that the synchronic structure of language has always been subjugated to its diachronic existence and this, perforce, has contributed to shaping it. Thus words (signs) have naturally acquired a non-arbitrary value within a particular system of linguistic representation — poetry, for example — and they indicate this value by their very presence in the structure. Fineman adds, speaking specifically of rhyme (although his analysis is clearly true in a broader sense), that words can function as a form of deictic indicating the properties of the texts within which they occur. Bonnefoy's careful distinction between 'stone' and 'brick' can be read in similar fashion. Much though he would have us read 'stone' as a sign pointing to the extra-linguistic through the intentionality with which writer and reader address it, because our system differentiates between 'poetic' and 'non-poetic' language, the word 'stone' itself acts as a proto-deictic pointing to structure, to the 'poeticity' of the text. Objectively, 'stone' has obtained this capacity through the historical evolution of language and the codes the community has come to accept as 'naturally' devolving to it. Indeed, this code is so well-integrated into Bonnefoy's work that it is perfectly reproduced by the critical community, which frequently points to his compelling tendency to limit his vocabulary to 'essential words', bearers of a universal message, and reads that as confirming the gravitas and importance of his work. Allegory, Fineman argues, has a similar indexical function: 'all the levels of allegory, up through and including the thematic [...] display themselves and each other with resoundingly poetic and emphatically structural effect'.[43] His unambiguous parallel between allegory and the motivated nature of the linguistic sign derives from allegory's particular position at the intersection of metaphor and metonymy. What allegory can do, perhaps better than other rhetorical tropes, is project the Jakobsonian metaphoric axis onto the metonymic axis because, as de Man argues, it 'corresponds to an authentically temporal destiny'.[44] And if it is true, as Fineman, Owens, and others argue, that allegory is misrepresented when it is equated with metaphor alone, then a singular matter of concern for us is the way in which allegory combines metaphor and metonymy to produce something that resonates with Bonnefoy's conversion of his philosophy of *présence* into language.

*   *   *   *   *

'Why allegory?' is the inevitable question asked in the wake of Bonnefoy's description of *présence* through the fragmentary, dying leaf. The answer resides in two potent characteristics of allegory: first, its tendency to recuperate the past and reinvest it with value; second, its inherent desire to mould both the reader and his or her reading. From the perspective of these latent goals, allegory can be seen not as a rhetorical ornament but rather as something essential to Bonnefoy's purpose, as indeed is the essay. The notion of fragmentation so frequently foregrounded by Bonnefoy carries over into another connection between allegory and essay, for both refer to other texts and sources, and these oblique roots often appear in fragmentary form in both. Indeed, just as Bonnefoy's choice of the word *présence* sketches out a continuum, anchoring his lexical choice to a series of historical moments that are both theological and philosophical, so is the word 'allegory' frequently theorized as looking back towards a textual origin. As Owens writes, 'in allegorical structure, then, one text is *read through* another, however fragmentary, intermittent, or chaotic their relationship may be'.[45] More globally, Bloomfield enlarges the scope of the backward glance of allegory by stating that 'one of the basic functions of allegory is to make literary documents relevant'. That said, Bloomfield himself recognizes that although it is largely determined by them, allegory is perhaps not limited solely to textual origins but includes the past in general: 'the allegorical or historical interpretative mind is continually telling us that the past is relevant and the quotations of the past apply today'.[46] This idea of giving renewed value to the past finds substantive echo in Bonnefoy's work: it is certainly worth noting that one of Bonnefoy's most academic productions was the editing of a two-volume *Dictionnaire des mythologies*. And from the recuperative perspective of allegory, it is striking that the stated objective of that work is to give renewed meaning and accessibility to a number of traditional narratives that were originally oral. The adamantly thematic orientation of the work diverges from the alphabetical organization normally associated with dictionaries and has an explicit purpose hinting at the moral potential of allegory: that of vesting the past with revived meaning while connecting it to present concerns.

Indeed, a number of critics suggest that one of the capital functions of allegory is to retrieve, almost to salvage, the past, particularly inasmuch as it is in constant danger of disappearing, or of losing its pertinence.[47] Naturally, for the reader of Bonnefoy, it is difficult to avoid connecting these ideas with the frequent references to the idea of salvation or redemption that constellate his work. The ready transposition of these particular terms suggests that it is possible — as Walter Benjamin suggests, and Owens reiterates — to see allegory not as a rhetorical flourish but more properly as a state of mind that pertains to a particular perception of the world. Owens writes:

> Allegorical imagery is appropriated imagery; the allegorist does not invent images but confiscates them. He lays claim to the culturally significant, poses as its interpreter. And in his hands the image becomes something other (*allos* = other + *agoreuei* = to speak). He does not restore an original meaning that may have been lost or obscured; allegory is not hermeneutics. Rather, he adds another meaning to the image. If he adds, however, he does so only to replace: the allegorical meaning supplants an antecedent one; it is a supplement. This is why allegory is condemned, but it is also the source of its theoretical significance.[48]

To properly understand the notion of (re)appropriating extant pieces, as well as that of supplement and how they work with *présence* in Bonnefoy's mindscape, we must return to his allegorical leaf passage and the specificity of his choice: why, indeed, a leaf? Why not a bird, a fence, or a stone? If it is true, as Owens suggests, that the allegorist does not invent images, then there must be identifiable textual sources for the image of the leaf, as indeed there were for the salamander image of *présence*. That is precisely what is shown by a reading that delves almost archaeologically into Bonnefoy's work.

★   ★   ★   ★   ★

The leaf image is, of course, striking, but Bonnefoy's 'I will say allegorically: it is the fragment of the dark tree' immediately provokes a number of questions. Why, for instance, does he use the definite article 'the' when referring to an unknown tree which is only later identified as 'ivy'? And in point of fact, why specifically ivy? This last question provides the simplest entry point, for ivy, like many plants, has symbolic import: since pagan times, its physical qualities — evergreen and clinging — has caused it to be associated with eternity and attachment. Two texts, a very early, uncollected essay and a poem from *Douve* indicate Bonnefoy's awareness of this symbolic value. His choice of ivy in 'Les Tombeaux de Ravenne', an essay whose main point is to disassociate the ideas of eternity and immortality from that of the concept is thus significant. Indeed, the fact that the ivy leaf of 'Les Tombeaux de Ravenne' should bear the burden of showing immediacy becomes completely congruent with the larger project carried by the essay, for Bonnefoy subverts the timelessness associated with ivy to show the very opposite: the passage of time and through it, mortality. Similarly, the notion of attachment symbolically carried by ivy is undone in the text by the explicit description of the leaf as being broken off from the larger whole.

The anti-conceptuality the ivy leaf assumes in 'Les Tombeaux de Ravenne', its explicit allegorization, and the undoing of the notion of attachment all connect Bonnefoy's leaf image to the more global characteristics of allegory suggested by Owens and others. For the over-determination of certain points suggests that Bonnefoy's choice is predicated, whether consciously or not, on principles that are, in the end, linked not only to the theoretical notions that subtend allegory — particularly as these latter encompass the notion of making the past relevant — but also, and more pertinently, to the ferocious opposition *présence* brings to bear on concept. Indeed, the deictic over-determination of the leaf ('*this* leaf') suggests its association with a previously identified object. This, in turn, allows us to seek the links between Bonnefoy's image and references it makes to an identifiable textual past, and subsequently to turn to the question of a 'supplemental' allegorical meaning contained in the Bonnefoyian text.

The two connections mentioned above appear particularly compelling. The first one uses Bonnefoy's very early essay, 'Sur le concept de Lierre' (1951), and the second is contained in a poem from *Douve*. These two very different texts combine with the leaf passage from 'Les Tombeaux de Ravenne' to show how the notion of *présence* serves as a multi-level link between poetry, prose, and essay. As we saw earlier, 'Les Tombeaux de Ravenne' provides an explicit and even violent rejection of the concept. Twice, Bonnefoy repeats the virtually identical question: 'de quelle chose sensible [...] de quelle pierre qui soit au monde le concept n'est-il détourné?' [Is there any sensate thing [...] any stone in the world from which the concept has not turned away?] (*I*, 20). The answer comes near the end of the essay: the concept has turned away from the real things of the world because the concept is an illusion:

> C'est lui ce premier voile des vieilles métaphysiques. Il s'agit d'être en regard de lui l'incroyant et l'athée. Car il est faible comme un dieu. Et qu'on ne dise point qu'en son absence, et dans ce débris de lierre que j'ai tenu, dans le passage et l'écume, toute vérité devient impossible. (*I*, 29)

> [It is the primary veil of the old metaphysics. One must, with regard to it, be an unbeliever and an atheist. For it is weak as a god. And let it not be said that

without it, in these scraps of ivy that I have held, in the passing and the foam,
all truth becomes impossible.]

But between the questions and the answer the paradigmatic leaf passage has
occurred. More importantly, it has set a leaf — this particular leaf — as the very
antithesis of concept, and has confirmed the idea that the absence of concept cannot
be equated with the absence of truth.

'Sur le concept de Lierre' is a brief, though dense and abstruse essay published
by Bonnefoy in 1951 in the short-lived journal *Troisième Convoi*. It was reprinted in
Jacques Ravaud's 1998 critical collection, *Yves Bonnefoy*, and provides some elements
of response to the question of why, grammatically, the anti-conceptual leaf in 'Les
Tombeaux de Ravenne' is so highly determined. The earlier essay appears to be
the starting point of a much larger project that was never developed: it is subtitled
'Prolegomenes', and this subtitle itself bears the number '1', suggesting the intention
of future sections that never materialized. The essay makes overt reference to the
philosophical opposition between Hegel and Kierkegaard (we know that Bonnefoy
was working on a thesis on Baudelaire and Kierkegaard at that time) but develops
it no further than to suggest that the opposition fails because both lines of thought
remain mired in the concept. 'Sur le concept de Lierre' is unusual, not only because
of the highly theoretical nature of the argument, but also because of its very
particular style, located somewhere between poetic discourse and argument. In his
Yves Bonnefoy à l'horizon du surréalisme, Arnaud Buchs provides an excellent analysis
of the essay, identifying it as the theoretical framework buttressing Bonnefoy's
rejection of surrealism. Buchs remarks judiciously that because of the nature of
Bonnefoy's argument, the 'concept de Lierre' evoked in the title finds its logical
conclusion in silence.[49] For our purpose here several points stand out to show how
the allegorical quality attributed to the leaf in 'Les Tombeaux de Ravenne' relies
on 'Sur le concept de Lierre' as a source. The first is that in contrast to the fierce
opposition between leaf and concept of 'Les Tombeaux de Ravenne', the very title
'Sur le concept de Lierre' seems to associate the two. The second point concerns the
grammar of the title, where the absence of article, combined with the capitalization
of 'Lierre' suggests that it is treated as a proper name. Does this equate 'ivy' with
the genus, making of it the generic representative of an entire category? Or does it
rather suggest some obscure onomastic properties attributable to the word, similar
to those Bonnefoy used in his proto-novel, *Agent secret*, whose protagonists bore
names such as Douve, Plaque, and Ruine?

The question remains unanswerable because the last and most fascinating point
is that despite the title, at no point in the text is there any mention of 'ivy' as a
concrete object, the entire text discussing only the abstract notion of the concept.
Therefore the only reference to the real object hovers in a strange no-man's land
between hyper-determination, if we interpret 'Lierre' as a proper name, or complete
genericity, if we take it as the undefined representative of a kind. Naturally, the
complete absence of ivy in the body of the text raises the question of why it should
be missing. Did Bonnefoy intend, in a never-written section of the same essay, to
introduce and clarify the relationship between 'ivy' and 'concept'? The point is

moot (and we will return to this later), for he allowed the essay to be reprinted in a much later collection of texts, suggesting its stand-alone significance. 'Sur le concept de Lierre' thus suggests strongly that the ivy occurring in the subsequent texts must be seen as mentally associated with concept seen in this earlier text.

Several lines from the second poem in *Douve* allow us further insight into how anterior textual sources provide the allegorical substratum for the leaf in 'Les Tombeaux de Ravenne'. In that poem, the speaker, responding to the 'imperfect drunkenness of living' describes a highly metaphysical scene and then reports the reactive speech of a 'you':

> L'été vieillissant te gerçait d'un plaisir monotone, nous méprisions l'ivresse imparfaite de vivre
> 'Plutôt le lierre, disais-tu, l'attachement du lierre aux pierres de sa nuit : présence sans issue, visage sans racine'
> 'Dernière vitre heureuse que l'ongle solaire déchire, plutôt dans la montagne ce village où mourir.'
> 'Plutôt ce vent...'

> [The dying summer had chapped you with listless pleasure, we felt only scorn for the marred joys of living.
> 'Rather ivy,' you would say, 'the way it clings to the stones of its night: presence without exit, face without roots.'
> 'Last radiant windowpane, ripped by the sun's claw, rather in the mountains this village to die in.
> 'Rather this wind...'] (*P*, 46; *D*, 47)

The poetic strategy of incorporating reported speech demonstrates how *présence* connects poetry and essay in Bonnefoy's work. The whole of *Douve* contains only a few instances of direct speech materialized by quotation marks. (Indeed, before the 1975 *Dans le leurre du seuil*, this use was exceedingly rare in Bonnefoy's poetry: there is no direct speech in *Hier régnant désert*, and only one instance in *Pierre écrite*.) In *Douve*, the first moments of reported speech occur in the above poem, and the subsequent ones are found in the salamander poem cycle near the end of the volume. Significantly, each of these poetic episodes has its memorable essayistic counterpart; both use image to show *présence*: leaf, in 'Les Tombeaux de Ravenne', and salamander in 'La Poésie française et le principe d'identité'. Not only does the reported speech thus provide an immediate link between them, but it also offers a 'material' connection between the first and last essays contained in the first volume of *L'Improbable*, and reveals a pattern where 'textual pasts' support the emergence of allegory in both instances.

In the above *Douve* poem, the effect of the reported speech is heightened by the fact that there are three distinct statements, each enclosed within its own set of quotation marks, and each governed by the repeated 'rather'. Although each of the statements expresses a desire connected to *présence*, the semantics of 'rather' demonstrates a tentative quality which appears surprising, considering Bonnefoy's strong position on *présence*. A genetic study of the prior textual source demonstrates, however, an increasing decisiveness. Indeed, a facsimile of the first manuscript copy of the poem shows that the early version contains only one set of quotation marks enclosing all the lines of direct speech.[50] Typography thus clearly has import, recalling other instances of Bonnefoy's semantic use of it. The effect of the three sets of quotation marks in the later versions of the poem visually draws attention to language and anchors it in temporality, which, as we saw, is one of the defining characteristics of allegory. That point is reinforced by Fineman's suggestion that:

> If the particular signifiers of allegory become vehicles of a larger structural story they carry but in which they play no part, they are at the same time ostentatiously foregrounded by the very structurality that becomes immanent in them. There is no clearer example of this than that of rhyme [...] and the resulting literary effect is exactly that we hear the sound of the sound rather than the meaning of the meaning. The same holds for the other metrical and intonational means of marking poetic periods as isochronic, all of which render 'the time' of the speech flow experienced.[51]

This is precisely the effect created by the triple repetition in the poem, foreshadowing, and perhaps even propelling, its allegorical transformation in 'Les Tombeaux de Ravenne', whose roots, it is now clear, lie in a textual past of Bonnefoy's own writing. Along similar lines, and supplementing the allegorical turn taken by the image of ivy, the incantatory '*this* leaf' repetition seen in the poem momentarily checks the flow of the text. This, Owens suggests, is a characteristic of allegory, for the reader must pause his or her progression along the x-axis of narrative in order to examine the repetition stacked along the y-axis.[52] These technical points actively support the image of the leaf itself, whose progression through the two earlier texts brings it to its central and most memorable position in 'Les Tombeaux de Ravenne'.

Just as ontogeny recapitulates phylogeny, the passage of Bonnefoy's image through time recapitulates the hybridity of allegory, showing it as a trope capable of fusing conceptualization and a poetic description. In 'Sur le concept de Lierre', the capitalized 'Lierre' is linked in an indecipherable manner — positive? negative? — to the idea of concept, making it difficult to apply to this early text Née's hypothesis that metonymy and the proper name are the governing structures of Bonnefoy's thought. The lower-case 'lierre' of the second poem of *Douve* (chronologically later in time) supplements the information of 'Sur le concept de Lierre' and undergoes a form of de-conceptualization by being associated with *présence* and the characteristics of living ivy ('the way it clings to the stones of its night'). Finally, in 'Les Tombeaux de Ravenne', the generic notion of ivy is entirely subsumed in the physical presence of a fragment of ivy. And though it appears to have a strong metaphorical dimension (leaf equals *présence* via the idea of death), Née argues that it cannot be given this value alone, for attaching the value of metaphor to the relation between leaf and *présence* would create nothing more than an analogical connection between the signifying surfaces of the two terms; and such a connection, because it deliberately ignores deeper existential connections carried by their metonymic interaction, is by its very nature false: the leaf, Bonnefoy would have it, is not *like présence*, it *is présence*.

Finally, then, the answer to 'why allegory?' resides in its necessity, that is, in the fact that its characteristics make allegory into something that is not mere rhetorical embellishment but rather something essential to Bonnefoy's purpose.

First, allegory's desire to retrieve the past, supplementing it, and giving it new value speaks directly to his recycling of the 'ivy' image from older texts within his own corpus. The all-important question of the past plays into the second characteristic of allegory: its ability to blur the metaphoric and metonymic paradigm. Indeed, the crucial point is that the ivy images 'salvaged' by the 'Les Tombeaux de Ravenne' text exist as a contiguous set in the past of Bonnefoy's writing. It is precisely this contiguity that allows him to transform what is essentially a metaphorical relation of similitude into one that becomes predominantly metonymic and thereby more theoretically apt to transmit his philosophical position.

★   ★   ★   ★   ★

The idea of *necessity* points to other characteristics of allegory that factor into Bonnefoy's compulsion to convey the idea, and even the fact, or act, of *présence* through writing. Indeed, beyond the trope of fragmentation, allegory also suggests a number of characteristics linking it with the preoccupations governing the essay. Some of these considerations connect the technical, linguistic principles defining allegory to implications that are rather more psychological in nature. The Jakobsonian reading of allegory shows this perhaps most clearly. As Fineman very cogently points out, the interplay between allegory, metaphor, and metonymy necessarily has an impact on both writer and reader. The effect of this commingling between the tropes is to legitimate the allegorical structure itself, thus engendering specific behaviour patterns associated both with writing and reading allegory. Fineman writes:

> It is always the structure of metaphor that is projected onto the sequence of metonymy, not the other way around, which is why allegory is always a hierarchizing mode, indicative of timeless order, however subversively intended its contents might be. This is why allegory is [...] an inherently political and therefore religious trope, not because it flatters tactfully, but because in deferring to structure it insinuates the power of structure.[53]

The idea of implicating allegory in systems of power and hierarchy may come as a surprise after seeing the importance of *allos agorein* and of fragmentation, both of which seem to suggest a certain reluctance to impose categorical affirmations overtly. However, the deferring to hierarchy points to the latent ambivalence regarding systems and their potential undoing that Bonnefoy's work projects. It is surely not by chance that this self-same ambivalence is identified by Angus Fletcher as one of the key psychological characteristics of allegory: 'allegory always demonstrates a degree of inner conflict, which we call "ambivalence"'.[54] Indeed, when placed in parallel with Fineman's comment on the hierarchical nature of allegory, the thematic insistence on fragmentation that is so patently present not only in Bonnefoy's leaf, but also in the way Phèdre's voice is described, shows that allegory provides the same double polarity we saw occurring in the essay. Both forms demonstrate a constant tension between elements that play into the notion of systems and those that seek to break out of that very system.

Further, allegory can potentially accommodate highly divergent motivations (from purely narrative all the way to clearly didactic) because of its inherent capacity to reiterate the value of structures. This, it seems to me, suggests a parallel between Bonnefoy's use both of allegory and of the essay. Indeed, the net effect given by Fineman's decrypting of the hierarchical substratum of allegory goes beyond structure to reveal a psychological dimension that, at least in part, provides a justification for Bonnefoy's need to use allegory. This allows us to read Bonnefoyian allegory as a form of writing that not only can more easily accommodate his imperative to transmit *présence*, but also can simultaneously be seen as the expression of a latent anxiety concerning the transmission of his message. Fletcher has suggested rather convincingly that from a psychological, and even Freudian, perspective, 'the proper analogue to allegory is the compulsive syndrome' because as far as explicitly allegorical texts are concerned, 'fear of not reaching [the] goal is' for the allegorical character 'even greater than fear of the particular terrors along the way'.[55] Fletcher is, of course, referring to true allegorical figures, whose function it is to behave as characters in a fiction, and he is careful to point out that the compulsive pattern refers to the behaviour of the characters and the unfolding of the narration, and can by no means be construed as a comment on the author. However, it must be said that as his chapter on 'Psychological Analogues' progresses, the line between allegorical figure, author, and even reader seems to become increasingly blurred, this conflation providing useful elements to understand the undercurrents initiating the allegorical mode in Bonnefoy's work.

Clearly, the idea of some form of compulsion requiring the use of allegory harmonizes well with the drive to express *présence* that comes across so clearly in Bonnefoy's writing. There is an overwhelming sense of urgency that marks statements such as 'il faut que la ruine ne s'installe pas sur les sociétés de la présence et du sacré, il faut en perpétuer la mémoire, il faut les faire revivre' [ruin must not be allowed take root in the societies of presence and of the sacred; the memory of these things must be perpetuated, we must make them live again] (*YB*, 132). In the wake of that urgency, it can be argued that the compulsive fear of not reaching the goal of transmitting *présence* dovetails seamlessly with some of the more controlling modes also attributed to allegory. For if the sense of compulsion originates in the writer, allegory also provides the rhetorical means to try to ensure that the message effectively reaches its target. Indeed, as Fletcher himself points out:

> The step from the compulsive to the compulsory is but short, and [...] allegorical works present an aesthetic surface which implies an authoritative, thematic, "correct" reading, and which attempts to eliminate other possible readings; they deliberately restrict the freedom of the reader.[56]

Fletcher's point is particularly apt for the leaf passage in 'Les Tombeaux de Ravenne', for the allegorizing mode is so obviously foregrounded there by the explicit and seemingly gratuitous allusion to allegory that any other reading modes are made impossible. This is notably the case of symbol or metaphor, either of which the leaf description might rather naturally evoke. The question then becomes one of determining how the idea of compulsion and control that appears to be so apposite to the allegorical construction of the leaf passage functions with respect to the objective of transmitting *présence*, especially inasmuch as a certain contradiction appears in the fact that Bonnefoy's own descriptions of *présence* identify it with an experience that can only occur spontaneously and thus, a fortiori, never be imposed or forced.

The answer to that problem is linked, I would suggest, to yet another feature that puts allegory and the essay into close parallel with each other: their potential didacticism. In the most ordinary sense, the moralizing dimension of allegory is well-known. Allegory, as has repeatedly been demonstrated, is intended to teach readers something about some other element that is, in reality, located deeper within it, or, more frequently, elsewhere: the tribulations of Christian and his cohort of helpers and hinderers in *A Pilgrim's Progress* are meant to show readers that salvation lies within their grasp also. In that particular example, the allegorical dimension of the text is so obviously emphasized that it is virtually impossible to read it in any other manner. Hardly any freedom is left for the reader to remain, for instance, simply at the narrative surface of the text. It is precisely this intent to control that constitutes the basis for much of the disfavour with which allegory is frequently met.

However, in contradistinction to this rather negative perception of the didacticism of allegory, which is, in truth, a powerful *lieu commun* of critical theory, there is another aspect that Maureen Quilligan most judiciously points out in *The Language of Allegory*. Her analysis allows us to combine Bonnefoy's profound attentiveness to the function of language with his use of allegory in a way that meshes more closely with the concern he so frequently expresses for finding a writerly place of exchange. Inverting the 'normal' didacticism that denotes a point external to the allegory and frequently implies, whether overtly or at a more subliminal level, the 'moral improvement' of the reader, Quilligan writes instead that 'the final focus of any allegory is its reader and [...] the real "action" of any allegory is the reader's learning to read the text properly'.[57] And though her use of the adjective 'properly' clearly reiterates a latent form of moral value, the idea that allegory can teach us not only to be better readers, but also allow us to enter more fully into the thought of the writer is an important one. This vision is, I would argue, far more in keeping with any latent objectives Bonnefoy might have in so pointedly using allegory as the focal point of the leaf passage. Indeed, Quilligan's argument reinvests the didactic tendency of allegory with a positive value that links it quite coherently with Bonnefoy's central preoccupations. She suggests that after reading an allegory, we realize:

> What kind of readers we are, and what kind we must become in order to interpret our significance in the cosmos. Other genres appeal to readers as human beings; allegory appeals to readers as readers of a system of signs, but this may be only to say that allegory appeals to readers in terms of their most distinguishing human characteristic, as readers of, and therefore as creatures finally shaped by, their language.[58]

To extend the argument, we might say that learning how to read can serve as a precondition to learning how to be. And it is precisely this reading of allegory that provides the *raison d'être* for Bonnefoy's essays. Perhaps *présence* is possible neither in the poetic text, nor in the essays, but through the model provided by allegory his essays have the function of teaching us how to read.

That is exactly what Bonnefoy seems to be doing with the leaf passage. Recalling Owens's observation that allegory tends to arrest the narrative in its place because the reader must interrupt the narrative flow in order to examine the metaphoric implications of the images presented, we see that Bonnefoy's description of *présence* literally materializes Owens's suggestion.[59] The text indeed gives the impression of coming to a standstill in order to delineate 'the act of presence' that is successively described from three different angles: beginning with the voice of Phèdre, the definition of *présence* expands into the allegory of the leaf, but does not stop at the allegorical infrastructure. Just as in the 'Dédicace', where the text extends beyond the 'poetry' of the middle section, in the leaf passage of 'Les Tombeaux de Ravenne', the description of *présence* continues beyond the rhetorical and poetic construction of allegory. By doing so, it intimates that allegory is a mandatory precondition to the representation of *présence* because such an evanescent notion cannot adequately be described in ordinary language: its 'true' description can only come after the 'allegorical training' of the reader.

Benjamin's suggestion that allegory is *necessary* proves useful here because he shows it as providing 'the synthesis which is reached in allegorical writing as a result of the conflict between theological and artistic intentions, a synthesis not so much in the sense of a peace as of a *treuga dei* between conflicting opinions'.[60] Allegory thus reconciles the theo-philosophical axis of Bonnefoy's *présence* with its artistic dimension in a momentary 'truce', which is itself an act. Indeed, the allegory we find in the second (leaf) paragraph is not simply an allegorical description, but can also be read as a true performative in the Austinian sense. Like the 'I dedicate' of the 'Dédicace' the allegory is actually performed in the opening sentence, where saying 'I will say allegorically' creates a reading which would not otherwise exist. It is the performance of this act that engenders the textual creation of the allegory and produces a highly poeticized text that will eventually lead, at the very end of the leaf passage, to the 'true' description of *présence*, which reads as follows:

> Qu'est-ce que la présence? Cela séduit comme une œuvre d'art, cela est brut comme le vent ou la terre. Cela est noir comme l'abîme et pourtant cela rassure. Cela semble un fragment d'espace parmi d'autres, mais cela nous appelle et nous contient. Et c'est un instant qui va mille fois se perdre, mais il a la gloire d'un dieu. Cela ressemble à la mort...
>
> Est-ce la mort? D'un mot qui devrait jeter ses feux sur la pensée obscure, mot cependant rendu méprisable et vain: c'est l'immortalité. (I, 27)

> [What is presence? It seduces like a work of art, it is brute like the wind or the earth. It is black like the abyss, and yet it reassures. It seems like a fragment of space among so many others, but it calls to us and holds us. And it is an instant that a thousand times will be lost, but it has the glory of a god. It resembles death...
>
> Is it death? Of a word that should cast its fire over obscure thought, a word nonetheless rendered contemptible and futile: it is immortality.]

Though extremely challenging to interpret, these paragraphs do get us closer to what Bonnefoy means by *présence*. They clearly mesh with other seminal texts from *L'Improbable*. Here again we see the incantatory repetition of a key word or grammatical structure: in the 'Dédicace' as in 'Dévotion', it was the preposition 'à'; in the leaf paragraph, the expression 'cette feuille'; here it is the demonstrative 'cela' [it]. Here also, Bonnefoy calls upon deixis to structure the text, and uses the physical disposition of the writing semantically, separating the statement 'It resembles death...' from the question that immediately follows it, 'Is it death?'. Finally, the juxtaposition of art and nature, seen here in the apposition of 'a work of art' and 'the wind or the earth', echoes not only the similar apposition of 'a poetry desired' and 'of rain, of waiting, and of wind' in the 'Dédicace', but also in the parallel between Phaedra and leaf that begins the passage.

What is immediately striking in the passage is that for all the grace and poetry of the definition, the fundamental meaning of *présence* remains obscure. Indeed, much like the 'improbable' of the 'Dédicace', this passage deliberately thematizes paradox, for if the gist is clear, the primary impression one receives is one of contradiction. From the passage, one can deduce that *présence* is an object of artistic production, while also being an element of the natural world; it exists in a temporality, yet is simultaneously a-temporal; it is fragmentary, but capable of totalization; finally, it is both death and immortality. Here, as in so many other instances, Bonnefoy's deliberate use of paradox is the key to understanding the culmination of the passage. For if the notion of paradox appears clearly in the apposition of such antinomic elements as art and nature, time and timelessness, etc., it is completely integrated, both thematically and grammatically, into the complicated final sentences: 'It resembles death... Is it death? Of a word that should cast its fire over obscure thought, a word nonetheless endered contemptible and futile: it is immortality' (*I*, 27). The cusp of the paradox comes with the last response to the original question 'What is presence?' 'It resembles death', Bonnefoy answers, the ellipsis at the end suggesting the possibility of multiple other descriptions. This materially visible ellipsis has a didactic function, for it prefigures the more important grammatical ellipses, warning the reader of their presence. Once again, Bonnefoy's purposeful use of typography is poetic, and uses the visual separation of logically connected segments to make the last sentences carry the focal weight of the passage. These sentences are set apart, mobilizing the reader's attention not only on the triangular relation between *présence*, death, and immortality, but also giving visual primacy to the last word, 'immortality', through the deictic focalization created by the colon.

Though the section as a whole gives a good demonstration of the destabilizing density and even obliqueness of Bonnefoy's prose, it is really his use of syntax, particularly of syntactic suppression, that produces the sense of paradox rather remarkably conveyed by the passage. Indeed, the only way to understand the second sentence, 'Of a word that should cast its fire over obscure thought, a word none-theless rendered contemptible and futile', the reader must re-insert the elided words 'it is the death' to obtain: '[it is the death] of a word which should cast its fire...'. Only by doing this can one gain an understanding of the challenging last fragment, 'it is immortality'. The problem is exacerbated by the fact that the sentence 'Of a word that should cast its fire' does not immediately strike the reader as lacking an introduction because it begins as a perfectly logical, albeit poetic construction. It continues, however, with an apposition, 'a word nonetheless rendered contemptible and futile' rather than the expected subject and verb, thus greatly complicating the reader's task, since the sentence diverges radically from the expected grammatical direction. Solving the problem requires the reader to fill the ellipsis and reintroduce something of the order of: 'this word is immortality'. And in a final perturbing element, though the colon creates a logical connection between 'word' and 'immortality', this link is substantively undercut by Bonnefoy's reintroduction of the demonstrative 'it is', whose answer to the initial question blurs the different parts of the text. The eliding, combined with the construction of the sentence, thus generates the strong sense of ambiguity that permeates the text, for it complicates the syntax to such a point that a hasty reading might mistakenly amalgamate the initial question 'What is presence?' with what appears to be the answer at the end, 'it is immortality'. In reality, of course, the answer is exactly the opposite of what might be gathered from the text, even by a relatively attentive reader: *présence*, Bonnefoy is telling us, is the death of immortality, in other words the complete reversal of conventional metaphysics. The question, of course, is why he allows such a high degree of ambiguity on a matter that is obviously of capital importance to him.

A return to allegory provides some elements of a solution. In the allegorical passage, it is precisely because the leaf has been ravaged that it is no longer within reach of destruction. In other words, its destruction has provided a paradoxical form of immortality, but this immortality is accessible only through the agency of the 'I' whose sensate awareness of the leaf ('I hold it in my hand [...] I hear its unceasing voice') confers the power of salvation it obtains: 'this leaf is pure presence, and thus my salvation' (*I*, 27). This returns us, of course, to the paradoxical duality of *présence*, inevitably vacillating between transience and immortality, and this is exactly what Benjamin attributes to allegory when he writes that 'an appreciation for the transience of things, and the concern to rescue them for eternity, is one of the strongest impulses in allegory'.[61] It is striking that all the elements Benjamin describes are perfectly enacted in Bonnefoy's leaf passage. The textual existence of Bonnefoy's leaf, filtered through the revitalization of 'Sur le concept de Lierre' and the second poem from *Douve*, imparts a form of immortality to it. This would be true even for a single text, but in the case of *L'Improbable*, its multiple printings over the past fifty years reinforce the idea of a form of textual immortality, confirming Benjamin's suggestion that textual immortality can be seen as the *raison d'être* of allegory.

Thus, from many perspectives allegory provides Bonnefoy with powerful tools to reinforce the ideas that he so obviously feels the moral obligation to transmit. And yet, allegory is by no means the perfect solution, for its tendency toward didacticism and control is also risky, potentially leading to the reader's rejection of the message. For it cannot be denied that allegory intrinsically contains a value judgement that

Fletcher underscores when he writes, 'frequently didactic in aim, allegories raise the question of value *directly* by asserting certain propositions as good and others as bad'.[62] Indeed, in the leaf passage, there is absolutely no ambiguity about which propositions are given positive value: the assertion that 'this leaf is pure presence, and consequently, my salvation' (I, 27) clearly indicates a moral stance that is reinforced by the highly positive status of the word 'salvation'. Bonnefoy's repeated use of an overtly theological vocabulary provides a highly significant connection with some of the more 'religious' themes that subtend allegory. Indeed, it is perhaps impossible to evaluate adequately the didacticism that allegory projects if one does not also consider the notion of the sacred and of redemption associated with it. From this perspective, a clear parallel emerges between these manifestly theological considerations and much of Bonnefoy's discourse on the value of poetic language.

Concerning the sacred, Quilligan very interestingly suggests that the horizontal rather than vertical reading that allegory imposes leads to the textual development of a sense of the sacred.[63] She does not expand on this idea, but a possible hypotext for her statement is found in Benjamin's comment that: 'it will be immediately apparent, especially to anyone who is familiar with allegorical textual exegesis, that all of the things which are used to signify derive, from the very fact of their pointing to something else, a power which makes them appear no longer commensurable with profane things, which raises them to a higher plane, and which can, indeed, sanctify them'.[64] In part, this feeling is doubtless linked to the non-substitutability of the terms used, in the sense that when words cannot be replaced by synonyms, they acquire an absolute quality that parallels the manner in which theological systems work. The Bonnefoyian example of the word *présence* intersects particularly aptly with this analysis: not only is it very difficult to interchange it with a synonym having a similar or identical meaning, but through the diachronic determination of *présence*, a text built around it would naturally tend to demonstrate a reticulation of words that are metonymically linked to the original term. This is precisely what happens in Bonnefoy's work, where the general use of a theological vocabulary is rendered necessary by the initial choice, resulting in the frequent use of terms such as 'salvation', 'sacred', 'redeem', 'communion', 'sacrifice' etc. that are so familiar to his readers.

And it is this vocabulary, or rather the more profound moral significance that it bears, that finally suggests an explanation for the usefulness of allegory's didactic potential. Why does Bonnefoy need the didacticism? Again, probably not because of its intrinsic appeal, but rather because of what he perceives as the vital importance of *présence*, and the absolute necessity of conveying this importance in spite of the alienating possibility of language. His writing reflects a clear sense of anxiety and distress about the historical loss of the power of language — and poetic language in particular — to link human beings to each other. He writes in the essay 'L'Analogie suprême':

> Après tant de siècles où l'expression poétique a été la voix principale de la conscience publique [...] voici en effet que la civilisation a changé, [...] voici que le besoin de totalité cohérente et de plénitude a été sacrifié, dans la nuit de plus

en plus dense de la pensée conceptuelle, au développement des sciences et des technologies de plus en plus autonomes. (*E*, 171)

[After so many centuries during which poetic expression was the principle voice of public conscience [...] civilization has indeed changed [...] and the need for a coherent whole and for plenitude have been sacrificed in the ever-deepening gloom of conceptual thought and the development of increasingly autonomous sciences and technologies.]

It is this strong reticence regarding the contemporary 'scientific' world that finally shows allegory's importance: it provides a means to limit the disintegration of models of signification and restore past meaning. Owens echoes Benjamin when he indicates that allegory is, par excellence, a mode of redemption because it has the:

capacity to rescue from historical oblivion that which threatens to disappear. Allegory first emerged in response to a similar sense of estrangement from tradition; throughout its history it has functioned in the gap between a present and a past which, without allegorical reinterpretation, might have remained foreclosed. A conviction of the remoteness of the past, and a desire to redeem it for the present — these are its two most fundamental impulses.[65]

The importance of this scrutiny of the past, which then serves as a springboard to the present provides another decisive parallel with the essay, which also frequently looks backward to an already-existing cultural element to find the material for its own existence. Bonnefoy's need for the essay is clearly shown by the sheer number he has written. In terms of his own rhetoric, however, allegory obtains a privileged position because its particular location at the intersection of the metaphoric and metonymic axes of expression enable it better to re-evaluate the capacities of language. And, in point of fact, it is its double capacity of aiming for a sense of redemption while pointing to the problematic interaction between language and reality that doubtless commands Bonnefoy's interest in it. Thus, Owens's more general perspective on allegory and redemption meshes seamlessly with the language-oriented analysis that Quilligan gives of the redemptive nature of allegory:

Perhaps language cannot redeem language, so that poetry cannot redeem society; fiction may only entertain. But all allegorists do aim at redemption, and because they must work with language, they ultimately turn to the paradox at the heart of their own assumptions about words and take the final focus of their narratives as not merely the social function of language, but in particular, the slippery tensions between literalness and metaphor. They scrutinize language's own problematic polysemy.[66]

This polysemy described by Quilligan is, as we have seen, one of the governing leitmotivs of Bonnefoy's work. It occurs not only in the very constitution of allegory and essay, but also echoes the thematic construction of the earlier collections of poetry. In *Douve*, for instance, the polysemy of the name of the central character combines with the multiple ways in which she/it is shown over the course of the poems: landscape, woman, cadaver, etc. Similarly, *Pierre écrite* contains a plethora of different poems whose single name, 'Une Pierre', suggests the plurality of descriptions and definitions a single word can contain. The net effect of such a strategy replicates for the reader the larger framework of fragmentation and unity that is created in Bonnefoy's work through his drive to reveal the unified and unifying structure that subtends our world, while acknowledging its polysemy and our ineluctably fragmented perception of it. It is this combination of ephemerality and persistence that provides one of the most striking connections with the theorization of allegory, and bring us to the final point of this chapter: a return to Bonnefoy's rejection of 'critique-allégorique', a denial he bases on the 'thievish' quality of its attempt to gain knowledge of an author's work ('tentative de connaissance par effraction', *VP*, 325). The danger of this form of criticism is, for him, the 'risk of losing completely the object one wishes to seize'; it is thus to be opposed to the valuable and respectful 'critique-symbole' which reads no more into an author's work than what he has put into it (*VP*, 325). I proposed to position myself as a 'bad reader' in order to show that allegory has multiple extensions in Bonnefoy's work, taking it far beyond a fortuitous incidence found in a few scattered examples. I propose now to go one step further and use allegoresis to show how that position of 'bad reader' is in reality not so far removed from the 'good reader' whom Bonnefoy desires.

As I suggested, his act of collecting a number of his essays to be parts of an integrated whole provides a structure whose result is to show the path he himself took in developing his notion of *présence*. Though partially masked by the characteristics intrinsic to the essay, his teleological objective is fundamentally didactic, functioning all the better for remaining subliminal. Reading the collected essays as a whole reveals Bonnefoy's ambition to provide a lasting contribution to the community and thereby give it perhaps the means to transform itself. His project is in large part made possible by the humble 'persona' the essay projects and its minimizing of the 'I' at its core. Incontrovertibly, however, that 'I' exists. In a 1989 interview on the ethics of the essay, Starobinski described the pleasure of writing essays as that of 'reaching myself through roundabout paths'.[67] The trope he uses is familiar and well-worn, for since Montaigne, part of the conceit of the genre of the essay is the serendipitous nature of its self-discovery. Though his position is undoubtedly true of a number of essayists, and is perhaps also true for essays whose textual life remains dispersed through different media, the temporally aggregated organization of Bonnefoy's collected essays suggests that this may be less the case for his work, where the collecting itself, beyond its intellectual objectives, brings together the different parts of a subject that has constructed itself over time. Lukács, as usual, gives the best description of this subject: 'The hero of the essay,' he tells us, 'was once alive, and so his life must be given form; but this life, too, is as much inside the work as everything is in poetry'.[68] Perhaps Bonnefoy does not see himself as a hero, but one of the paradoxical limitations of a contemporary poetry that has abandoned the effusions of the lyric 'I' is its difficulty in showing the person behind the poetry. Clearly, the essay is better equipped to 'give form to the life of the essayist', and though Bonnefoy's action in collecting his essays may have begun with the didactic aim of showing *présence*, the nature of the essay first transforms that collecting into a carefully structured 'biography', which itself provides the allegorical training required to read Bonnefoy's collected essays allegorically, as a masked autobiography.

★   ★   ★   ★   ★

Bonnefoy's heartfelt 's'arracher aux mythes du moi' [wrench oneself from the myths of the ego] (*YB*, 331) provides an indicator of his position. Though his life of the mind is well known to his readers, he remained, as critics who were also his friends remark, very disinclined to put his private life on public display. In fact, it is almost amusing to see that one of the few changes in the third (1990) edition of *L'Improbable* is the appearance in the front matter of the briefest of biographies, contained in seven pithy sentences:

> Né le 24 juin 1923, à Tours.
> Études secondaires, puis de mathématiques et de philosophie à Tours, Poitiers et Paris.
> À Paris depuis 1944. Voyages, notamment en Méditerranée et en Amérique.
> Travaux sur l'histoire de formes et des moments de la poétique.
> Invitations de diverses universités à partir de 1960. Depuis 1981, professeur au Collège de France. (front matter; no pagination)

> [Born in Tours on the 24th of June, 1924.
> Studies at the secondary level, then of mathematics and philosophy at Tours, Poitiers, and Paris.
> Settled in Paris since 1944. Travel, notably around the Mediterranean and in America.
> Work on the history of forms and on the moments of poetics.
> Invited lecturer at various universities from 1960. Since 1981, professor at the Collège de France.] (*I*, 9)

This mini-biography appeared originally in the back matter of the 1982 Gallimard edition of *Poèmes* in a two-page section rather bombastically entitled 'La Vie et l'œuvre d'Yves Bonnefoy', a title which again causes amusement because the 'biography' occupies barely a fifth of the textual space. This imbalance, which skews heavily in favour of the work, and the brevity of the biographical statement are tellingly eloquent of Bonnefoy's humility, his strong desire to avoid mingling his personal life with the interaction he established with the world through his writing. More profoundly perhaps, it also connotes a philosophical gesture which tends to subsume the personal in the universal, which allows individuals, he says, 'dans l'assomption même de notre rien, d'accéder à l'universel' [through the very acceptance of our nothingness, to attain the universal] (*E*, 82). In some senses, however, this 'universality' is reductive, necessarily excising parts of lived reality. Hence, an interesting counterpoint to the rarity of personal anecdote in Bonnefoy's work is found in Née's comment (quoted in Chapter 3)[69] regarding the covert referentiality of Bonnefoy's work. Née cites the 'great glass houses reflecting the sky' (*P*, 180) from the poem 'Dévotion' and identifies them as a poetic description of New York engendered by a metonymic relationship of contiguity connecting an experienced reality and the images that appear in the writing.[70] Though this situation is perhaps entirely germane to the 'universalizing' tendencies so frequent in poetry, it is far less characteristic of the essay, which can more easily integrate a unabashedly individual vision correlated with an 'I' that overtly assumes its subjectivity. Despite this possibility, what is notable in Bonnefoy's essays is the relative paucity of biographical anchors; any real-life contiguity that might have been plainly perceptible from the writer's position is rendered virtually impossible to discern from the exterior. This is a theoretical position that Bonnefoy fully espouses. Indeed, in his discussion on metonymy, one of the rights he specifically claims for the writing subject is that of remaining silent on the details of incidents that have given rise to poetry, in order to allow them their metonymic potential to 'break the closed constructions of metaphor' (*E*, 51). Bonnefoy's intentional minimizing of his own subjectivity (and of subjectivity in general) coalesces in a polarity that is recurrent in his work: the opposition between a *moi* perceived as sealed off in its own narcissism and a *je* open to engagement with the real world. That expression, 's'arracher aux mythes du moi', summarizes a struggle, omnipresent in his work, to find a balance between the subject and his or her artistic production; this struggle is most notably seen in his treatment of biography. An early reflection appeared in a 1955 critical essay discussing a biography of Degas. Bonnefoy praises the biographer, writing that 'Sa biographie a la qualité de discretion. Elle ne s'attache qu'à cette part de la vie qui a trait à l'oeuvre et la vérité gagne toujours à des limitations de ce genre' [his biography has the quality of discretion. It hews to that part of life that relates to the work; truth always gains through limitations of this type] (*I*, 167).

Bonnefoy's encomium, lauding the truth shown by discretion, is echoed in his own reticence in divulging personal information. It is only in his later biographical reflections that his position becomes clearly consolidated. In 1991, he published his monumental biography of Alberto Giacometti. Its unusual subtitle, *Biographie d'une œuvre*, is emblematic and recapitulates much of Bonnefoy's own quest to re-evaluate the creator-creation dichotomy. Noteworthy is the fact that Bonnefoy did not write an analysis, a commentary, or a study of Giacometti's work, nor did he put the artist on the same plane as his artistic production by using, for instance, a title commonly given to such books: 'Giacometti and His Work'. In his analysis of *Alberto Giacometti*, critic Jean-Michel Maulpoix comments on the surprising nature of Bonnefoy's title:

> Ordinarily, people write the biography of an author or an artist, that is, the story of a perishable being who created objects that were less ephemeral than he. Writing the biography of an oeuvre means inverting the perspective and focusing attention less on the circumstances of the life of the creator than on the durable objects into which this life was converted [...]. It means not writing the life of an ephemeral being, but rather his successive encounters with what Malraux would have called his 'share of eternity'.[71]

In many ways, Maulpoix's keen analysis of the reversal of the relation between that which is fleeting and that which persists substantiates the way in which Bonnefoy uses the essay in his work, for it is the malleability of the essay, its 'collectibility', that allows it simultaneously to mimic the function of biography while remaining true to itself, that is to say, tentative, advancing only a low-key subjectivity.

So what does Bonnefoy's title, 'biography of a work', indicate? On the one hand, it shows a desire to efface the subject, that is, the artist producing the work, but on the other hand, this effacing itself highlights the useful value of the artwork. By focusing on the work itself, Bonnefoy underscores the lasting worth it acquires by becoming an object that can be shared by the community. Indeed, by using the word 'biography' in connection with the work and not the man, Bonnefoy 'gives life', reintegrating *bios* into Maulpoix's 'durable objects' and signifying thereby that both the artist and his art can harbour life. That duality recapitulates the elsewhere-pointing so typical of allegory and allegoresis, inviting the reader to construct a meaning predicated on semantic categories lying outside the text. But it also references the double capacity of *présence* to be felt both in the ephemeral nature of the lived life and through the manner in which the intellect has transformed that experience into a durable artistic element. Arguably, however, and especially from the standpoint of a philosophy of *présence*, this 'I' must also go out to encounter the world, especially insofar as much of what Bonnefoy claims for poetry is its desire to create authentic exchanges between that 'I' and 'you' which are for him the enduring markers of *présence*.

True ambivalence thus characterizes Bonnefoy's position, which simultaneously shows two sides: a philosophical imperative to express his subjectivity warring with a personal reticence to do so. Philippe Lejeune, in his comment that 'it is impossible for the autobiographical vocation and the passion for anonymity to coexist in the same person', seems to suggest that such a duality is impossible.[72] His position is perhaps true for pure autobiography. The essay, however, can circumvent this difficulty, for its strength lies precisely in its ability to maintain an equilibrium between the characteristics it shares with autobiography (the conflation between narrator, character, and subject) and its own thoroughly essayistic discourse centred on an external cultural object. This generic capacity to be subjective while simultaneously downplaying subjectivity is, of course, present in the single essay. However, it is vastly amplified, as we saw, by Bonnefoy's decision to organize his essays into structured collections. That structuring is also singular because it takes place over time. In other words, Bonnefoy did not just decide belatedly to create the collections. On the contrary, the broader collecting of *L'Improbable* is anchored in a temporal axis. To this, we must add the additional structuring that each collection further underwent through multiple re-editions, some of which included significant changes. These changes are the mute indicators of the structural and organizational principles that Bonnefoy brought to bear on the essays. Thus if we return momentarily to the Giacometti text, the subtitle *Biographie d'une œuvre* maps perfectly onto Bonnefoy's collections of essays, whose careful construction clearly shows biographical dimensions playing out on a chronological scale that reproduces the movement of the subject through time. The subtitle's focus on the *œuvre* shows its lasting usefulness; similarly, as we also saw, Bonnefoy's collected essays work on a didactic scale meant to guide the reader to a better understanding of *présence*. Now, armed with this better understanding, we can take our insight one step further, and extend the allegorical competencies we learnt in the essays to convoke allegoresis, and read this structured 'biography' of Bonnefoy's work as a shrouded autobiography. This, in short, not so surprising for as Smith reminds us, 'what, in fact, is being named and reinforced in postmodern allegory is the figure of the author'.[73] That author also needs to be a presence in his own work.

Allegory, we know, is bound to time along a number of different vectors that include: its projection along the syntagmatic axis of the linguistic structure, its revitalizing of textual pasts, and its concern with origins and the permanence of structure. As Fineman indicates, 'the motive for allegory emerges out of recuperative originology'.[74] And though Bonnefoy attempted to stave off an allegorical reading of his work, such a reading is nonetheless supported by a reticulation of choices and modifications so dense that it seems improbable that he should not have been aware of it (or even engineered it). In point of fact, this concern for textual origins is one of the more striking and unusual characteristics of Bonnefoy's work, with the quest for origins appearing as a frequent theme in his comments there: 'the true beginning of poetry,' he writes, lies in 'une force en nous plus ancienne que toute langue, une force notre origine, que j'aime appeler la parole' [a force in us that is more ancient that all language, a force that is our origin, and that I like to call speech] (*E*, 34). Along similar lines, in that vivid image drawn from folk tales, Née described the textual 'little white stones' that Bonnefoy casts behind him to help him find his way back to his own existence.[75] Given, however, the conscious and explicitly formulated publishing decisions that Bonnefoy carefully made available to readers through peritextual matter (the notes and bibliographical appendices), it is unclear whom the little white stones are really meant to help.

A case in point is the 1978 collection, *Poèmes*. Bonnefoy's statements indicate that it is far more than a simple compilation of his then-extant poetry. Rather, it resembles much more a constructed artefact whose purpose is to describe the origins and trajectory of his poetic project. Indeed, much as he does for his essay collections, he provides in the back matter to *Poèmes* an indication of the transformations undergone by the formerly single volumes of poetry. Readers thus learn that *Douve*, *Pierre écrite*, and *Dans le leurre du seuil* are to be found unchanged from their original editions. However, for *Hier régnant désert*, Bonnefoy explains that he has deliberately eschewed a more recent 1970 edition in order to return to the original version, thus, he says, allowing readers to understand better the sequence of the developments that link the different volumes of poetry (*P*, 336). This pattern of providing origins is even more strikingly foregrounded by Bonnefoy's republishing of early, incomplete texts such as the essay 'Sur le concept de Lierre', or the extant chapters of *L'Ordalie* that survived his own destruction of it. In both these cases, the texts appear as fragments, albeit of a diametrically opposed nature. Blanchot's comments on the novel fragment furnish a useful theoretical frame, particularly his observation that fragments are inevitably considered against the backdrop of 'a whole that either was so earlier or will be so later'.[76] These two Bonnefoy texts occupy precisely those two opposing positions, with 'Sur le concept du Lierre' explicitly presented, as we saw, as the 'prologomenes' of a work to come, and the two chapters of *L'Ordalie* as the fragments of a work that is no more.

Bonnefoy's choices are all certainly legitimated by a concern for truth and accuracy. This, indeed, is what comes across both in the note appended to the reprinting of *L'Ordalie* (in *Rue traversière* (1977), 197–201) and in the brief interview transcribed at the end of *Le Cœur-espace: 1945, 1961*, itself a 2001 reprinting of the very different 1945 and 1961 versions of the poem 'Le Cœur-espace'. In response to the interviewer's question about the autobiographical dimension of the poem, Bonnefoy evokes, among other fragments of memory, the power that poetic words had over his rather book-less childhood. He further explains that with few exceptions, he keeps the traces of all stages of the evolution of his work in order, he says, to be able to return to them to decipher the zones that had remained obscure.[77] One cannot quarrel with the tenacity of this desire to understand the more opaque aspects of the images created by his mind, nor indeed, with the honesty he demonstrates by providing works towards which he no longer felt any intellectual allegiance. By his own assessment, these texts are intended to show earlier positions that his own later evaluation analysed as erroneous. The didactic dimension of such an approach is patent.

Yet in this, as in so many other domains, Bonnefoy confronts us with the paradoxical nature of his reality. Beginning with the essays collected, organized, and re-organized by him over four decades, so many elements evoked throughout this chapter sustain the need for an allegorical reading that reveals the autobiographical backdrop of his work. In addition to the essays, we can add the reprintings of poetry and prose texts that make the full arc of his intellectual and poetic development available to readers, showing even its fits and starts and its self-examination. Finally, the peritextual commentary that accompanies so much of his work contributes to the reader's structuring, understanding, and even rethinking of the texts. Examined under the allegorical microscope, these decisions all seem forcefully to evoke the guiding voice of the author and thus the authorial person himself, for they show that by consciously mooring all these elements in time, Bonnefoy reproduces his own temporal progression in a manner that replicates the function of autobiography. This, of course, begs the question of its presence in his work.

Several elements undergird Bonnefoy's autobiographical impulse; they appear, it seems to me, as a response to certain failings Bonnefoy perceived in contemporary literary practice, particularly with respect to the projection of an auctorial voice. The most conspicuous of these is the 'crisis of the lyric voice' evoked in Chapter Two in reference to the rising star of the essay and the corresponding decline of lyric poetry. Stamelman indeed highlights the general tendency of contemporary poetry to downplay the individual voice, remarking in his article 'The Syntax of the Ephemeral' that 'in the poetry of Bonnefoy, Dupin and du Bouchet, the poet's presence is tenuous, if non-existent'.[78] Yet one of the premises of a philosophy of *présence* is the reality of that *présence*, with as its corollary the quest for the means to express it. This position thus enters into conflict with an assumed poetic 'I', but also with some of the more basic tenets of deconstructionism, namely, the impossibility of origin and, to cite Barthes's well-known expression, the 'death of the author'. As I showed earlier, Bonnefoy is viscerally opposed to these stances and the alienation they engender. Indeed, the opposition he brings to bear against 'allegorical criticism' in the essay, 'Quelque chose comme une lettre', that we saw earlier consolidates that hostility, which is a latent but omnipresent aspect of his work. Against that criticism which derides the presence of the author as a tyrannical demonstration of authority, Bonnefoy asks, 'qu'avons-nous fait depuis le début de l'humanité sinon vouloir être l'origine et non simplement un aspect du sens qu'a commencé le langage?' [what have we done since the beginning of humanity but desire to be the origin, and not just an aspect of the meaning that language engendered?] (*E*, 62). Bonnefoy's autobiographical impulse is thus both a logical riposte to the circulation of these ideas in the contemporary literary landscape, and that desire to be a demonstrable 'I'.

This brings us back to the convoluted problem of the bad readers we are being in deliberately contravening Bonnefoy's instructions, and using allegoresis to interpret his work. To this, one might respond that he was at great pains to integrate into his work all the elements discussed above; each required non-negligible amounts of reflection, publishing decisions, and revisions. Our allegorical reading of the autobiographical dimension of his collected essays is thus the logical result of a process that I assume he himself generated because, again, it seems unlikely that he would have been unconscious of such a high concatenation of indicators evoking the authorial voice. We can add to the above Lejeune's comment that 'the deep subject of autobiography is the proper name'.[79] 'Deep' is indeed the proper adjective to apply to Bonnefoy's work. Through his collected essays and their peritexts (and also his collected interviews, but that would be the subject of another book), Bonnefoy has succeeded in making the reader produce the proper name, his own. Arguably, we have only been able to do this because we were primed to do so through the example of the fairy. Both, I find, are an extraordinary achievement.

But does that make us into the good readers he wants? Not yet, I would argue, for in another demonstration of the circular reading learnt by reading his essays, in order to be those truly good readers, we need also to pay attention to the forms — essay and peritext — he uses to give us information. Thus the truly good reader who has assimilated the lessons so unobtrusively given by Bonnefoy will use allegoresis to move beyond autobiography and see that essay and peritext have semantic meaning inasmuch as they point deictically to a specific structure which readers must identify and decode. That structural meaning has become familiar to us, as it resides in the generic characteristics of the essay whose unobtrusiveness and humility are aspects we saw to be central to its definition. By its very nature, then, the essay counters the vainglorious quality autobiography might contain. Similarly, the peritextual spaces we have seen Bonnefoy using to such subtle effect are located at the margins of the work, they literally *are* marginal, making them the material figuration of the 'supplement' that allegory is also said to be. But Bonnefoy has subverted their supplemental 'non-necessity' by making them the bearers of a significant portion of our understanding, allowing us perhaps to extrapolate a similar function for allegory in his work: it transforms the supplemental into the necessary. Both essay and peritext encapsulate then a relation to paradox and duality that comprises the glinting reality of all parts of Bonnefoy's work. His collected essays are both autobiography and not-autobiography; the peritexts are both marginal and central; deixis is both a simple word and something more, *présence* is both experience and idea. And the good readers that we have become are those who have understood that to experience life is to embrace paradox, because that is the true nature of reality.

Notes to Chapter 4

1. Bonnefoy, *The Lure and the Truth of Painting*, trans. by Stamelman, p. xi.
2. Ibid., p. xi.
3. Riendeau, 'La Rencontre du savoir et du soi dans l'essai', p. 92.
4. René Descartes, *A Discourse on Method*, trans. by John Veitch, Everyman's Library (London: Dent, 1949) <https://www.gutenberg.org/files/59/59-h/59-h.htm> [accessed 29 July 2022].
5. de Obaldia, *The Essayistic Spirit*, p. 33.
6. As a reminder of what I indicated in the Preface and earlier chapters, *L'Improbable* is a pluri-edition work. The first version (1959) contained eight essays plus the poem, 'Dévotion'. *Un rêve fait à Mantoue* (1967), was Bonnefoy's second collection of essays. It contained thirteen essays plus a narrative text very much resembling the 'récits en rêve' [dream narratives] he would later publish. These two texts, along with four additional essays were fused into the 1980 book entitled *L'Improbable suivi de Un Rêve fait à Mantoue*. Comments found in a note to *Vérité de parole* indicate that Bonnefoy considered the latter to be the 'definitive' version of *L'Improbable*.
7. Née, *Rhétorique profonde d'Yves Bonnefoy*, p. 1.
8. Genette, *Thresholds of Interpretation*, trans. by Lewin, p. 2.
9. Ibid., p. 21.
10. Ibid., pp. 316, 317.
11. Ibid., p. 8.
12. de Obaldia, *The Essayistic Spirit*, p. 18.
13. Georgia Johnston, 'The Whole Achievement in Virginia Woolf's *The Common Reader*', in *Essays on the Essay: Redefining the Genre*, ed. by Alexander Butrym (Athens: University of Georgia Press, 1989), pp. 148–58 (p. 148).
14. Gouvard, 'Éléments pour une grammaire de la poésie moderne', p. 3.
15. Lukács, *Soul and Form*, p. 14.
16. Gérard Genette, *Seuils* (Paris: Seuil, 1987), p. 8.
17. Gasarian, *Yves Bonnefoy*, p. 9.
18. Paul Éluard, *L'Amour, la poésie* (Paris: Gallimard, 1929), p. 18.
19. Austin, *How to Do Things with Words*, p. 8.
20. Patrick Née, 'Art et essai: l'exemple majeur d'Yves Bonnefoy', in *Le Quatrième Genre: l'essai*, ed. by Patrick Née (Rennes: Presses universitaires de Rennes, 2018), pp. 213–34 (p. 227).
21. Obaldia, *The Essayistic Spirit*, p. 101.
22. Lukács, *Soul and Form*, p. 18.
23. Craig Owens, 'The Allegorical Impulse: Toward a Theory of Postmodernism', *October*, 12 (Spring 1980), 67–86 (p. 70).
24. Serge Canadas, 'Celui qui s'éveille et qui rêve encore', *Critique*, 43 (December 1987), 1044–63 (p. 1057).
25. Ibid.
26. Joel Fineman, 'The Structure of Allegorical Desire', *October*, 12 (Spring 1980), 46–66 (p. 51).
27. Owens, 'The Allegorical Impulse', p. 75.
28. Angus Fletcher, *Allegory: The Theory of a Symbolic Mode* (Ithaca, NY: Cornell University Press, 1964), p. 1 (my emphasis).
29. Roman Jakobson and Morton Halle, *The Fundamentals of Language* (The Hague: Mouton, 1956), pp. 81–82.
30. Daniel Chandler, *Semiotics, the Basics*, 2nd edn (London: Routledge, 2007), p. 127.
31. Guillaume Apollinaire, *Alcools* (Paris: Gallimard, 1966), p. 7.
32. Hugh Bredin, 'Roman Jakobson on Metaphor and Metonymy', *Philosophy and Literature*, 8.1 (1984), 89–103 (p. 101).
33. Oswald Ducrot and Tzvetan Todorov, *Dictionnaire encyclopédique des sciences du langage* (Paris: Seuil, 1972), p. 354.

34. Jakobson and Halle, *The Fundamentals of Language*, p. 61.

35. Née, *Yves Bonnefoy*, pp. 49–50. James McAllister makes much the same point in his 'Metonymy and Metaphor in Yves Bonnefoy's Poetry', *French Forum*, 19.2 (May 1994), 149–60.

36. Née, *Yves Bonnefoy*, pp. 50, 49. Regarding the question of name and naming that are so central in Bonnefoy's thought, it is, of course, noteworthy that *metonym* means 'change of name'.

37. James McAllister, 'Metonymy and Metaphor in Yves Bonnefoy's Poetry', p. 150.

38. Bredin, 'Roman Jakobson on Metaphor and Metonymy', p. 102.

39. Fineman, 'The Structure of Allegorical Desire', p. 50.

40. Owens, 'The Allegorical Impulse', p. 74.

41. It must be noted, however, that Benveniste's refutation concerns more particularly the relation between the signifier and the signified, but that between the sign and the object, which is subject to 'the action of various historical factors': Émile Benveniste, 'The Analysis of Structure and Meaning: The Nature of the Linguistic Sign', in *Debating Texts: A Reader in Twentieth-Century Literary Theory and Method*, ed. by Rick Rylance (Milton Keynes & Philadelphia: Open University Press, 1987), pp. 77–81 (p. 80).

42. Fineman, 'The Structure of Allegorical Desire', p. 53.

43. Ibid.

44. Paul de Man, *Blindness and Insight* (Minneapolis: University of Minnesota Press, 1983), p. 206.

45. Owens, 'The Allegorical Impulse', p. 69.

46. Morton W. Bloomfield, 'Allegory as Interpretation', *New Literary History*, 3.2 (Winter 1972), 301–17 (pp. 301, 302).

47. Maureen Quilligan, *The Language of Allegory: Defining the Genre* (Ithaca, NY: Cornell University Press), p. 64. Owens also makes much the same point ('The Allegorical Impulse', p. 68).

48. Owens, 'The Allegorical Impulse', p. 69.

49. Buchs, *Yves Bonnefoy à l'horizon du surréalisme*, p. 341.

50. de Lussy and Bonnefoy, *Yves Bonnefoy*, p. xx.

51. Fineman, 'The Structure of Allegorical Desire', pp. 51–52.

52. Owens, 'The Allegorical Impulse', p. 72.

53. Fineman, 'The Structure of Allegorical Desire', p. 51.

54. Fletcher, *Allegory*, p. 301.

55. Ibid., p. 287.

56. Ibid., p. 305.

57. Quilligan, *The Language of Allegory*, p. 24.

58. Ibid.

59. Owens, 'The Allegorical Impulse', p. 72.

60. Walter Benjamin, *The Origin of German Tragic Drama*, trans. by John Osborne (London: Verso, 2003), p. 177. *Treuga dei* , 'truce of god', is a cessation of hostilities that is imposed by religion.

61. Benjamin, *The Origin of German Tragic Drama*, trans. by Osborne, p. 223.

62. Fletcher, *Allegory*, p. 306.

63. Quilligan, *The Language of Allegory*, p. 28.

64. Benjamin, *The Origin of German Tragic Drama*, trans. by Osborne, p. 175.

65. Owens, 'The Allegorical Impulse', p. 68.

66. Quilligan, *The Language of Allegory*, p. 64.

67. Alain Grosrichard and Judith Miller, 'Entretien avec Jean Starobinski, l'essai et son éthique', *La Cause du désir*, 102.2 (2019), 21–32, para. 3 <https://doi.org/10.3917/lcdd.102.0021> [accessed 7 December 2021].

68. Lukács, *Soul and Form*, p. 11.

69. Née, *Rhétorique profonde d'Yves Bonnefoy*, p. 7.

70. Ibid.

71. Jean-Pierre Maulpoix, 'Giacometti par Yves Bonnefoy: "biographie d'une œuvre"' <https://www.maulpoix.net/giacometti_par_yves_bonnef.htm> [accessed 2 January 2022].

72. Philippe Lejeune, *On Autobiography*, trans. by Katherine Leary, (Minneapolis: University of Minnesota Press, 1989), p. 20.

73. Smith, 'The Will to Allegory in Postmodernism', p. 119.

74. Fineman, 'The Structure of Allegorical Desire', p. 49.
75. Née, 'Art et essai', p. 227.
76. Blanchot, *L'Entretien infini*, p. 451.
77. Yves Bonnefoy, *Le Cœur-espace: 1945, 1961* (Tours: Farrago, 2001), p. 51.
78. Stamelman, 'The Syntax of the Ephemeral', p. 115.
79. Lejeune, *On Autobiography*, trans. by Leary, p. 20.

AFTERWORD

❖

Beyond the Good Reader

A final question remains: is it enough to be, or to have become, the good reader that Bonnefoy's essays have trained us to be? In spite of the high level of abstraction that Bonnefoy's writing evinces, there is a pragmatic grounding to it that spurns the airy heights of a language imbued with itself. And if his primary mission is the expression and transmission of *présence*, with the essay qua essay allowing him to expand and reinforce that goal, there is also, as I suggested earlier, the fact that the teleological objective of showing *présence* imperfectly masks the larger aim of making a mark on and perhaps even transforming the readers, and through them, society. Bonnefoy, in his essay 'Lever les yeux de son livre', obliquely suggests as much when he so emphatically exhorts readers to 'lift their eyes from their book' and 'interrupt' their reading in order to see that 'il y a, au dehors, du temps, du lieu, du hasard, des choix à decider, de la mort, mais aussi bien, en cela, un monde' [outside, there is time and contingency, there are places and choices to be made, there is death, but also, withal, a world] (*E*, 229). In a larger sense, however, it is not so much the experience that matters for the readers as the change in how they understand their relation to the world. And in the end, the goal of reader transformation veils in turn a yet greater objective, or, to use a more Bonnefoyian terminology, a hope, namely that of providing a means for society to change itself by embracing a poetry finally able to furnish it with the means for its transformation (*YB*, 4).

The path toward the goal remains, nonetheless, uncertain. Paradoxical as it may seem, and despite Bonnefoy's insistence on 'interrupting' reading to turn toward experiencing real life, he speaks, in the same essay, of our absolute need for 'les mots élaborés par les œuvres' [the words that are forged in literature], for a language able to counter the social and even political ills of society (*E*, 234). Clearly, he would have wanted these words to be those of poetry. Just as clearly, however, as his sometimes urgent comments indicate, he was aware not only of the diminishing social force of poetry, but also of the fact that a purely lyrical poetry centred around the experience of the speaking 'I' has a very reduced power to communicate and to build a like-minded community in the world of today. The high ambition he had for poetry remains thus mired in a double contradiction encompassed both by the problematic referentiality of language, and by the ever-dwindling impact of poetry. Indeed, in the present literary landscape, poetry has come to be viewed as a particularly hermetic and intrinsically self-referential genre, giving rise to the general perception that for large swathes of people it no longer creates a space for proper communication. We have come far indeed from Alexander Pope's contention, in the introduction to his well-known poem *An Essay on Man*, that the poetic form is the clearest and most concise means to seize and retain the reader's attention.[1] The paradox of Pope's title, turning a poem into an essay, thrusts into sharp light the conundrum that Bonnefoy faced: can the poetic form today seize and retain the reader's attention in order to build communities of readers capable of inflecting what he saw as the dangerous atomization of the world? It is no accident that the titles of several of his later books *La Communauté de traducteurs* (2000) and *La Communauté des critiques* (2010) refer to these possible communities, calling for their help to reinstate poetry in its central place. These later essays carry on the work initiated in *L'Improbable*, reinforcing the idea that it is the potential failure of poetry that motivates Bonnefoy's urgent commitment to the essay and its greater communicative power for contemporary readers. He writes:

> Terre, ce qu'on appelle la poésie
> T'aura tant désirée en ce siècle, sans prendre
> Jamais sur toi le bien du geste d'amour.[2]

[Earth, the thing we call poetry | Will have desired you so intensely in this century, harvesting | Never from you the grace of the act of love.]

Communication and connection are indeed the crux of the matter: 'Au cœur de l'interruption, la communication', he writes (*E*, 232). Both for writer and reader, the essay is the very figure of this interruption. It breaks into the tasks of writing poetry and reading it in order to reconnect the individual with the real world. In the essay 'Lever les yeux de son livre', Bonnefoy very wittingly describes how a fleeting reference to the King of Asine causes Georges Séferis to abandon his reading of the *Iliad*. Seferis, he writes is 'moins celui qui trahit une œuvre mais le meilleur des lecteurs possibles' [is less someone who betrays a work, than the best of all possible readers] (*E*, 232). Indeed, we know that this reading engendered one of Seferis's most celebrated poems, 'Le Roi d'Asiné', which in turn, gave rise to Bonnefoy's own *Le Nom du roi d'Asiné*. The true goal, thus, is one we have seen from the earliest of his writings: poetry as act, as the impetus towards action. Though we saw how we could become good readers by learning how to pay a focused quality of attention to the language, to the syntax and structures that poetic language can create, for Bonnefoy, our learning through language cannot remain sterile and individual. The essence of *présence* is a shared attention and action. It is the conjoined act of poetry and of the essay to impel us to take the action of seeking *présence* in the world that surrounds us. 'Une grande œuvre,' says Bonnefoy, 'est bien moins la réussite d'une personne que l'occasion qu'elle donne aux autres de recommencer la recherche' [A great work far less the accomplishment of an individual than the possibility it gives to others to set off on the same quest] (*E*, 231).

Notes to the Afterword

1. Alexander Pope, *An Essay on Man, Moral Essays and Satires* (London: Cassell, 1891) <https://www.gutenberg.org/files/2428/2428-h/2428-h.htm> [accessed 25 June 2022].
2. Yves Bonnefoy, *Ce qui fut sans lumière, suivi de Début et fin de la neige* (Paris: Gallimard, 1991), p. 15.

BIBLIOGRAPHY OF WORKS CITED

❖

ACKE, DANIEL, *Yves Bonnefoy, essayiste: modernité et présence* (Amsterdam & Atlanta, GA: Rodopi, 1999)

ADORNO, THEODOR, 'The Essay as Form', in *Notes to Literature*, trans. by Shierry Weber Nicholsen, 2 vols (New York: Columbia University Press, 1991–92), I, 1–23

——*Prismen: Kulturkritik und Gesellschaft* (Munich: Deutscher Taschenbuch, 1963)

ALLISON, DAVID B., 'Derrida's Critique of Husserl and the Philosophy of Presence', in *Veritas (Porto Alegre)* (2005), 89–99

APOLLINAIRE, GUILLAUME, *Alcools* (Paris: Gallimard, 1966)

ARGYROS, ALEX, 'The Topography of Presence: Bonnefoy and the Spatialization of Poetry', *Orbis Litterarum*, 41 (1986), 244–64

AUSTIN, J. L., *How to Do Things with Words*, ed. by J. O. Urmson and Marina Sbisà, 2nd edn (Cambridge, MA: Harvard University Press, 1975)

BARTHES, ROLAND, *La Chambre claire* (Paris: Gallimard, 1980)

——*Essais critiques* (Paris: Seuil, 1991)

BAUDELAIRE, CHARLES, *Œuvres complètes de Charles Baudelaire, tome 2* (Paris: Michel Lévy frères, 1868) <http://catalogue.bnf.fr/ark:/12148/cb30066456s>

BEITCHMAN, PHILIP, 'The Fragmentary Word', *SubStance*, 12.2 (1983), 58–74

BELLE-ISLE LÉTOURNEAU, FRANCINE, 'L'Essai littéraire: un inconnu à plusieurs visages', *Études littéraires*, 5.1 (April 1972), 47–55

BENJAMIN, WALTER, *The Origin of German Tragic Drama*, trans. by John Osborne (London: Verso, 2003)

BENSMAÏA, REDA, *Barthes à l'essai* (Tübingen: Gunter Narr, 1986)

BENVENISTE, ÉMILE, 'The Analysis of Structure and Meaning: The Nature of the Linguistic Sign', in *Debating Texts: A Reader in Twentieth-Century Literary Theory and Method*, ed. by Rick Rylance (Milton Keynes & Philadelphia: Open University Press, 1987), pp. 77–81

——*Problèmes de linguistique générale* (Paris: Gallimard, 1966)

BEREK, PETER, 'Interpretation, Allegory, and Allegoresis', *College English*, 40.2 (October 1978), 117–32

BERG, CHRISTIAN, 'Le Chemin interdit par la déesse', in *Yves Bonnefoy: poésie, art et pensée. Colloque international 9 11 mai 1983*, ed. by Yves-Alain Favre (Pau: Publications de l'Université de Pau et des pays de l'Adour, 1983), pp. 165–93

BLANCHOT, MAURICE, *L'Entretien infini* (Paris: Gallimard, 1969)

BLOOMFIELD, MORTON W., 'Allegory as Interpretation', *New Literary History*, 3.2 (Winter 1972), 301–17

BOMBARDE, ODILE, 'La Pensée du rêve', in *Yves Bonnefoy: poésie, recherche et savoirs. Actes du colloque de Cerisy-la-Salle*, ed. by Daniel Lançon and Patrick Née (Paris: Herman, 2007), pp. 547–77

BONNEFOY, YVES, *The Act and the Place of Poetry*, trans. by John T. Naughton (Chicago: University of Chicago Press, 1989)

——*Alberto Giacometti: biographie d'une œuvre* (Paris: Flammarion, 1991)

——*L'Arrière-pays* (Geneva: Skira, 1972)

——'Le Carrefour dans l'image', in Arnaud Buchs, *Yves Bonnefoy à l'horizon du surréalisme: la réalité à l'épreuve du langage* (Paris: Galilée, 2005), pp. 11–32

——*Ce qui fut sans lumière, suivi de Début et fin de la neige* (Paris: Gallimard, 1991)

——*Le Cœur-espace: 1945, 1961* (Tours: Farrago, 2001)

——*La Communauté des critiques* (Strasbourg: Presses universitaires de Strasbourg, 2010)

——*La Communauté des traducteurs* (Strasbourg: Presses universitaires de Strasbourg, 2000)

——*Correspondance*, ed. by Odile Bombarde and Patrick Labarthe (Paris: Belles Lettres 2018)

——'Entretien avec Fabien Scotto', *Europe*, 890–91 (June–July 2003), 49–63

——*Entretiens sur la poésie* (Neuchâtel: La Baconnière, 1981)

——*Entretiens sur la poésie (1972–1990)* (Paris: Mercure de France, 1990)

——*L'Heure présente, précédé de La Longue chaîne de l'ancre et suivi de Le Digamma* (Paris: Gallimard, 2014)

——*Hier régnant désert* (Paris: Mercure de France, 1958)

——*L'Improbable* (Paris: Mercure de France, 1959)

——*L'Improbable, suivi de Un rêve fait à Mantoue* (Paris: Gallimard, 1983)

——*L'Improbable, suivi de Un rêve fait à Mantoue* (Paris: Gallimard, 1992)

——*The Lure and the Truth of Painting*, trans. by Richard Stamelman (Chicago: University of Chicago Press, 1995)

——*Le Nom du roi d'Asiné* (Fontaine-les-Dijons: Virgile, 2003)

——*Le Nuage Rouge: essais sur la poétique* (Paris: Mercure de France, 1977; repr. 1992)

——*On the Motion and Immobility of Douve*, trans. by Galway Kinnell (Newcastle upon Tyne: Bloodaxe Books, 1992)

——*Poèmes: Du mouvement et de l'immobilité de Douve, Hier régnant désert, Pierre écrite, Dans le leurre du seuil* (Paris: Mercure de France, 1978)

——*Récits en rêve* (Paris: Mercure de France, 1987)

——*Rue traversière* (Paris: Mercure de France, 1977)

——*La Vérité de parole* (Paris: Mercure de France, 1988)

BORGES, JORGE LUIS, *Historia universal de la infamia* (Madrid: Alianza, 1998)

BOUQUET, SIMON, 'Benveniste et la représentation du sens: de l'arbitraire du signe à l'objet extra-linguistique', *Linx*, 9 (1997), 107–23 <https://doi.org/10.4000/linx.1008>

BREDIN, HUGH, 'Roman Jakobson on Metaphor and Metonymy', *Philosophy and Literature*, 8.1 (1984), 89–103

BRETON, ANDRÉ, *Nadja* (Paris: Gallimard/Folio, 1965)

BROOKS, CLEANTH, *The Well-wrought Urn* (New York: Harcourt Brace, 1947)

BUCHS, ARNAUD, *Une pensée en mouvement* (Paris: Galilée, 2008)

——*Yves Bonnefoy à l'horizon du surréalisme* (Paris: Galilée, 2005)

BÜHLER, KARL, *Sprachtheorie* (Jena: Gustav Fischer, 1934)

BUTRYM, ALEXANDER (ed.), *Essays on the Essay: Redefining the Genre* (Athens: University of Georgia Press, 1989)

BUTTERS, GERHARD, '"L'absente d'aucun bouquet" — Stéphane Mallarmé repris par Yves Bonnefoy', *Studia Neophilologica*, 54 (1982), 141–50

CANADAS, SERGE, 'Celui qui s'éveille et qui rêve encore', *Critique*, 43.487 (1987), 1044–63

CAVALLINI, CONCETTA, *Langage et poésie: lire Yves Bonnefoy* (Millau: Alain Baudry, 2009)

CHANDLER, DANIEL, *Semiotics, the Basics*, 2nd edn (London & New York: Routledge, 2007)

CHUNG, CHIN-YI, 'Deconstruction and the Transformation of Husserlian Phenomenology', *Kritike*, 2.2 (December 2008), 77–94

COHEN, RICHARD A., 'Levinas: Thinking Least about Death — Contra Heidegger', *Self and Other: Essays in Continental Philosophy of Religion*, ed. by Eugene Thomas Long (= special issue of *International Journal for Philosophy of Religion*, 60.1–3 (December 2006)), 21–39

COLERIDGE, SAMUEL TAYLOR, *The Statesman's Manual* (Burlington, VT: Chauncey Goodrich, 1832)

COMBE, DOMINIQUE, *Poésie et récit: une rhétorique des genres* (Paris: José Corti, 1989)

CRAWSHAW, ROBERT, 'The Essay as Performance', in *The Modern Essay in French*, ed. by Charles Forsdick and Andy Stafford (Bern: Peter Lang, 2005), pp. 219–32

DE MAN, PAUL, *Allegories of Reading* (New Haven, CT: Yale University Press, 1979)

——*Blindness and Insight* (Minneapolis: University of Minnesota Press, 1983)

DENIS, BENOÎT, *Littérature et engagement: de Pascal à Sartre* (Paris: Seuil, 2000)

DERRIDA, JACQUES, *Of Grammatology*, trans. by Gayatri Chakravorty Spivak (Baltimore, MD: Johns Hopkins University Press, 1976)

——'The Parerga', trans. by Craig Owens, *October*, 9 (1979), 3–41

DESCARTES, RENÉ, *A Discourse on Method*, trans. by John Veitch, Everyman's Library (London: Dent, 1949)

DUBRUNQUEZ, PIERRE, 'La Fonction ontologique de l'image chez Yves Bonnefoy', *Revue d'esthétique*, 7 (1984), 85–90

DUCROT, OSWALD, and TRISTAN TODOROV, *Dictionnaire encyclopédique des sciences du langage* (Paris: Seuil, 1972)

EDIE, JAMES M., 'Husserl vs. Derrida', *Human Studies*, 13.2 (1990), 103–18

ÉLUARD, PAUL, *L'Amour, la poésie* (Paris: Gallimard, 1929)

FAUSKEVAG, SVEIN EIRIK, 'Yves Bonnefoy et le réalisme poétique', in *Yves Bonnefoy: poésie, art et pensée. Colloque international 9–11 mai 1983*, ed. by Yves-Alain Favre (Pau: Publications de l'Université de Pau et des pays de l'Adour, 1983), pp. 455–68

FAVRE, YVES-ALAIN (ed.), *Yves Bonnefoy: poésie, art et pensée. Colloque international 9–11 mai 1983* (Pau: Publications de l'Université de Pau et des pays de l'Adour, 1983)

FINEMAN, JOEL, 'The Structure of Allegorical Desire', *October*, 12 (Spring 1980), 46–66

FLETCHER, ANGUS, *Allegory: The Theory of a Symbolic Mode* (Ithaca, NY: Cornell University Press, 1964)

GAGNEBIN, MURIELLE, *Yves Bonnefoy: lumière et nuit des images* (Seyssel: Champ Vallon, 2005)

GASARIAN, GÉRARD, *Yves Bonnefoy: la poésie, la présence* (Seyssel: Champ Vallon, 1986)

GELAS, BRUNO, 'Figures et fonction de la voix', in *Yves Bonnefoy: poésie, art et pensée. Colloque international 9–11 mai 1983*, ed. by Yves-Alain Favre (Pau: Publications de l'Université de Pau et des pays de l'Adour, 1983), pp. 383–97

GENETTE, GÉRARD, *Seuils* (Paris: Seuil, 1987)

—— *Thresholds of Interpretation*, trans. by Jane E. Lewin (Cambridge: Cambridge University Press, 1997)

GIGUÈRE, RONALD GÉRALD, *Le Concept de la réalité dans la poésie d'Yves Bonnefoy* (Paris: Nizet, 1985)

GLAUDES, PIERRE (ed.), *L'Essai: métamorphoses d'un genre* (Toulouse: Presses universitaires du Mirail, 2002)

GOMEZ DE BAQUERO, EDUARDO, *El renacimiento de la novela española en el siglo XIX* (Madrid: Mundo Latino, 1924)

GORDON, ALEX L., 'From *Anti-Platon* to *Pierre écrite*: Bonnefoy's "Indispensable" Death', *World Literature Today*, 53.3 (Summer 1979), 430–40

GOUVARD, JEAN-MICHEL, 'Éléments pour une grammaire de la poésie moderne', *Poétique*, 129 (2002), 3–31

——'Métrique et variations dans *Hier régnant désert* d'Yves Bonnefoy', *Semen*, 24 (2007), 2–20

GRAY, J. GLENN, 'Heidegger's "Being"', *Journal of Philosophy*, 49.12 (June 1952), 415–22

GROSRICHARD, ALAIN, and JUDITH MILLER, 'Entretien avec Jean Starobinski, l'essai et son éthique', *La Cause du Désir*, 102.2 (2019), 21–32, para. 3 <https://doi.org/10.3917/lcdd.102.0021>

GUILLEMETTE, LUCIE, and JOSIANE COSSETTE, 'Déconstruction et différance', *Signo*, ed. by Louis Hébert, para. 2.2.1 <http://www.signosemio.com/derrida/deconstruction-et-differance.asp>

HALL, MICHAEL L., 'The Essay and Discovery', in *Essays on the Essay: Redefining the Genre*, ed. by Alexander Butrym (Athens: University of Georgia Press, 1989), pp. 73–91

HAMON, PHILIPPE, 'Le Sujet lyrique et l'ironie', in *Le Sujet Lyrique en Question*, ed. by Dominique Rabaté, Joëlle de Sermet, and Yves Vadé (Bordeaux: Presses universitaires de Bordeaux, 1995), pp. 19–25

HARMON, WILLIAM, and C. HUGH HOLMAN, *A Handbook to Literature*, 8th edn (Upper Saddle, NJ, & London: Prentice Hall, 1999)

HEGEL, GEORG FRIEDRICH WILHELM, *The Phenomenology of the Mind*, trans. by James Black Baillie (New York: Harper Colophon, 1967)

HEIDEGGER, MARTIN, *Lettre sur l'humanisme*, trans. by Roger Munier (Paris: Aubier Montaigne, 1964)

——*Poetry, Language, Thought*, trans. by Albert Hofstadter (New York: Harper & Row, 1971)

HOCQUARD, EMMANUEL, 'Cette histoire est la mienne (Petit Dictionnaire autobiographique de l'élégie)', in *Le Sujet Lyrique en Question*, ed. by Dominique Rabaté, Joëlle de Sermet, and Yves Vadé (Bordeaux: Presses universitaires de Bordeaux, 1995), pp 273–86

HORI, VICTOR SOGEN, 'Translating the Zen Phrase Book', *Bulletin of the Nanzan Institute for Religion and Culture*, 23 (1999), 44–58

HUET-BRICHARD, MARIE-CATHERINE, 'L'Avant-texte de l'essai (XIXe-XXe siècles)', in *L'Essai*, ed. by Glaudes, pp. 29–46

HUSSERL, EDMUND, *L'Origine de la géométrie*, introduction and trans. by Jacques Derrida (Paris: Presses universitaires de France, 1962)

JACKSON, JOHN EDWIN, *Yves Bonnefoy*, Poètes d'aujourd'hui, 229 (Paris: Seghers, 1976)

JAKOBSON, ROMAN, and MORRIS HALLE, *Fundamentals of Language* (The Hague: Mouton, 1956)

JASPER, DAVID, 'La Même Voix, toujours : Yves Bonnefoy and Translation', in *Translating Religious Texts: Transgression and Interpretation*, ed. by David Jasper (New York: St Martin's Press, 1993), pp. 106–21

JOHNSTON, GEORGIA, 'The Whole Achievement in Virginia Woolf's *The Common Reader*', in *Essays on the Essay: Redefining the Genre*, ed. by Alexander Butrym (Athens: University of Georgia Press, 1989), pp. 148–58

JOSSUA, JEAN-PIERRE, *Pour une histoire religieuse de l'expérience littéraire*, 4 vols (Paris: Beauchesne, 1985)

KAZIN, ALFRED, *The Open Form: Essays for Our Time* (New York: Harcourt Brace, 1970)

KORHONEN, KUISMA, *Essaying Friendship: Friendship as a Figure for the Author-reader Relationship in Essayistic Textuality from Plato to Derrida* (Helsinki: Yliopistopaino, 1998)

LARROUX, GUY, 'L'Essai aujourd'hui', in Glaudes, Pierre, *L'Essai: metamorphoses d'un genre*, ed. by Pierre Glaudes (Toulouse: Presses universitaires du Mirail, 2002), pp. 459–72

LEJEUNE, PHILIPPE, *On Autobiography*, trans. by Katherine Leary (Minneapolis: University of Minnesota Press, 1989)

LEMIRE, LAURENT, 'Interview d'Yves Bonnefoy, poète', *Amateur idées*, 23 March 2009 <http://www.amateur-idees.fr/Site/suite.php?art=86>

LEUWERS, DANIEL, *Yves Bonnefoy* (Amsterdam: Rodopi, 1988)

LEVINSON, STEPHEN, 'Deixis', in *The Handbook of Pragmatics*, ed. by Laurence R. Horn & Gregory Ward (Malden, MA: Blackwell, 2006), p. 11

LEWIS, C. S., *The Allegory of Love: A Study in Medieval Tradition* (New York: Galaxy, 1966)

LUKÀCS, GEORG, *Soul and Form*, trans. by Anna Bostock (Cambridge, MA: MIT Press, 1974)

LUSSY DE, FLORENCE, and YVES BONNEFOY, *Yves Bonnefoy: livres et documents*, exhibition catalogue (Paris: Bibliothèque nationale de France, 1992)

LYOTARD, JEAN-FRANÇOIS, *La Phénoménologie* (Paris: Presses universitaires de France, 1954)

MACÉ, MARIELLE, *Le Temps de l'essai* (Paris: Belin, 2006)

MADOU, JEAN-POL, 'La Poétique d'Yves Bonnefoy: un défi au nihilisme mallarméen', in *Yves Bonnefoy: poésie, art et pensée. Colloque international 9–11 mai 1983*, ed. by Yves-Alain Favre (Pau: Publications de l'Université de Pau et des pays de l'Adour, 1983), pp. 27–39

MAILHOT, LAURENT, 'The Writing of the Essay', trans. by Jay Ludtz, *Yale French Studies*, 65 (1983), 74–89

MALLARMÉ, STÉPHANE, *Poésies* (Paris: Gallimard, 1979)

MARTIN, BERNARD, 'Lev Shestov: A Russian Jewish Existentialist', *Theology Today*, 23.3 (October 1966), 386–402

MAULPOIX, JEAN-PIERRE, 'Giacometti par Yves Bonnefoy : "biographie d'une œuvre"' <http://www.maulpoix.net/giacometti_par_yves_bonnef.htm>

—— 'Introduction à la lecture de l'œuvre d'Yves Bonnefoy' (2005) <http://www.maulpoix. net/Oeuvre%20de%20Bonnefoy.htm>

MAURIN, MARIO, 'On Bonnefoy's Poetry', *Yale French Studies*, 21 (1958), 16–22

MCALLISTER, JAMES, 'Metonymy and Metaphor in Yves Bonnefoy's Poetry', *French Forum*, 19.2 (May 1994), 149–60

MERGER, FRANCK, *Les Planches courbes* (Paris: Bréal, 2005)

MONTAIGNE, MICHEL DE, *Œuvres complètes* (Paris: Seuil, 1967)

MONTE, MICHÈLE, '*Runes* de Jean Grosjean et *La Grande Neige* d'Yves Bonnefoy: de l'étrangeté pragmatique à la lecture allégorique', in *Sens et présence du sujet poétique*, ed. by Michael Brophy and Mary Gallagher (Amsterdam: Rodopi, 2006), pp. 227–41

NAUGHTON, JOHN T., 'The Notion of Presence in the Poetics of Yves Bonnefoy', *Studies in Twentieth & Twenty-First Century Literature*, 13.1 (1989), 43–59

—— *The Poetics of Yves Bonnefoy* (Chicago: University of Chicago Press, 1984)

NÉE, PATRICK, 'Art et essai: l'exemple majeur d'Yves Bonnefoy', in *Le Quatrième Genre: l'essai*, ed. by Patrick Née, Rennes: Presses universitaires de Rennes, 2018), pp. 213–34

—— *Rhétorique profonde d'Yves Bonnefoy* (Paris: Hermann, 2004)

—— *Yves Bonnefoy* (Paris: Association pour la Diffusion de la Pensée Française, 2005)

—— *Yves Bonnefoy, penseur de l'image* (Paris: Gallimard, 2006)

NIETZSCHE, FRIEDRICH, *The Portable Nietzsche*, trans. by Walter Kaufmann (New York: Viking, 1977)

OBALDIA, CLAIRE DE, *The Essayistic Spirit* (Oxford: Clarendon Press; New York: Oxford University Press, 1995)

OTHEGUY, RICARDO, 'Saussurean Anti-nomenclaturism in Grammatical Analysis', in *Signal, Meaning, and Message*, ed. by Wallis Reid, Ricardo Otheguy, and Nancy Stern (Amsterdam: Johns Benjamins, 2002), pp. 373–403

OWENS, CRAIG, 'The Allegorical Impulse: Toward a Theory of Postmodernism', *October*, 12 (Spring 1980), 67–86

PAQUETTE, JEAN-MARCEL, 'De l'essai dans le récit au récit dans l'essai chez Jacques Ferron', in *L'Essai et la prose d'idées au Québec*, ed. by Paul Wyczynski, François Gallays, and Sylvain Simard (Montreal: Fides, 1985), pp. 621–42

—— 'Prolégomènes à une théorie de l'essai', *Kwartalnik Neophilologiczny*, 33.4 (1986), 451–54

PASCAL, BLAISE, *Œuvres complètes* (Paris: Seuil, 1963)

PEARRE, ANJA, 'Le Bouddhisme et la poésie contemporaine: Yves Bonnefoy', *Dalhousie French Studies*, 46 (Spring 1999), 167–77

POPE, ALEXANDER, *An Essay on Man, Moral Essays and Satires* (London: Cassell, 1891) <https://www.gutenberg.org/files/2428/2428-h/2428-h.htm>

QUILLIGAN, MAUREEN, *The Language of Allegory: Defining the Genre* (Ithaca, NY: Cornell University Press, 1979)

RACINE, JEAN, *Phaedra*, trans. by Bruce Boswell <https://www.gutenberg.org/files/1977/1977-h/1977-h.htm>

RAVAUD, JACQUES (ed.), *Yves Bonnefoy* (Cognac: Le Temps Qu'il Fait, 1998)

RICHARD, JEAN-PIERRE, *Onze études sur la poésie moderne* (Paris: Seuil, 1981)

RIENDEAU, PASCAL, 'La Rencontre du savoir et du soi dans l'essai', *Etudes littéraires*, 37.1 (2005), 91–103

SALLIS, JOHN, 'Heidegger/Derrida — Presence', *Journal of Philosophy*, 81.10 (October 1984), 594–601

SAROCCHI, JEAN, 'L'Essai, un drôle de genre', in *L'Essai: métamorphoses d'un genre*, ed. by Pierre Glaudes (Toulouse: Presses universitaires du Mirail, 2002), pp. 17–28

SAUSSURE, FERDINAND DE, *Course in General Linguistics*, trans. by Wade Baskin (New York: McGraw-Hill, 1959)

SERÇA, ISABELLE, 'Roman/essai: le cas Proust', in *L'Essai: métamorphoses d'un genre*, ed. by Pierre Glaudes (Toulouse: Presses universitaires du Mirail, 2002), pp. 83–106

SHESTOV, LEV, *Athènes et Jérusalem*, trans by Boris de Schloezer (Paris: Aubier, 1993)

——*In Job's Balances*, trans. by Camilla Coventry and C. A. Macartney [1932], ed. by Bernard Martin (Athens: Ohio University Press, 1975) <http://shestov.phonoarchive.org/ijb/jb1_5.html >

SLOANE, THOMAS, *Encyclopedia of Rhetoric* (Oxford & New York: Oxford University Press, 2001)

SMITH, PAUL, 'The Will to Allegory in Postmodernism', *Dalhousie Review*, 62.1 (1982), 105–21

STAMELMAN, RICHARD, *Lost Beyond Telling* (Ithaca, NY: Cornell University Press, 1990)

——'The Syntax of the Ephemeral', *Dalhousie French Studies*, 2 (October 1980), 101–17

STAROBINSKI, JEAN, 'Peut-on définir l'essai ?', in *Approches de l'essai*, ed. by François Dumont (Quebec: Nota Bene, 2003)

STEINER, GEORGE, *Real Presences* (Chicago: University of Chicago Press, 1989)

SUSINI-ANASTOPOULOS, FRANÇOISE, *L'Écriture fragmentaire* (Paris: Presses universitaires de France, 1997)

THÉLOT, JÉRÔME, *Poétique d'Yves Bonnefoy* (Geneva: Droz, 1983)

TRACY, H. L., 'The Lyric Poet's Repertoire', *Classical Journal*, 61.1 (October 1965), 22–26

VERNIER, RICHARD, *Yves Bonnefoy ou les mots comme le ciel* (Tübingen: Gunter Narr, 1985)

WINSPUR, STEVEN, 'Bonnefoy Cartésien?', *French Forum*, 9.2 (1984), 236–50

——'The Poetic Significance of the Thing-in-itself', *SubStance*, 41 (1983), 41–49

WOOLRIDGE, PAUL, 'Activist Essayism' (2007) <http://www.ucl.ac.uk/opticon1826/currentissue/article/RfP_Art_A_H_Paul_Essay.pdf>

ZUBIATE, JEAN-PIERRE, 'Essai et poésie au XXe siècle', in *L'Essai: metamorphoses d'un genre*, ed. by Pierre Glaudes (Toulouse: Presses universitaires du Mirail, 2002)

INDEX

❖

.

www.ingramcontent.com/pod-product-compliance
Lightning Source LLC
Chambersburg PA
CBHW050745100426
42739CB00016BA/3442